The Anglo-Saxon Cross

THE CROSS IN THE LIFE AND LITERATURE
OF THE ANGLO-SAXONS

by William O. Stevens
Yale Studies in English, XXII

with a new preface by Thomas D. Hill

SOME ACCOUNTS
OF THE BEWCASTLE CROSS
Between the Years 1607 and 1861

by Albert Stanburrough Cook
Yale Studies in English, L

with a new preface by Robert T. Farrell

ARCHON BOOKS

1977

Yale Studies in English, vols. 22 and 50

Library of Congress Cataloging in Publication Data

Main entry under title:

The Anglo-Saxon cross.

    Reprint of the 1904 ed. of W. O. Steven's The cross in the
life and literature of the Anglo-Saxons, and of the 1914 ed. of
A. S. Cook's Some accounts of the Bewcastle Cross between the
years 1607 and 1861, published by H. Holt, New York, which
were issued as v. 22 and 50, respectively, of the Yale studies in
English; with new prefaces.
    Includes bibliographies.
    1. Crosses. 2. Anglo-Saxon literature—History and criticism.
3. Bewcastle cross. I. Stevens, William Oliver, 1878–1955. The
cross in the life and literature of the Anglo-Saxons. 1977. II.
Cook, Albert Stanburrough, 1853–1927. Some accounts of the
Bewcastle Cross between the years 1607 and 1861. 1977. III. Series:
Yale Studies in English; 22 [etc.].
BV160.A53   1977   246'.558   76–23238
ISBN 0–208–01555–8

First published 1904 and 1914
Reprinted with permission in
unabridged editions in one volume
as an Archon Book, an imprint of
The Shoe String Press Inc.
Hamden, Connecticut

Printed in the United States of America

Contents

PART I

THE CROSS IN THE LIFE AND LITERATURE OF THE ANGLO-SAXONS

A New Preface

William O. Stevens' *The Cross in the Life and Literature of the Anglo-Saxons* is a book which remains useful despite the fact that his scholarship is (necessarily) dated and that many of his specific conclusions are either debatable or clearly wrong. The range of material which Stevens surveyed, and his habit of quoting or paraphrasing original texts at some length, make this book almost an anthology of texts pertaining to the Cross in the early medieval period in England. Again, the fact that Stevens was concerned with the Cross in the "life" as well as the "literature" of the Anglo-Saxons meant that he surveyed a body of materials with which most specialists in Old English literature are not generally familiar. And yet the use of the Cross in charms or in the penitentials is, potentially at least, very relevant to our understanding of such poems as the *Dream of the Rood* or *Elene*. The strength and usefulness of Stevens' book lies precisely in the fact that he recognized that his topic did not lend itself to conventional divisions and that he covers virtually every conceivable aspect of the use of the Cross in Old English literature, history, law, liturgy, magic, sculpture and art. The book is not absolutely comprehensive, but it remains a helpful guide to an extensive and heterogeneous body of material.

Even a general critique of those of Stevens' conclusions and comments which no longer seem tenable would be out of place and in a sense almost impertinent since, for the modern student of Anglo-Saxon literature, history, or religious life, Stevens' book is chiefly useful as a guide and survey of primary sources. Inevitably, in using a book which was published over seventy years ago, the reader will find it necessary to consult recent scholarship to see what is the cur-

rent state of the question in any given instance, and I am
providing a *brief* annotated bibliography which is intended
to supplement Stevens' bibliography. I am not, however,
attempting to provide anything like a comprehensive bibliography on the topics which Stevens treats so that the
reader, if he wishes to cover any specific question in detail,
should consult one or more of the standard bibliographies
such as the *CBEL*, Fred C. Robinson's *Old English Literature: A Select Bibliography*, Toronto Medieval Bibliographies (Toronto: University of Toronto Press, 1970), or
Wilifred Bonser, *An Anglo-Saxon and Celtic Bibliography,
450–1087*, (Berkeley and Los Angeles, 1959). For more recent
work the annual bibliographies in the journal *Anglo-Saxon
England* are very useful. I am also deliberately excluding
most discussions of the Cross in Old English art or sculpture
since these topics are covered by my colleague R. T. Farrell
in his preface to Albert S. Cook's book, *Some Accounts of
the Bewcastle Cross* in the "Yale Studies in English" series.
On the Cross and the symbolism of the Cross in patristic and
medieval Christianity, the fundamental text (which Stevens
did not mention) is the work of the 17th century Jesuit
scholar, Jacobus Gretser, whose book *De Sancta Cruce* (vols.
I–III of his *Opera*; Ratisbourne: Peez and Bader, 1734) is a
comprehensive treatment of crucifixion as punishment and
the Cross as a Christian symbol. While this work is indexed,
its very comprehensiveness makes it somewhat forbidding. It
consists of over 1200 folio pages of Latin, and if my own
experience is at all typical, the process of finding one's way
around in it—let alone mastering it—can be time-consuming.

Some other useful renaissance compilations of materials
concerning the Cross are Justus Lipsius, *De cruce* (Amstelodamus [Amsterdam]: Andrea Frisius, 1670); and Honoratus
Nicquetus, S.S., *Titulus sanctae crucis seu historia et myste-
rium tituli sanctae crucis . . . domini nostri Iesu Christi*
(Antverpia [Antwerp]: Andrea Frisius, 1672); Thoma Bar-
tholinus, Casp. F., *De cruce Christi (Amstelodamus [Amster-
dam]*: Andrea Frisius, 1670). In the editions which I have
had the opportunity to examine, these three works are
bound together. There is, as far as I am aware, nothing quite

comparable to Gretser on the Cross in modern scholarship; but a useful and very intelligent introduction to aspects of the symbolism of the Cross in patristic and medieval Christianity is the chapter "The Mystery of the Cross" in Hugo Rahner, *Greek Myths and Christian Mystery*, trans. Brian Battershaw (London: Burns and Oates, 1963) 46–68. For discussion of the specific problem of the history of the Cross, the legendary stories of its past, etc., see E. C. Quinn, *The Quest of Seth for the Oil of Life* (Chicago: University of Chicago Press, 1962). For discussion of medieval hymns on the Cross, see Joseph Szöverffy, "Crux Fidelis . . . Prolegomena to a History of the Holy Cross Hymns," *Traditio* XXII (1966) 1–41, and for more general studies of Cross symbolism see Eleanor Simmons Greenhill, "The Child in the Tree: A Study of the Cosmological Tree in Christian Tradition," *Traditio* X (1954) 323–71 and R. E. Kaske, "A Poem of the Cross in the Exeter Book: 'Riddle 60' and "The Husband's Message," *Traditio* XXIII (1967) 41–71 (while concerned with a specific text, the so-called "Husband's Message" in *The Exeter Book*, this article provides a convenient survey of several important themes in medieval Cross lore and provides useful bibliographical information). Two further studies concerned with the symbolism of the Cross from the perspective of art history are those of Aloys Grillmeier, S.J., *Der Logos am Kreuz* (Munich: Max Huebner, 1956), and Adolf Katzenellenbogan, "The Image of Christ in the Early Middle Ages," in *Life and Thought in the Early Middle Ages*, ed. Robert S. Hoyt (Minneapolis: The University of Minnesota Press, 1967).

The two Old English poems which are primarily and explicitly concerned with the Cross, the *Dream of the Rood* and *Elene* perhaps deserve special consideration here. *Elene* has been edited by P. O. E. Gradon for Methuen's Old English Library (London: Methuen, 1958) and has been discussed as literature in a number of recent articles. See particularly T. D. Hill, "Sapiential Structure and Figural Narrative in the Old English 'Elene' " *Traditio* XXVII (1971) 159–77, Catharine A. Regan, "Evangelicalism as the Informing Principle of Cynewulf's 'Elene' " *Traditio* XXIX (1973) 27–52, and Gordon A. Whatley's Harvard dissertation, *Wisdom and Bondage: An Interpretation of Cynewulf's 'Elene'* (1973). The *Dream of the Rood* has recently been reedited by M. J. Swanton in the Old and Middle English Texts series (New York: Barnes and Noble, 1970). Swanton's edition is a very full and careful one which provides a full listing of the copious recent periodical literature which deals with the *Dream of the Rood*. There are two articles, however, which have been influential enough to deserve special mention, Rosemary Woolf, "Doctrinal Influences on the *Dream of the Rood*," *Medium Aevum* 27 (1958) 137–53 and J. A. Burrow, "An Approach to the *Dream of the Rood*," *Neophilogus* 43 (1959) 123–33.

In conclusion, the most important point for the reader to bear in mind in using this book, is that the problems with which Stevens was concerned are really very much unresolved. The idiosyncracies of the *Dream of the Rood*, the relationship of *Elene* to its Latin source or sources, the rationale for the use of the Cross in the Old English charms, possible allusions to the Cross in the vernacular riddles, all these questions and a variety of other related problems in Old English literature, history, religious thought need to be reexamined and rethought. And Stevens' book on *The Cross in the Life and Literature of the Anglo-Saxons* is still of use to those who wish to work on these problems.

THOMAS D. HILL

PREFACE

The Old English poems, *Elene,* the *Dream of the Rood,* and the Doomsday Vision in the *Christ,* express a remarkable spirit of veneration for the Cross. The purpose of this study is to furnish a setting for these poems with respect to this devotion to the Cross. It is to find what were the ideas of the Cross inherited with Christianity; how much these ideas entered into the life and thought of the Anglo-Saxons; whether, in brief, this sentiment must be regarded as peculiar to Cynewulf and the poet of the *Dream of the Rood,* or whether it was more or less characteristic of the civilization to which these poems belong. It is also to discover whether this spirit found expression in forms other than poetry, whether it was more predominant at one time than another, and to account, if possible, for its existence.

These questions, and others suggested by them, will be taken up in the following pages; and, in attempting to provide a background for the Old English poetry of the Cross, I hope that some light may be thrown on the cultural history of this early and comparatively obscure period.

The translations of Old English prose that I have used are frequently quoted direct from the versions that accompany the texts in the editions cited. In the case of the poetry I have used Garnett's translation of the *Elene,* Whitman's of the *Christ,* and the *Translations from Old English Poetry,* edited by Cook and Tinker, which includes a translation of the *Dream of the Rood* by Miss Iddings.

Preface

In the references to texts and authorities, the abbreviations in the foot-notes should be recognized without special mention. Where the name of an author only is cited, the work is the only work facing his name in the bibliography, in the edition there mentioned. Some texts of the *Patrologia Latina* are reprints from other editions. In these the paging of the original is preserved by black-faced numerals. As the references in the indices of these volumes is to the original rather than to the actual paging, I have followed that system here.

CONTENTS

CHAPTER I

VARIETIES OF CROSS-WORSHIP

The event of supreme importance in the history of the worship of the cross as an emblem of the Christian faith was the conversion of Constantine, which occurred in the year 312. This was the starting-point for all the adoration of the cross in the Middle Ages, and the one event which at a bound lifted the emblem from disgrace, and crowned it with glory and honor.

Up to that time the cross had been the Christian's reproach. While to him it was associated with the sacrifice of his Redeemer, to the world it meant only shame and misery. And because, with Paul, he gloried in the cross of Christ, he was taunted with being a 'worshiper of the cross' (*crucicolus*), a term which the Fathers resented and repudiated. So, to avoid the charge of staurolatry, and to save the symbol of the faith from the sport and malice of the pagans, the early Christians as a rule refrained from open representations of the cross. Instead, they used emblems, the 'cruces dissimulatæ,' such as the letter Chi, the anchor, the so-called Swastika cross, and, chief of all, the famous Chi Rho monogram.

But after the vision of the cross in the heavens, and the subsequent conversion of the Emperor, the cross needed no longer to remain in hiding. Shortly after his conversion Constantine forbade magistrates or great land-owners any longer to use the cross as an instrument of punishment. So, while at first the ideas of ignominy were yet too freshly associated with the cross for it to be exalted publicly, and the monogram remained the favorite emblem, it came to pass that, as actual scenes of crucifixion faded from memory, the monogram steadily receded, and the cross came to the front. By the time of the conversion of the Anglo-Saxons

the cross had replaced its former associations of shame by
those of honor, its praises were sung like those of a god,
and it was ' adored ' by a formal ceremony of the church.
In the year 597, the missionary band led by Augustine
landed in Kent, and established the Christian faith once
more on British soil.   Then followed a period of some four
centuries and a half before the coming of the Normans.
It is in the remains of this period that we must look for
the ideas of the cross as they prevailed among the Anglo--
Saxons.

Without a minute knowledge of the literature and rituals
of the Roman, the Gallic, and the British churches it is
impossible to define the sources for all the Anglo-Saxon
ideas and practices under this head.   But it is possible to
give the facts as they are found, and to examine them in
the light of such a general survey of the previous history
of the Christian church as may be gained from authoritative
works of reference.   We may take as a starting-point the
legendary history of the cross.

I. THE CROSS IN LEGEND

(a) The Wood of the Cross

The root of the mediæval legends of the True Cross is in
the Apocryphal Gospel of Nicodemus.   Just after the
announcement is made in hell that Christ is on his way to
release the prophets and patriarchs, Seth, at his father's
bidding, relates the ancient prophecy made to him by the
archangel Michael (14. 3-8) :

I, Seth, when I was praying to God at the gates of Paradise,
beheld the angel of the Lord, Michael, appear to me, saying, I am
sent unto thee from the Lord; I am appointed to preside over human
bodies. I tell thee, Seth, do not pray to God in tears and entreat
him for the oil of the tree of mercy wherewith to anoint thy father
Adam for his headache, because thou canst not by any means obtain
it till the last day and times, namely till five thousand and five
hundred years be past. Then will Christ, the most merciful Son
of God, come on earth to raise again the human body of Adam, and

at the same time to raise the bodies of the dead, and when he cometh he will be baptized in Jordan. Then with the oil of mercy he will anoint all those who believe on him; and the oil of his mercy will continue to future generations, for those who shall be born of water and the Holy Ghost unto eternal life. And when at that time the most merciful Son of God, Christ Jesus, shall come down on earth, he will introduce our father Adam into Paradise, to the tree of mercy.

From this story developed during the Middle Ages a rich and varied body of legends, the general tenor of which runs as follows: When Adam fell sick unto death, he bade his son Seth go to the gate of Paradise and beg for a drop of the healing oil from the Tree of Life. But the archangel Michael answered Seth with the prophecy of the Messiah, and gave him instead a twig (according to some accounts a seed, in others three seeds) from the Tree of Life. When Adam died, Seth buried him on Golgotha, exactly where the cross of Christ was to stand. The seed, or shoot, he planted in Jerusalem, where it grew into a great tree. In Solomon's time it was cut down, on account of its beauty, to be used in the building of the temple; but as it proved always too short or too long to fit any place whatever, it was rejected, and finally thrown over the brook Kedron for a foot-bridge. When the Queen of Sheba visited Solomon she refused to set foot upon it, declaring that one day it would cause the destruction of the Jews. Accordingly, Solomon caused it to be thrown into the pool of Bethesda, to the waters of which it imparted healing virtues. Finally, at the time of the trial of Christ, the beam came to the surface, and the Jews took it and made of it at least the upright part of the cross.

The Gospel of Nicodemus is found in an Old English translation, and the story of Seth's visit to Paradise was doubtless always familiar. But it is not till the fourteenth century that we find this elaborate story developed.[1] During the Anglo-Saxon period there seems to have been no

---

[1] Morris, *Legends of the Holy Rood.*

legend of the wood itself. In the *Dream of the Rood,* for example, there is no hint of the tree planted in Jerusalem, cut down by Solomon, and taken from the Pool of Bethesda for the Crucifixion. The Rood itself speaks, saying:

> It was long, long ago . . . .
> Yet I recall, when, at the forest's edge,
> I was hewn down, and from my stem removed.[1]

As to the kind of wood of which the cross was composed, there was a wide divergence of opinion. Chrysostom, for example, had applied the words of Isaiah: 'The glory of Lebanon shall come unto thee, the fir tree, the pine tree and the box together, to beautify the place of my sanctuary; and I will make the place of my feet glorious,'[2] to the different parts of the cross. And finally, in the Golden Legend, the version is given which has survived the rest, namely, that the upright part of the cross was of cedar, the cross-beam of cypress, the piece on which the feet rested of palm, and the slab on which the title was fastened of olive.

But at the period which we are studying, or at least among the Anglo-Saxons, there seems to have been no canon in the matter. The quotation from the *Dream of the Rood* just cited shows that the author of that poem did not conceive of the cross as made of more than one kind of wood. (Pseudo.?) Bede, however, says:

> The cross of the Lord was made of four kinds of wood, which are called cypress, cedar, pine, and box. But the box was not in the cross unless the tablet was of that wood, which was above the brow of Christ, on which the Jews wrote the title, 'Here is the King of the Jews.' The cypress was in the earth and even to the tablet, the cedar in the transverse, the pine, the upper end.[3]

But he is not quite sure about the box, and in the Riddle on the Cross[4] there is a totally different enumeration. There the parts are described as ash or maple,[5] oak, the 'hard yew'

[1] ll. 28-30.   [2] 60. 13.
[3] *Patrolog. Lat.* 94, *Collectanea* 555.
[4] No. 56. *Bibl. der A. S. Poesie,* Wülcker-Grein.
[5] *hlin,* the meaning of which is doubtful.

and the 'dark holly.' Evidently the question was still a matter for individual speculation.

In his *Book of the Holy Places,* Bede speaks of the relic of the True Cross preserved at Constantinople as possessing a wonderful fragrance: 'A chest containing the relic is laid on a golden altar and exposed to view. As long as it remains open on the altar a marvelous odor spreads through the whole church, for an odoriferous liquor like oil flows from the knots of the holy wood, the least drop of which cures every complaint with which a man may be afflicted.[1] So, according to the *Martyrology,* the fragrance is ' a wonderful odor, as winsome as if there were collected there all kinds of flowers.'[2] Ælfric, also, in his account of the Exaltation of the Cross, dwells on this fragrance of the cross:

> There was also another marvel, so that a winsome odor steamed from the Holy Cross when it was on its way home throughout the land, and filled the air; and the people rejoiced on account of their being filled with the odor. No perfume could give out so delightful a smell.[3]

This idea of fragrance may have originated in the lines of Fortunatus,

> Funde aroma cortice
> Vincens sapore nectare,[4]

but possibly it can be traced back further.

(b) Relics of the True Cross in England

In the metrical homily by Ælfric on the Exaltation of the Cross, quoted above, the writer says: ' It is, however, to be known that it—the cross—is widely distributed by means of frequent sections to every land. But the spiritual signification is always with God, ever incorruptible, though the tree be cut in pieces.' But there are not many references to relics of the True Cross finding their way to England during

---

[1] *Opera,* ed. Giles, 4, 440. [2] *Mart.* 648.
[3] *Æ. H.* 1. 108-13. [4] 'Vexilla Regis' 2. 25-6.

the Anglo-Saxon period. In his life of St. Felix, Bede relates the havoc made by a conflagration that threatened an entire town. While the people were at church praying for assistance, Felix went home and, ' taking a small splinter of the wood of our Lord's cross, threw it into the midst of the fire. Immediately the flames subsided, and the small fragment of wood effected what so many men with abundance of water had not been able to accomplish.' Æthelstan received a piece of the cross, enclosed in a crystal, from King Hugh of Brittany,[1] and Pope Marinus[2] gave a fragment to King Alfred.

The so-called Brussels Cross bears these lines in Old English, reminiscent of the *Dream of the Rood:*

> Rood is my name. Once long ago I bore,
> Trembling, bedewed with blood, the mighty King.

From this it must be inferred that the wood was regarded as a fragment of the True Cross. This wood is bound together by strips of silver, as Ælfric says the cross was adorned by Helena after the Invention.[3]

It is evident, however, that relics of the True Cross had not yet become numerous in England during the period we are studying, and were regarded as gifts appropriate for kings and popes to bestow and receive.

(c) The Vision of Constantine

But the most popular legends of the cross were those that clustered about the vision of Constantine, including the stories of the Invention and the Exaltation, which were always associated with it. The famous story of the appearance of the cross in the heavens is connected with the victory of Constantine over Maxentius on the 28th of October, 312. It was the defeat and death of Maxentius upon this battle-field that made Constantine Emperor of the West. The story of the vision as told by Eusebius, which accord-

[1] Wm. Malmesb. p. 397.   [2] *A.-S. Chron.* A. 883.   [3] *Æ. H.* 2. 306.

ing to his account was related to him by the Emperor himself, and ratified by an oath, is the best known. He says of
Constantine that—' about midday, when the sun was beginning to decline, he saw with his own eyes the trophy of a
cross of light in the heavens above the sun and bearing the
inscription, " Conquer by this." At this sight, he himself
was struck with amazement, and his whole army also, which
. . . witnessed the miracle.' [1]

Lactantius, Rufinus, and Sozomen tell only of a dream
in which Constantine saw the cross and its accompanying
inscription. And the Old English poem *Elene*,[2] the anonymous eleventh-century homily on the Invention of the Cross,
and Ælfric's sermon on the Invention,[3] all tell of the cross as
appearing in a dream in the early morning rather than as an
apparition in the sky shortly after midday. The fact that
these three Old English versions—one of the eighth, and the
others of the eleventh century—agree in this important variation, shows that the accounts which the Anglo-Saxons had
of the vision of Constantine were not taken directly, at least,
from Eusebius, but had come from one of the other
three, Lactantius, Rufinus, or Sozomen. According to
Professor Cook,[4] 'Ælfric derives his information on the
subject from Rufinus' version of Eusebius.' It is probable
that this was also the source for the other two Old English
accounts.[5]

---

[1] Tr. Cook, *Christ*, p. 90.
[2] Morris, *Legends of the Holy Rood.*
[3] *Homilies*, 2. 302.
[4] *Christ* 19.
[5] Two minor variations may be noted: 1. Ælfric adds a detail
omitted by the rest: 'He [Constantine] bade then be forged of
beaten gold a little rood, which he laid on his right hand, fervently
praying the Almighty Ruler that his right hand might never be
polluted with the red blood of the Roman people.' 2. There is a
variation in date between the *Elene* and the anonymous homily:
the former sets the year as 233 A. D.; the latter, 133 years 'after
Christ's passion and ascension to heaven.'

(d) The Invention of the Cross

Closely linked with the legend of the vision of Constantine is that of the Finding of the True Cross by Helena, the mother of the emperor, and that of the Exaltation of the Cross, or the restoration of the cross to its place of honor in Jerusalem by Heraclius. Both were familiar to the Anglo-Saxons. The two most detailed accounts of the Invention are Cynewulf's poem *Elene,* of the eighth century and an anonymous homily of the eleventh, both of which have just been quoted among the chief sources of the Constantine legend. The *Elene* tells the story with great spirit. The expedition is described as a magnificent emprise, the aim of which was to gain the most precious object in the world. The whole has a distinctly warlike coloring, and suggests an expedition of viking warriors; but the story is the same as that of the well known legend. The details of the narrative of the homily vary scarcely at all from those of the *Elene* version.[1]

(e) The Exaltation of the Cross

The chief account in Old English of the Exaltation is Ælfric's homily on that subject.[2] In this, the course of the story is the same as that of the accepted legend of the church. If there be any original contribution to the story it is in the elaboration of details, and in the speeches put into the mouths of the characters. One is significant enough for quotation:

[1] The few may be noted. In the *Elene* the element of perfume, which is dwelt upon by almost all, is omitted. It is 'a vapor like smoke' which reveals the hiding place of the crosses. In the homily it is 'the sweetest smell of all the most precious perfumes.' In the *Old English Martyrology* the brief paragraph under May 3d combines the smoke and the perfume. "There came up a smoke of delightful smell from the ground where the cross was found." Again, in the homily, it is a voice from heaven that bids Helena forge the nails on her son's bridle; in the *Elene* it is the advice of an elder of Jerusalem.

[2] *Homilies,* 3, 144.

And then the Emperor exclaimed with joy: ' O thou marvelous rood on which Christ deigned to suffer, and quench our sins with his precious blood! O thou rood shining more than the stars, glorious on this earth! Greatly art thou to be loved, O holy and winsome tree that wast worthy to bear the prize of all the earth! Be mindful of this assembly which is here gathered for the honor of God!'

This ardent devotion, as we shall find, was not peculiar to Ælfric.

To review briefly the legend of the cross: We find that as yet there was no legend of the tree of the cross, and no canon of belief as to the varieties of wood of which the cross was composed. But of the history of the cross after the crucifixion there is abundant material; evidently the stories of Constantine, Helena, and Heraclius were perfectly familiar. The differences in these versions from the older stories are of small importance, the greatest variation from the accepted legend being the story of the vision of Constantine, which does not follow the original account of Eusebius.

II. THE CROSS IN THE CHURCH

(a) The Church Edifice

The home of the cross was naturally the church. The cruciform church edifice had been known from a very early period. Indeed, whether the plan was at first consciously adopted out of reverence for the symbol of Christ, or whether it was the natural modification of the old Roman basilica, there are remains of churches of the epoch of Constantine which have for their ground-plan the cross.

Among the Anglo-Saxons, ' all the churches,' says Lingard, ' mentioned by the most ancient Saxon writers are of a square or quadrilateral shape, and were probably built after the plan of the basilica at Rome, " in quadrum " (Bede, *Hist.* 2. 14), " templum quadratum " (Alc. *Op.* 2. 530). But Æthelwold, a monk of the monastery of St. Peter on the east coast of Bernicia, who wrote about the year

810, mentions not only a square but a cruciform church, the first of that form noticed in our annals (Æthel. *De Abbat. Lind.* 120-22).'[1]

But according to another record,[2] Oswald built his church *in modum crucis* in memory of the victory of Heavenfield, and indeed upon the battle-field itself. In this case there was, of course, special significance in building the church cruciform, because it was the cross which gave Oswald the victory. But if the record is reliable, it shows that the cruciform church was not unknown in the early history of the faith among the Anglo-Saxons. Later, however, the practice became more common, and remains of cruciform churches of our period—for example, that of Stow in Lincolnshire, and that at Dover—exist to this day. But the practice did not become conventional till about the time of the Crusades.

After the edifice had been completed, it was consecrated throughout by the cross. The bishop marked a cross with chrism at various places on the walls, and afterwards on these spots crosses were carved or painted, and sometimes crosses of metal were affixed. The altar-stone also was consecrated at the four corners and at the centre, and at these places as well crosses were carved. All this was in accordance with a custom of the church which has been traced to the fourth century.[3] The legend of Edward the Confessor tells how Westminster was dedicated by angels who ' sprinkled ' and ' marked ' it ' with twelve crosses.'[4]

(b) The Altar-Cross

The cross that held the place of honor within the church was that upon the altar. The custom of placing a cross upon the altar is very old, though it did not become general till the ninth century, and then it was the plain cross, and

---

[1] *Hist. and Antiq.* 1. 371.
[2] *Hist. Church of York*, 1. 434.
[3] This rite is given in detail in the Egbert *Pontifical.*
[4] *Ann. Cambr.* 237.

not the crucifix. In fact, the plain cross was on the altar more often than the crucifix till as late as the sixteenth century.[1] In the Anglo-Saxon church there was generally, at any rate, an altar-cross which either stood upon the altar or was suspended over it. It was, in the richer churches at least, of the most precious materials, for the cross was the symbol of the Redeemer, and as such nothing was too precious to lavish upon it.[2]

(c) The Altar-Cross as a Crucifix

In speaking of the crucifix among the Anglo-Saxons, Rock says: ' Before all and above all other images in their estimation was that of the crucifix. The figure of Christ was frequently of the purest gold, a masterpiece of workmanship, and fastened by four nails to a cross of wood overlaid with plates of gold in which were set precious stones.'[3] Now it is noteworthy that in the long prayer offered at the consecration of the cross in the Egbert *Pontifical,* while the gold, the wood, the crystal, etc., are mentioned, there is no reference whatever to a crucified figure. It runs:

' Radiet hic Unigeniti Filii tui splendor divinitas in auro, emicet gloria passionis in ligno, in cruore rutilet nostræ mortis redemptio, in splendore cristalli nostræ vitæ purificatio.'

The word *cruore,* by the way, suggests that the cross was painted red. This was a very ancient custom in Rome,[4] and it is not unlikely that it was practised in England. Aside from the word just referred to, in the charters a boundary cross is sometimes mentioned as a ' red cross;'[5] the *Dream of the Rood*[6] and the *Christ*[7] represent the cross

---

[1] Seymour, p. 209.
[2] For the significance of this ornament, see the prayer quoted below.
[3] 1. 305.
[4] Ebert, *Ueber den Traum,* etc., p. 83.
[5] Earle, *Charters,* p. 291, No. 909.
[6] 1. 24.   [7] 1. 1101.

2

as bloody or red; and some of the ancient consecration-crosses have vestiges of red paint.[1]

In the same *Pontifical* is an adoration-ceremony, containing a prayer to be said when the cross is adored, and this might seem at first glance to indicate that there was a figure of the Savior upon the altar-cross:

Domine Jesu Christe, adoro te *in cruce ascendentem, spineam coronam in capiti portentem;* deprecor te ut ipsa crux liberet me ab angelo percutiente. Domine Jesu Christe, adoro te *in cruce vulneratum,* felle et aceto potatum; deprecor te, ut tua mors sit vita mea.

But the prayer continues:

Domine Jesu Christe, adoro te *descendentem ad inferos, liberantem captivos,* . . . *ascendentem in caelum, sedentem ad dextram Patris;* . . . *adoro te venturum in judicio,* etc.,

showing that these conceptions of Christ have no reference to anything upon the actual cross.

This is confirmed by the fact that all Anglo-Saxon crucifixes represented the Savior, not with a thorny crown, but with the diadem of a king.[2] The older tradition generally prevailed, representing Christ as ruling in majesty, not suffering in agony. The 'spineam coronam in capiti portantem' of the prayer could not in any case refer to a crucifix. Further, an illumination which pictures Cnut presenting a great golden jeweled altar-cross to the Abbey of New Minster (Hyde Abbey)[3] represents this cross as without the crucified figure. All this evidence, negative and positive, together with the fact that plain altar-crosses, rather than crucifixes, prevailed in Christian Europe generally till as late as the sixteenth century, makes it almost certain that among the Anglo-Saxons the altar-cross was always plain.

(d) The Crozier as a Crucifix

In speaking of the crozier, or archiepiscopal cross, Rock affirms that 'while it is frequently shown in monuments as

[1] *Archæologia* 48, 456.
[2] Rock 1. 306. Note also legend of Dunstan, *Vita S. Dunst.*, Rolls Series, 5, 63. p. 113.
[3] *Palæog. Soc. Facs.*, Series 2, Vol. 1, pl. 16.

a mere cross without any kind of image upon it, still we have good reasons for believing that not unoften it bore on each of its two sides a figure of our Lord hanging " nailed to the rood." '[1] But the ' good reasons ' that he adduces are a manuscript drawing of the twelfth century, and a grave-brass of the fifteenth. The drawing of Archbishop Elga, already referred to, represents him as holding a crozier which is plain. Indeed, among all the facsimiles of Anglo-Saxon manuscripts that I have seen I have not found a single picture of a crucifix, and while there is plenty of evidence that crucifixes were known in England before the Norman invasion, they were certainly not in use during the whole of the Anglo-Saxon period, and it is useful for our purpose to make some distinction.

(e) The Crucifix

As early as the fifth century there were beginnings of a tendency to represent Christ's person without relation to the cross. To the early Christian a realistic representation of the person of Christ would have savored of idolatry, and to represent him crucified, an act of sacrilege. But there was evidently a craving for some visible representation of the Atonement. At first the Lamb was used as the symbol of the Divine Sacrifice, employed in conjunction with the cross in a great many varieties of combination,[2] which reached their climax in the eighth and ninth centuries.[3]

But long before the eighth century another step had been taken. The cross was depicted in union with ideal portraits of the Savior, generally as a beautiful youth holding a cross in his hands.[4] In a manuscript of the sixth century a cross is drawn with a bust of Christ surmounting the top, and similar figures have been found in painting and mosaic.[5]

[1] 2. 232.
[2] Walcott, *Sacred Archæology,* p. 341; Didron, *Christ, Icon.* s. v. Lamb. [3] Ibid.
[4] Seymour, p. 158.
[5] Jameson, *History of Our Lord,* p. 320.

The transition from this ideal portrait of Christ over the cross to the entire figure outstretched and nailed thereon is a short one. The earliest picture of the crucifixion comes from the Orient; it is in a Syrian manuscript of the Gospels, dating from the year 586.[1] Not long after this, Pope Gregory the Great presented Theodolinda with a cross of gold on which the crucifixion is represented in enamel, the work of a Greek artist.[2] But pictures of the crucifixion were still very rare a hundred years after. The council ' Quinisextum in Trullo,' of the year 692, gave formal sanction to the custom of representing the actual figure of Christ instead of the symbolical figure of the Lamb,[3] but most representations of the crucifixion were still in painting or mosaic.

So, as we have seen, at the time of the mission of Augustine representations of the crucifixion must have been extremely rare, as it was nearly a hundred years after when the custom received the formal sanction of the Church. It is therefore absurd to call the silver cross that figured in the procession of Augustine a crucifix—as Miller does, for example, in his translation of Alfred's Bede. The passage in the Ecclesiastical History is as follows:

'Bǣron Crīstes rōde tācen, sylfrene Crīstes mǣl mid him.'

Here ' Crīstes rōde tācen sylfrene Crīstes mǣl,' translates Bede's 'crucem (pro vexillo ferentes) argenteam.' Miller translates the Old English thus: ' They bore the emblem of Christ's cross—*and had a silver crucifix with them*'—a translation not warranted in the least.[4]

The faith was introduced into England before crucifixes were known, and when pictures of the crucifixion, even in painting or mosaic, were very rare. Still it is too much to say, with the writer in the *Dictionary of Christian Antiquities*, that up to the time of Charlemagne ' all representations of the crucified form of our Lord alone, as well as pictures,

---

[1] Cutts, *Hist. Early Christ. Art*, p. 198.
[2] Martigny, p. 227.
[3] ibid.
[4] Bede, *Eccles. Hist.*, E. E. T. S. 95-96, p. 59.

reliefs, and mosaics, in which that form is the central object of the scene, may be considered alike symbolical, and without historical realism or artistic appeal to the emotions.' Bede [1] mentions among the treasures brought by Benedict Biscop from Rome in 678 a painting of the serpent raised up by Moses, paralleled by one of the Son of Man ' in cruce exaltatum.' This is the earliest example of a picture of the crucifixion in England that we have; still it is not a crucifix.

One of the earliest examples of an actual crucifix in western Europe is that which Charlemagne presented to Pope Leo III, of the date 815.[2] But that it was not an object of worship in the Gallican church of that time seems clear from the tenor of the famous capitularies on the subject of image-worship, published by the Emperor some years before.

The earliest mention of a crucifix in England is one in the legend of St. Dunstan,[3] belonging therefore to the tenth century. But it is not unlikely that after the final victory of image-worship in the great iconoclastic controversy, crucifixes gradually found their way into England during the latter part of the ninth century.

According to Lingard,[4] after the burning of the Abbey of Medeshamstede (Peterborough), and the massacre of the monks by the Danes, the victims were buried in one wide grave; on the surface a small pyramid of stone was placed, bearing a record of the disaster, and opposite the pyramid, to protect the spot from being profaned, a cross was erected on which was engraved the image of Christ. As the massacre took place in the year 870, it shows that the carving of an image upon the face of the cross was already practised in the latter part of the ninth century.

On stone crosses belonging in all probability to the tenth century is frequently carved a rude image of the Savior.[5]

---

[1] *Hist. Abb.,* Sec. 9, in *Op., Hist.,* ed. Plummer, p. 373.
[2] *Dict. Christ. Antiq.,* p. 514.
[3] *Vita S. Dunst.,* auctore Osberno; Rolls Ser. 63, 113.
[4] *Hist. Antiq.,* etc., 2. 234.
[5] *Brit. Arch. Journ.,* 44. 300.

In documents[1] of the late tenth and eleventh centuries there are references to the crucifix, showing that by that time it had come into general use. In the tomb of Edward the Confessor was found a golden crucifix.[2]

It is not improbable, as Rock supposes, that the image may have been carved on processional and archiepiscopal crosses in the tenth and eleventh centuries, though as yet I have found no evidence to prove it. But the altar-cross continued plain certainly till the Norman Conquest, and probably for several centuries after.

Ælfric makes no allusion to the crucifix, but orders his flock to pray to the cross,[3] and it is evident that in his day the cross was the significant thing, whether or not an image was upon it—and it was the cross that was adored. It was still, as in its ancient uses, the emblem of the Savior. This is further brought out by the Old English words for the cross, which wholly ignore the presence of an image. It is the '*rōd*'—the '*rood*' or '*cross*'; or the *Crīstesmǣl*, the symbol of Christ; a *rōde tācn* '*rood token*'; or '*Crīstestācn*,' and so on, not one of the terms having the special significance of a crucifix. The word '*Crīstesmǣl*' is most frequently translated 'crucifix,' but for no reason that I can discover. The word means only the 'symbol of Christ,' which is the precise significance of the cross in the early church. This word is frequently used to designate the plain cross-mark signed at the end of charters[4] to represent the sign of the cross, and, in short, is found over and over again where it must mean simply a cross.[5]

In conclusion, we may say that the crucifix was practically unknown in England before the ninth century and that it

---

[1] e. g. *A. S. Chron.* 1070; see also *AA. S. Ethelred, AA. SS. Boll. Junii* 4. 571, and *AA. SS. Boll. Junii* 2. 329 (Margaret of Scotland).

[2] *Archeologia* 3, 390.

[3] *Canons of Ælfric*, ed. Thorpe, *A. S. Laws*, p. 449.

[4] e. g. *A. S. Chron.* E. 656, 963.

[5] e. g. Oswald's Cross, Alfred's *Bede*, p. 154; sign of cross, *Lchdm.* 2. 294.

did not come into general use till about a hundred years before the Conquest.

(f) Ceremonial Honoring of the Cross

The two festivals of the cross, the Exaltation and the Invention (September 14 and May 3 respectively), were both observed in the Anglo-Saxon church, at least from a period which is covered by the Egbert *Pontificial,* since it contains benedictions for use on those days.[1] In the Anglo-Saxon church these were single feast-days; later in the Sarum use the Invention became a double feast.

The ceremony of the Adoration of the Cross was celebrated by the Anglo-Saxons, as by the rest of the Christian church, on Good Friday. The ceremony is given in full by Rock (v. 3, pt. 2, pp. 88 ff.),[2] but here we need only the opening. In the following quotation I have substituted ' cross ' for ' crucifix ' (which Rock uses throughout), for reasons already discussed:

' A muffled cross was held up by two deacons, who stood half-way between the choir and the altar. From this spot they carried this veiled rood toward the altar, before which they laid it down on a pillow. After due time this cross was unshrouded by the two deacons, who, in doing so, uttered in a low chant " Behold the wood of the Cross." Then barefoot, as he and all the other clergy were from the very beginning of the day's service, whoever happened to be the celebrant, whether bishop, abbot, or priest, came forward, and halting thrice on the way to throw himself on the ground, in most lowly wise kissed the cross. After him followed the clergy, then the people, to offer this same token of homage to their crucified Lord. All the while this kissing of the cross was going on, the choir sang the

[1] pp. 86, 89.
[2] Also, *Concordia* 2. 76 ff. (cf. Durand, *Rationale* 6. 77. 21, p. 229) and 182, 184 ff., 385, 665, 735, 833, 870, 895; *Durham Ritual* 93. 150.

anthems—*Ecce lignum crucis, Crucem tuam adoramus, Dum
Fabricator mundi,* and the hymn *Pange, lingua.*
' It was also the custom of the celebrant to repeat, besides
the seven penitential psalms, a prayer before the cross. All
the sacramentaries contain prayers to be said when the
cross is adored.'

Following the ceremony of adoration on Good Friday
was another, which, according to Rock, was ' not insisted on
for general observance,' but was a rite which might follow
the prayer of adoration. This ceremony is worth quoting
because it shows how literally the cross was the ' symbol
of Christ.' In this very simple liturgical drama the cross
plays the role of Christ's person in the burial and resurrection. I quote the description in Fosbroke's *British Monachism:*[1]

> Because on that day was the burial of our Savior, an image of a
> sepulchre was made on a vacant side of the altar, and a rail drawn
> around it, where the cross was laid until it should have been wor-
> shiped, . . . The deacon's bearers wrapping it in the places where it
> had been worshiped, i. e., kissed, brought it back to the tomb, sing-
> ing certain psalms, and there laid it with more psalmody. There it
> was watched till the night of Easter Sunday, by two, three, or four
> monks singing psalms. On easter day, the seven canonical hours
> were to be sung in the manner of the canons; and in the night, be-
> fore matins, the sacrists, because our lord rested in the tomb, were
> to put the cross in its place. Then during a religious service four
> monks robed themselves, one of whom in an alb, as if he had some-
> what to do, came stealingly to the tomb, and there, holding a palm
> branch, sat still till the responsory was ended; then the three others,
> carrying censers in their hands, came up to him, step by step, as if
> looking for something. As soon as he saw them approach, he began
> singing in a soft voice, ' Whom seek ye?' to which was replied by
> the three others in chorus, ' Jesus of Nazareth.' This was answered
> by the other, ' He is not here, he is risen.' At which words the
> three last, turning to the choir, cried, 'Alleluia, the Lord is risen.'
> The other then, as if calling them back, sang, ' Come and see the
> place,' and then rising, raised the cloth, showed them the place with-

---

[1] A fairly close translation from the *Regularis Concordia Monachorum* ascribed to Dunstan, or with more probability to Ethelwold
(*Anglia* 13. 426-428).

out the cross, and linen cloths in which it was wrapped. Upon this
they laid down their censers, took the cloths, extended them to show
that the Lord was risen, and singing an anthem, placed them upon
the altar.

(g) *Private Worship*

In the Canons of Ælfric it is written[1] that Christians
should " pray to the holy rood so that they all greet the rood
of God with a kiss." But in his sermon on the Invention
of the Cross, Ælfric says : ' Christian men truly should bow
to the hallowed rood in the name of Jesus, for although we
have not that on which he suffered, its likeness is neverthe-
less holy, to which we can ever bow in our prayers to the
Mighty Lord who suffered for men ; and the rood is a
memorial of his great passion, holy through him though it
grew in a wood. We ever honor it for the honor of Christ,
who redeemed us with love through it, for which we thank
him as long as we live.'[2]

Moreover, it is written in the life of Alcuin[3] that whenever he saw the cross he bowed towards it, whispering these
words :[4] ' Tuam crucem adoramus, Domine, et tuam glori-
osam recolimus passionem.' Ceolfrith also, ' worshiped '
the cross which accompanied him when he set out from
Wearmouth for Rome. The deacons of his church went
with him on board the vessel, carrying lighted tapers and a
golden cross. When he had reached the other side of the
river ' he worshiped the cross, then mounted his horse and
departed.'[5]

It is evident from these examples alone that the worship
of the cross was not restricted to the ' adoration ' of Good
Friday, or even to the customary devotion paid to it in the
church,[6] but was practised by individuals in private.

[1] *A. S. Laws,* ed. Thorpe, p. 449.
[2] *Hom.,* 2, 306.
[3] *Vita,* etc., *Patrolog. Lat.* 100.
[4] The same prayer is in the *Durham Ritual.* p. 140.
[5] Bede, *Hist. Abb.* 2. 392, ed. Giles.
[6] *Durham Rit.,* pp. 149-150.

(h) The Nature of the Adoration

But whatever this adoration may have amounted to in practice, in theory it was not a worship of the cross itself, Ælfric concludes his sermon for the fifth Sunday in Lent thus: ' Through the tree came death to us, since Adam ate the forbidden apple; and through the tree came to us again life and redemption. In the holy rood-token is our blessing, and to the cross we pray, *by no means however to the tree itself, but to the Almighty Lord* who hung for us on the holy rood.'[1] So also Alcuin, who was foremost in honoring the cross, says: ' We prostrate ourselves bodily before the cross, mentally before the Lord; we venerate the cross by which we were redeemed, and we invoke him who redeemed us.'[2] This is clearly indicated by the prayer of the Adoration ceremony, already quoted, and the same thing is true of all other prayers ' to be said when the cross is adored.' The cross was the visible symbol of Christ; to this the worshiper bowed his head, but in the words of his prayer he invoked Christ.

However, it was a distinction difficult to maintain, and, as we shall find later, the cross became, probably as a result of this adoration, endowed with a personality to the point of being deified. In the early days of the faith the Christian repudiated the name of ' cross-worshiper,' but at the time which we are studying there was no longer reproach in the name. Aldhelm, for example, calls himself ' worshiper of the cross ' as a synonym for Christian.[3]

III. THE SIGN OF THE CROSS

The visible, material cross—*crux exemplata*—was not more important in the service of the church and the life of the Christian than the cross in its invisible or imaginary

[1] *Homilies* 2. 240.
[2] *Patrolog. Lat.* 75. 479.
[3] Pref. *Liber de Virgin., Patrolog. Lat.* 89. 103. Lingard 2. 107 gives references to the author of the Life of St. Willibald, and one of his correspondents, who uses the same term.

form, the 'sign of the cross' or *crux usualis*. Long before
the Christian dared to expose the symbol of his Lord in out-
ward, visible form, this was his countersign among his
fellow-disciples, his profession of faith before his enemies,
and his comfort and resource for every event, from the
trivial details of daily life to the deepest experiences of joy
or sorrow.

The original method of making the sign was to mark a
cross on the forehead with the thumb or fore-finger.[1] The
same mark could also be applied to blessing parts of the
body or other objects. In the sixth century another method
had risen into favor, in which the hand was raised to the
forehead, then drawn down to the heart, then to the left
shoulder, then to the right.[2] These were the two chief
methods—the small cross and the large cross—and there
were in the making of the latter a variety of methods of
holding the fingers, with a corresponding variety of sig-
nifications.

Both the small and the large cross were known in
Anglo-Saxon England. In the Egbert *Pontifical* the sign
is referred to as made *cum pollice* or *cum digito*.[3] Alcuin,
in speaking of the celebration of the Mass, evidently has the
cross in mind.[4] Boniface says: 'Habete Christum in corde,
et signum sanctæ crucis in fronte,'[5] and there are many
other references to this small cross upon the brow. According to William of Malmesbury's account of the Life of St.
Dunstan, this usage persisted in his day; for, as the saint
beheld Edgitha making the sign frequently upon her brow,
he cried, 'May that hand never decay!' And it was proved

[1] Kraus, *Realencyl. Christ. Alt.* p. p. 252.
[2] ibid.
[3] Egbert, *Pontif.,* pp. 36. 40.
[4] *Patrolog. Lat.* 100. 499: 'Crucem in fronte ponit diaconus, . . .
deinde in pectore.'
[5] *Opera,* ed. Giles, 2. 97.

after her death that the hand that made the sign remained
uncorrupted.[1]

Possibly the long life of this earlier use among the
Anglo-Saxons was due to the great number of legends with
which they were familiar which went back to the time
when the small cross was the only one in use; and also to
their adherence to rituals which were probably of very early
origin. But in the Blickling Homilies Christians are ex-
horted to bless all their bodies seven times with Christ's
rood-token.[2] In this the reference seems to be to the large
cross. Ælfric describes this as follows: ' A man may wave
about wonderfully with his hands without creating any
blessing, unless he make the sign of the cross. In that case
the fierce fiend will soon be frightened on account of the
victorious token. With three fingers one must bless himself for the Holy Trinity.'[3]

By the same authority we are told that the sign of the
cross in its origin goes back to Christ himself;[4] therefore,
since the Savior gave this token to his disciples, it had the
added dignity of a sacrament.

(a) The Sign in Ritual

The idea which underlay the use of the sign in the ritual
of the church was its power to purify the person or object
so blessed from the presence of evil spirits. This is brought

---

[1] Zöckler, p. 247, refers to this princess as an example of self-in-
flicted cross-torture, that she scratched the sign of the cross upon
her forehead an innumerable number of times with her sharp thumb-
nail. The only reference to anything of the sort whatever is the
passage mentioned above, wherein I find no hint of anything beyond
the usual crossing of the forehead. The passage is as follows:
' Viderat eam sanctus Dunstanus in consecratione basilicæ beati
Dionisii . . . pollicem frequenter dextrum protendere et signum
crucis fronti a regione pingere.' Wm. Malm., *Gesta Pontif.,* p. 189.
[2] p. 47.
[3] *Homilies* 1. 462.
[4] ibid. 2. 508. Also *Gospel of Nicodemus,* ed. Thwaites, p. 17:
'And se Hælend . . . rōde tācen ofer Adam geworhte.'

out by what Alcuin and Wulfstan have to say on its use in baptism. ' The breast also,' says Alcuin, ' is anointed with the same oil, so that the entrance for the devil is closed by the sign of the Holy Cross. The shoulder-blades are also signed, so that there may be a defense on all sides.'[1] Wulfstan says: ' In the christening that one performs previous to baptism there is great significance. When the priest christeneth, he breathes on the man, then signs him *in modum crucis.* After that, through God's might, the devil becomes speedily much discouraged.'[2]

Of the use of the sign in particular rites there is no need of discussion here. As far as I can discover, its use in the various ceremonies of the Anglo-Saxon church was the same as in the Mother Church. It was used a countless number of times, giving sanctity and weight to every rite— common to all and uniting them all.

But its usefulness was not confined within the walls of the church or monastery. It was the Christian's ready weapon for every time of need. Alcuin says, explaining why Christ chose crucifixion rather than some other form of death: ' He did not wish to be stoned or cut down by a sword, because we should not be able to carry always with us stones or a sword with which we should be protected. But he chose the cross, which is expressed by an easy movement of the hand, and with which we may be protected against the wiles of the enemy.'[3]

It was first of all a defense against the assaults of the devil. Bede, in his letter to Bishop Egbert, advises him to remind his flock ' with what frequent diligence to employ upon themselves the sign of our Lord's cross,'[4] and so to fortify themselves and all they have against the continued snares of unclean spirits. He recommends it especially as a safeguard against evil thoughts.[5] Alcuin says that the first act

[1] *Patrolog. Lat.* 100. 127. [2] *Hom.,* p. 33.
[3] *Patrolog. Lat.* 75. 428. [4] *Opera,* ed. Giles, 1. 135.
[5] ibid. 9. 270.

upon waking in the morning should be to mark upon the
lips the sign of the cross.[1] Wulfstan says: 'Be ever thy
food and thy rest directed of God and blessed with the holy
cross.'[2]

If the sign had not as yet become prescribed in the rite of
supreme unction, the dying man himself fortified his passing spirit by the sign of hope. Bede, in his story of Cædmon's death, tells how the holy man, 'after he had signed
himself with the sign of the holy cross, laid down his head
upon the pillow, and fell asleep for awhile, and so in quiet
ended his life.'[3]

Belief in the efficacy of this sign was supported by a
great body of legends in which its powers as a talisman are
most conspicuous.[4] They point the moral that safety de-
mands that it should accompany every act of life, and show
that devils, the forces of nature, and the ills of the flesh,
are all subject to the wonder-working sign.

It is only to be expected that, if so many had been healed
of their ills in the past, the faithful and believing should
look for its salutary powers for their own benefit in the
present. So, very naturally, the sign of the cross invaded
the province of medicine. The position of the church in
regard to disease and cure by natural means was that dis-
eases were the work of demons, that mediums are useless
and contrary to what St. Ambrose declared was 'celestial
science—watching and prayer.'[5] Among the Anglo-Saxons,
however, the use of natural remedies was by no means
despised, as the three volumes of Cockayne's *Anglo-Saxon
Leechdoms* testify. Mingled with these natural remedies,
however, are prescriptions in which theology also has a

[1] *Patrolog. Lat.* (*Lib. de Psalm.*) 101. 468.
[2] *Homilies*, p. 250.
[3] *Eccles. Hist.* 4. 24.
[4] e. g. *Blickl. Hom.*, p. 243; Ælfric, *Hom.* 3. 170; Alfred's *Bede*,
p. 402, et al.
[5] Quoted by A. D. White, *Hist. Conflict Science and Theology*
2. 26.

find any reason for its being there. It comes sometimes in the middle of a charter, and it occurs frequently on the margin, especially on a line which contains the name of a king.[1] It appears sometimes in the middle of a word, especially ' cru+cis,'[2] and always in the middle of the word in the sacramentary where a sign of the cross is to be made, as, for example, ' bene+dicere,' ' sancti+ficare.'[3] It appeared also in literary documents, a custom that long survived the Conquest, the manuscript of the Morality *Everyman,* for example, beginning with a cross. In the manuscript of the ' Nine Herbs Charm,' also, the cross is on the margin on a line with the word ' worm,' perhaps for the same reason that the writer would have crossed himself at the name of the devil.

Nor was it restricted to writings on parchment; it is found preceding inscriptions on stone slabs and crosses, and on inscribed rings and jewels.[4] Apparently in all of these the use of the cross is a sort of invocation or ' saying grace,' a pious custom without rules or restrictions. Possibly it may have been used merely as a sign of good luck.

(d) The Cross on Coins

The cross had been stamped on the coins of Christian emperors of Rome from a very early time,[5] and its use in Anglo-Saxon England was probably introduced with the establishment of the Faith. At all events, it appeared upon coins as early as the *sceata* of Egbert, King of Kent (665 —674). These crosses were small and in relief, and therefore are evidently not applied for the purpose of dividing the coins into fragments, as was the case with the penny of later times. The significance of the cross on Anglo-Saxon coins

[1] *Codex Dipl.* 2. 296-7.
[2] e. g. Egbert, *Pontif.* 7.
[3] e. g. *Ibid.,* 16-17.
[4] e. g. Ruthwell Cross, Minster Lovel Jewel.
[5] According to Martigny, from the fourth century.

was doubtless the same as when it was first applied to the coins of Roman emperors, namely, that, by its sanctity, it pledged the value of the coin. It is akin, therefore, to the use of the cross as an oath on legal documents.

In this connection may be mentioned a few miscellaneous forms of oath in which the cross plays a part, though in these cases it is not the *sign* of the cross. Wulfstan swears by the cross in a way that is not found elsewhere among Anglo-Saxon writers. He says: ' We swear by the great power of Almighty God, and by the Holy Rood on which Christ suffered for the salvation of men, that what we say is true.'[1]

Among the laws for the taking of oaths, we find the following which mention the cross. Archbishop Egbert sets as a test of innocence of an accused person that he ' place above his head the cross of the Lord, and testify by the Eternal that he is free from guilt.'[2] Another form of oath, also, among Egbert's decrees, was to speak the vow with hands ' outstretched upon a rood.'[3] If an oath not spoken upon a cross was broken, the penalty was one-third of the penalty if the oath had been sanctified by the cross. In the hot-water ordeal, also, the prisoner was required to ' kiss the Book and Christ's rood-token.'[4]

The idea of the sacredness of the emblem is brought out in another way by the making of the sign of the cross in posture. The ancient method of prayer, that of standing with outstretched arms ' in the likeness of a cross,' was transplanted into England, and was used as the most solemn form of invocation. Bede tells how Cuthbert, at the request of Hereberht, prayed that both might die at the same time; ' then the bishop extended himself in the form of a cross and prayed, and at once was informed in spirit that the Lord had granted the request.'[5] It is related of St.

[1] *Hom.*, p. 214.
[2] Thorpe, *A. S. Laws*, p. 320.
[3] *Ibid.*, p. 229.
[4] Thorpe, *A. S. Laws*, p. 96.
[5] *Eccles. Hist.*, p. 372. Plummer.

Ecgburga that, when she wanted to show St. Guthlac how strongly she urged him to accept her gift of a leaden coffin and a winding sheet, having spoken her wish she stretched out her arms as if in prayer—'adjurans per nomen terribile superni Regis, seque ad patibulum Dominicæ crucis erigens' —as a sign of her earnest insistence. She instructed her messenger to deliver her message to Guthlac, and then place himself in the position of the cross, as he had seen her do.[1] This custom appears also in one of the charms, which directs the sufferer to 'chant *benedicite* with outstretched arms.'[2] Another method was, instead of standing, to kneel with the arms extended wide; and a third was to lie prostrate, with the arms extended as before.

But to stand or kneel *in cruce* was also a form of penance. Among the Canons of Edgar it is directed that the penitent 'cry to God and implore forgiveness, . . . and kneel frequently in the sign of the cross.'[3] But it was not till the eleventh century that we find the custom of laying the dying man outstretched upon a cross of ashes, and it was not till the Norman invasion that we find this famous mediæval custom to have been generally practised.

Up to this point we have found little or nothing peculiarly national in the aspect of cross-worship among the Anglo-Saxons, but there yet remain two forms, the pictorial arts and literature, which afford a wider opportunity for originality than ritual or legend.

IV. THE CROSS IN ART

(a) The Monogram

Before passing to the cross, a word may be said in regard to the use of the monogram. The Chi Rho monogram, as we have seen, was gradually supplanted by the cross, as the need of symbolism, and the actual scenes of crucifixion, disappeared. But it was often met with as an accompani-

---

[1] AA. SS. *Aprilis* 2, 47, q. Rock.   [2] *Lchdm.* I. 400.
[3] Thorpe, *A. S. Laws*, p. 415.

ment of the cross, and as one of the symbols of the faith, long after it had yielded to the cross.

In the England of the Anglo-Saxons, the monogram had but little meaning. It had already been outgrown by the church before Christianity was introduced among them. It was doubtless seen in Rome on old monuments, and it might easily have been transferred as a mark of the Faith upon Christian stones or documents in England. But these examples are comparatively rare. The church of Jarrow contained a tablet commemorating its original founding, in which the inscription is headed by the Chi Rho monogram. This event occurred in 686, and it is quite possible that Benedict Biscop may have imported the device along with the paraphernalia that he brought from Rome. But in the earliest documents it is not to be found, and the simple cross is used instead. It appears first in a charter dated 770,[1] taking the place of what might be termed the 'invocation' cross, at the very beginning of the document. It occurs only once again in a charter of the years 779,[2] where it is combined with the letters A and Ω. It occurs most frequently, however, in the charters of Edgar, in the tenth century. Just why it should have been fashionable in clerical circles at that particular time it would be difficult to say, unless it was a belated influence of the court of Charlemagne. In the time of Charlemagne the use of the monogram was revived, through the quickened interest in the early history of the Church, a result of that revival of letters of which his court was the centre. The Chi Rho, with the swastika and a few unimportant devices, occurs rarely on the coins of Anglo-Saxon kings.[3] The swastika may have been adopted from Teutonic paganism, where, as some say, it stood for the hammer of Thor, the so-called *hamarsmark*. On the other hand, more probably it may have come from an early Christian use kept alive in

[1] *Codex Dipl.* 2. 145.   [2] *Ibid.* 164.
[3] *Catalog Eng. Coins, A. S. Series*, Vol. 1, plate 47.

Ireland, as it is seen in some of the Irish illuminations. The same device is found also on some of the stone carvings of the Anglo-Saxon period, in the so-called ' Celtic ornament.' [1]

But the use of the Chi Rho disappeared in Europe at the end of the fifth century, [2] and the remains in England—excepting, of course, the late revival of its use on manuscripts referred to above—belong as a rule to British rather than to Anglo-Saxon Christianity. The emblem to which the Anglo-Saxons devoted their art was the cross.

(b) Monumental Crosses

The most striking feature of the art of the cross—and, indeed, of all art among the Anglo-Saxons—is the monumental cross of stone.

Monumental crosses had been set up in public places in Rome before the mission of Augustine. But for the origin of the ornamented stone crosses of the Anglo-Saxon we turn, not to Rome, but to the ancient customs of the pagan Celts.

The most exhaustive study of these stone crosses that I have found has been made by Mr. J. R. Allen in the pages of the *British Archæological Journal,* and I have followed his authority wherever I have been unable to verify his conclusions for myself.

According to him, the origin of stone crosses of the Anglo-Saxon era may be traced back to the gigantic monoliths of the preceding Celtic period. These rough, unhewn obelisks were erected to commemorate chieftains—probably such as were slain in battle—and the value of the tribute lay in the great size of the stone and the consequent difficulty in raising it.

At a later period, when writing became known, the rough pillar was inscribed, in oghams, or in debased Latin characters, on a smooth side of the stone. After the introduction of Christianity the symbol of the cross was, also, often en-

[1] e. g. Calverley, p. 128.   [2] Martigny s. v. *Monogram.*

closed in a circle, the emblem of eternity. From these rude Christian monuments developed the graceful and elaborately ornamented crosses of the later period. The tall shaft of these is all that remains of the obelisk, and, crowning this, the cross, generally coupled with the circle. 'Some of the oldest of these monuments,' says Allen, 'are still covered with interlaced work, but without the cross. A celebrated example is at Llantwit Major in Glamorganshire. . . . The Penrith crosses are a good instance of pillar-stones, differing very little in outline from the pagan monoliths.'[1]

The remains of the stone monuments which bear the cross incised, or are cruciform, may be roughly divided into two classes. First, the Pillar-Stones just described, which are only removed from the pagan monolith by the incision of the cross, but which sometimes bear other Christian marks or inscriptions. Secondly, the Interlaced Crosses, which are stones carved into the shape of the cross, erected upon a base, with more or less elaborate ornament upon the sides. Sometimes there is also an inscription, but both the lettering of the inscriptions and the details of ornament vary according to the locality. Let us examine these two classes in detail.

1. *Pillar-Stones.* These rude pillar-stones belong to the period when paganism was being superseded by Christianity. They are most common in Ireland; in Wales there are a hundred and seven; in Scotland, five; in Dorset, Devon, and Cornwall, thirty. Their geographical distribution points to their Celtic origin, with Ireland for their home.

The characteristics of this class are as follows. The stone is in its natural state, without dressing and without ornament. The cross is incised, and of the simplest form, generally two lines crossing at right angles, often inclosed in a circle. The inscription is in debased Latin capitals, or

[1] *Brit. Arch. Journ.* 34. 353.

in the Celtic language, in oghams. It is impossible to assign dates to these, as none of the names inscribed are known to history.

'That these rude pillar-stones belong to the transition period between paganism and Christianity is,' says Allen, 'almost certain, as they are only found either in connection with semi-pagan remains or upon the earliest Christian sites.' They bear still further evidence of Christianity: some have the Chi Rho monogram; some of the names mentioned are Scriptural or distinctly Christian; and some of these are specified as church-officers, as bishops, and as priests; and, finally, *Requiescat in Pace,* a formula that is purely Christian, is also found, besides the customary *Hic Jacet.*

These stones must be regarded as the oldest Christian monuments in the British Isles. They belong to a period antedating the Christian art of the Anglo-Saxons, and to a different race. They stand in an introductory position to the more important art of the cross-monument, introduced later among the Anglo-Saxons by Christian artists from Ireland. This is represented in our second division of Interlaced Crosses.

2. *Interlaced Crosses.* This term is applied by Allen, 'because,' he says, 'the leading feature in the ornament is a variety of patterns formed of interlacing hands or cords. The characteristics of this class are entirely different from those of the rude pillar-stones, and are as follows: 1. The stone is carefully dressed, and cut out into the shape of a cross, and often fixed into a stone socket. 2. There is a profusion of ornament of a kind described hereafter, generally arranged in panels enclosed in a bead or cable molding. 3. The formulas of these inscriptions are more varied, and generally to the effect that "A erected this cross to B; pray for his soul." 4. The language and lettering vary with the locality; the language being either Latin, Celtic, or Scandinavian, and the letters Irish minuscules and oghams (similar to the manuscripts of the same period) or

the runic letters of Northern Europe.' These crosses are found at over 180 different localities in Great Britain, varying anywhere from two or three to twenty-one feet in height.

The art of these stones is Christian; springing from Ireland, and spreading thence with the diffusion of the faith into Wales, Scotland, and England. It was considerably modified by the locality to which it was transplanted. For example, in the Isle of Man, and parts of Cumberland, Derbyshire and Yorkshire, the Celtic styles are mingled with Danish.[1] In the south of England the Saxon predominates.

'In purely Irish art,' says Allen,[2] 'the geometrical ornament consists of three separate kinds, namely, spiral-work, key-patterns, and interlaced work. Of these, the spiral-work is the most typically Celtic, and is copied from the British metal work of pre-Christian times, the spiral, with expanded trumpet-shaped ends, being unknown outside the stones in Ireland and Scotland, and in a few of the manuscripts executed in England and by Irish monks abroad. Key-patterns occur on stones in Ireland, Scotland, and Wales, and the north of England. Interlaced work is found on stones throughout the whole of Great Britain.

'In Wales and the south of England interlaced work predominates; in the north of England interlaced work and key-patterns are found in combination; and in Scotland interlaced work, key-patterns, and spiral are blended together in about equal proportions. The Northumbrian stones are characterized by scrolls of great beauty. On the Scandinavian stones are found scaly dragons and runic inscriptions, also patterns formed by interlaced rings. On the stones showing Saxon influence the interlaced work is badly executed, and in Wales this is also sometimes the case.'

Besides these styles of ornament, there are found also symbolical devices—the *triquetra,* the emblem of the Trin-

---

[1] *Brit. Arch. Journ.* 41. 267.   [2] *Ibid.*

ity, and the five bosses, representing the five wounds of the Saviour; and pictorial representations of men, birds, trees and animals, many of which also probably bore a symbolical meaning.

3. *Pictorial*

Of the pictorial decorations the most common are the crucifixion, hunting scenes, and portraits of the Evangelists. In some instances of the crucifixion, as the Halton and Burton Crosses,[1] the Virgin and John are pictured standing on either side of a plain cross. As the custom of representing Christ's person on the cross became general, the crosses sometimes became crucifixes, with rude carvings of a body, generally clothed in a long tunic, and with arms outstretched at right angles to the body. This was almost without exception upon the western face of the crosses, in accordance with the traditions of the position of Christ on the cross. Sometimes, as on some of the Cornish crosses, these crucified figures were evidently added at a date later than that of the erection of the cross. Another method was to insert a picture of the crucifixion-scene in one of the panels of ornamentation upon the shaft of the cross. In all of these the figure-carving is of the simplest and crudest description.

The most curious feature of the pictorial ornament is the representation of warriors and huntsmen on horseback, together with stags and hounds. These are found most frequently on crosses in Scotland; they occur in Ireland, but there they are placed more frequently upon the base, rather than the shaft of the cross.

These pictures of the chase appear so often that it is believed that they do not refer to contemporary events, or the occupation of the person in whose memory the cross may have been erected, but that they have a mystic, Christian significance, as the chase is repeatedly referred to by the Fathers as a commonly accepted symbol of the conver-

[1] Calverley, pp. 89, 186.

sion of sinners.[1] But the meaning is still a matter of conjecture.

The Evangelists were held in high honor at this period, and on several of the crosses they are portrayed in their symbolical characters as part man and part animal. These symbolical beasts grow out of the descriptions in the visions of Ezekiel and of the Apocalypse, and first appear in Christian art in the fifth century.[2] It is a curious fact, by the way, that while these symbols of the Evangelists appear in almost all the Celtic manuscripts of the Gospels, they do not appear on any of the crosses of Ireland or Wales.

There is a figure upon the Halton Cross that is unique, and has apparently not the least mystical significance. It is a blacksmith working at his forge, with the tools of his trade depicted all about him. On the crosses at Leeds, Dumfallandy in Perthshire, and Kirkholm in Wigtonshire, there are smith's tools introduced in the ornament. It is not unlikely that these served to show the trade of the deceased person to whom the memorial cross was erected. This custom of carving the tools of the trade upon the tomb or coffinstone goes back to the vaults of the Catacombs, but in England it is not till the Norman period that the custom became at all general.

In addition to the types of picture already mentioned, there are figures of men and women, birds, trees, and animals, the significance of most of which it is difficult to conjecture; these are impossible to classify. Many of them seem to depict scenes of pagan myth intermixed with the Christian, a class which will be reserved for discussion later.

4. *The Date of the Interlaced Crosses*

Mr. J. R. Allen, from whom we have already quoted much, has, in his discussion of the age of the *Ilkley Crosses*, reviewed such evidence concerning the interlaced crosses

[1] *Brit. Arch. Journ.* 42. 343. [2] *Ibid.,* p. 336.
[3] *Brit. Arch. Journ.* 46. 341.

of Great Britain and Ireland as gives any clue to their age, and arranged them according to the centuries in which they belong.

According to this table, five crosses belong to the seventh century, three to the eighth, while to the ninth belong all the crosses of the Isle of Man, two English crosses, two Scotch, and several Irish. To the tenth century he ascribes most of the Irish crosses, and to the eleventh and twelfth a few unimportant Irish crosses and slabs.

But this geometrical interlaced ornament, as we have already seen, was Irish in its origin, or at least it was so developed in Ireland as to gain a thoroughly national character. Then it was communicated to the Anglo-Saxons by Irish artists. It was used at first for manuscript decoration, and reached its perfection about the end of the seventh century in such work as that of the Lindisfarne Gospels. But the earliest dated stone in Ireland that bears any ornament whatever of this sort, is the tombstone of an abbot of Clonmacnois, who died in 806.[1] This has a single Greek fret around the cross. In Celtic metal-work there is no trace of this ornament before the ninth century, and the famous high crosses of Ireland, the best specimens of this kind of art, belong, undoubtedly, to the tenth.[2]

It seems strange, therefore, since Ireland was the teacher of England in these arts of ornament, that England should possess ornate crosses in the seventh century, covered with highly elaborated Celtic ornament, when Ireland herself had no trace of anything of the sort, either in stone or metalwork, before the ninth century, while her best specimens belong to a period a full century later.

Upon examining the evidence for the dating of the seventh and eighth century crosses in this list, we find that it is based entirely upon the reading of a name upon the cross. Granted, first, that the reading is correct (which in con-

[1] *Brit. Arch. Journ.* 41. 334.   [2] *Ibid.*, p. 336.

spicuous examples, as we shall see, it is not), the archæologist continues with two other assumptions: first, that
this name refers to a person of the same, or more often, of
a similar name known in history; and, secondly, that this
cross must have been erected immediately after that person's death.

In dating these crosses, Allen follows respectfully, though
doubtfully, the readings and conjectures of Stephens and
Haigh. But unfortunately these placed two of the most
elaborate and finished specimens in the seventh century, namely, the Bewcastle Cross and the Ruthwell
Cross. Upon the latter, Stephens read the inscription in
runes, *Caedmon me fawed,* which he interpreted ' Cædmon
made me; ' hence he assigned the cross to the time of Cædmon the poet. On the former he read, ' In the first year
of the king of this realm Ecgfrith; ' hence he set for it the
date 670.[1]

But Professor Cook, having made an investigation of the
verses inscribed on the Ruthwell Cross from the standpoint
of meaning, metre, diction, and phonology, reaches the conclusion that they must be a quotation from the eighth-cen-
tury poem, *The Dream of the Rood,* and gives the entire
matter of date its final word in his concluding paragraph:

On the basis of this phonological examination we have found
that, while the general aspect of the inscription has led many persons
to refer it to an early period, it lacks some of the marks of antiquity; every real mark of antiquity can be paralleled from the
latest documents. . . . We shall not hesitate, I believe, to assume that
the Ruthwell Inscription is at least as late as the tenth century. If
now we seek the opinion of an expert, Sophus Müller, on the ornamentation, . . . we shall find it to this effect: "The Ruthwell Cross
must be posterior to the year 800, and in fact to the Carlovingian
Renaissance, on account of its decorative features. The free foliage
and flower-work, and the dragons or monsters with two forelegs,
wings, and serpents' tails, induce him to believe that it could scarcely
have been sculptured much before 1000 A. D." Vietor has at length

---

[1] It may be remarked that Haigh made out a very different reading.
Archæol. Æliana, q. S. Bugge, p. 93, note.

proved that the *Caedmon me fawed* of Stephens' fantasy is non-existent, and we are free to accept a conclusion to which archæology, linguistics, and literary scholarship alike impel.[1]

The Bewcastle Cross is beyond question a product of[2] the same period as the Ruthwell, so that this also may be removed from the seventh to the end of the tenth century. With these may be grouped the Gosforth Cross also,[3] on account of its shape, size, and ornament. This, too, Stephens pronounced to be 'probably of seventh century date,' no doubt because it evidently belonged to the type of the Ruthwell Cross.

It is of the most importance that, instead of depending upon fancy and guesswork, we can determine with good reason the approximate date of an important cross like the Ruthwell. With this we can group others which have the same characteristics, and thus assign the close of the tenth century as an approximate date for the height of the development of the cross-monument in England. This tallies well with what we know of the cross-monument in Ireland.

There are two other guides.[4] First, as stated above, the scroll-and-foliage-element was derived from Frankish artists, who developed this style in the 'Carolingian Renaissance.' Secondly, the pictorial element (with the characteristic interlaced dragons or serpents) is a product of Scandinavian influence, and dates from the settlement and conversion of the Danes. These will help a great deal in determining the probable age of stones which bear no inscriptions whatever.

We have already disposed of the two most notable crosses which have been assigned to the seventh century. Let us examine the evidence for assigning other interlaced crosses to a period preceding the ninth century, when, as already noted, the interlaced ornament makes its first appearance on stone in Ireland.

[1] 'Notes on the Ruthwell Cross,' *Pub. Mod. Lang. Assoc. of America,* Vol. 17, No. 3.
[2] Bugge, p. 493.   [3] Calverley, p. 138.
[4] Westwood, Introd. v-ix; also *Arch. Journ.* 10. 278 ff.

The four remaining crosses which Mr. Allen assigns
to the seventh century are these, denoted by the locality in
which they are found. All four are in England: one at
Collingham, dated circa 651; Beckermet, 664; Yarm, 681;
Hawkeswell, 690.

Of the Collingham Cross, Allen says, it is 'inscribed in
runes to the memory of King Oswini, who was ruler of
the Deira in 651.' Here he follows Stephens,[1] who makes
it out: ' . . . Aeftar Onswini, cu . . . ' and refers it to
the King Oswini mentioned above. Anything deciphered
by Stephens from a practically illegible inscription may be
suspected after his reading of the Ruthwell Cross, to say
nothing of the assumption of the king in question. But in
this case the cross as depicted by Stephens has both the
marks of a late date already mentioned, for the scroll-work
and interlaced dragons are conspicuous in its ornament
at the expense of the earlier, purely geometric design. It
is certain, at all events, that this cross is not earlier than
the ninth century.

At Beckermet are two shafts of crosses, 'one of which,'
continues Mr. Allen, 'bears an inscription showing that it
marks the grave of Bishop Tuda. Bede mentions that
Tuda, Bishop of Northumbria, died of the plague in A. D.
664. . . . This cross is, therefore, probably one of the seventh century.' This reading was given by Rev. D. H.
Haigh, whom Stephens calls the 'learned Mr. Haigh,'[2] an
archæologist who could read on the Collingham Cross, for
example, eight lines of inscription, where even Stephens
himself could make out only the two words we have already
quoted. According to Mr. Haigh, the inscription on the
Beckermet cross reads as follows (translated):

> Here enclosed
> Tuda Bishop:
> the plague destruction before,
> the reward of Paradise after.[3]

---

[1] *Runic Monuments* I. 390.   [2] *Runic Monuments* I. 390, note.
[3] Calverley, p. 27.

'This, in conjunction with the story of Bede,[1] makes it seem inevitable that the cross belongs to the seventh century, and that it is, in fact, the burial stone of Bishop Tuda.'

This 'celebrated reading' was made in 1857. Two years later, Rev. John Maughan announced another reading and translation:

> Here beacons
> two set up
> queen Arlec
> for her son Athfeshar
> Pray for our
> souls.[2]

Then, after various attempts by different hands, R. Carr Ellison announced his reading in 1866:

> O, thou loved
> offspring Edith,
> little maid
> in slumber waned.
> Years XII. Pray ye for her soul.
> Year MCIII.

Finally in Calverley[3] is quoted the most recent version. Here the language is supposed to be 'Manx Gaelic,' and the author of this reading is a Mr. John Rogers:

> '(This cross was)
> made for
> John mac Cair
> he gone to
> rest in the keeping
> of Christ. Be gracious
> to him, O Christ.'

At this point the plague-stricken bishop of the seventh century has vanished rather completely, together with our confidence in any testimony from Mr. Haigh.

The fragment of a cross at Yarm may be dismissed

---

[1] *Eccles. Hist.* Bk. 3, chap. 26-27.
[2] *Archæologia Æliana* 6, 61, quoted by Calverley, p. 29.
[3] p. 31.

4

briefly. It is sufficient to quote the evidence in its favor. 'It bears an inscription showing that it was erected by " . . . berecht Bishop, in memory of his brother." Professor Earle, of Oxford, reads the name "Hireberecht"; but Professor Stephens makes it "Trumberecht" and identifies him with the Bishop of Hexham of that name, A. D. 681.' By similar 'identification' by the reading of 'St. Gacobus' on the shaft of a cross at Hawkeswell, it is supposed to commemorate a deacon of St. Paulinus mentioned by Bede. This concludes all the evidence for the existence of interlaced crosses before the eighth century.

Of the eighth century there are three, at Alnmouth, Harkness, and Thornhill. Of the Alnmouth fragment, Stephens gives a description on pages 461-2 of his *Runic Monuments*. All that he can make out is a few meaningless fragments of words, but Mr. Haigh (to quote Stephens) 'fills up the words thus,' and get an inscription which reads:

> (This is King E)Adulf's th(ruh)(grave-kist)
> (bid)(= pray)(for—the)Soul.
> Myredah me wrought
> Hludwyg me fayed (inscribed).

We have already seen something of Mr. Haigh's work at deciphering and 'filling up.' But because the forms of the letters on this fragment 'resembles those on the Ruthwell Cross,' he feels sure that it can not be later than the begining of the eighth century! The word *Adulf* that he reads and 'fills up,' he identifies, therefore, as the name of a King Aedulf of the early eighth century. This needs no comment.

The Harkness Cross fragments are on the site of an ancient monastery founded by St. Hilda of Whitby. Accordingly, on one, Mr. Haigh reads:

> Huaethburga, thy houses always remember thee, most loving mother. Blessed Aethilburga! For ever may they remember thee, dutifully mourning! May they ask for thee verdant rest, in the name of Christ, venerable mother.

On another,

> Trecea Bosa, Abbess Aethilburga pray for us.

These sound characteristic of Mr. Haigh. No. 3 is inscribed with the name ' Bugga.'

The persons named in this reading, who have been
' identified,' lived anywhere from the beginning to the end
of the eighth century. Stephens himself gives these fragments the dates 700-800. If we accept Haigh's reading,
it is perfectly reasonable to suppose that the stones
were erected in the ninth century, after the death of
the latest of the godly persons mentioned, who are asked
to pray for the souls of their friends who remain on earth.
However, there is no reason why we should accept a reading by Haigh until it has been confirmed by some one else.

For the two Thornhill fragments ascribed to the eighth
century, we have to depend again upon the readings of Mr.
Haigh.[1] Upon one he finds the name *Aethuini;* on another, the inscription: ' Eadred Isete aefte Eata Inne.' The
word *inne* presents difficulty at first, but as it is derived
probably from *innan,* ' to enter,' it must mean ' hermit,' i. e.,
a man who *enters* a cave. This is ' confirmed ' by a passage in Simeon of Durham. It is an entry, dated in the
middle of the eighth century, as follows: ' Eata obiit in
Craic apud Eboracum.' Of a date some twenty or twenty-
five years later, there is another entry: ' Etha anachoreta
feliciter in Cric obiit.' Doubtless if Etha died in Cric or
Craic, and was an anchorite, Eata, who died in the same
locality, must have been a hermit too, and probably ' they
were successive occupants of the same cell.' In the *Liber
Vitae* about the middle of the eighth century are the names
Aethelwini and Eadhelm. The former is undoubtedly the
same as the Aethwini of one fragment, and Eadhelm ' there
can be no difficulty in admitting as the full form of Eata.'
Hence, these stones belong to the eighth century. Still,

---

[1] *Yorkshire Arch. Journ.* 4. 426 ff.

the runes about Eata and Aethwini, Mr. Haigh admits, are
'not very legible.'

If we turn from this style of reasoning to the reproduction
of the stones themselves, we find the ornament on one side
is a conventional foliage, and on the other an interlaced
dragonesque design, both of which are accepted as the
marks of the ornament which, at any rate, belong to a time
after the Carolingian Renaissance and in the period of
Scandinavian influence.

So far we have found no trustworthy evidence for the
existence of the interlaced cross before the ninth century,
and there is nothing in the way of what would, at first,
seem the natural and reasonable supposition that the interlaced cross was a product of Irish influences, and that it
did not appear in England before the ninth century.

In our classification of crosses, we have made two divisions: the Pillar-Stones, with a simple cross incised, and the
Interlaced Crosses, with their cross-form and wealth of
ornament. But between these two lies an intermediary
class, where the monolith develops into the cruciform shape,
and is sometimes adorned with simple ornament. The
cross-fragment in Calverley, on page 81, another on page 6,
and a third on page 96, are probably examples of this class,
and there are a great many of them in Western Cornwall.
But they are unimportant for our consideration here, as
they simply bridge the step between the rude Pillar-Stones
and the Interlaced Crosses.

To contrast the plain incised cross upon the original pillar-stone with the elaborate ornament which adorned the
interlaced cross at the height of its development, I subjoin
Calverley's description[1] of the cross-column at Bewcastle:

The details are: *west* face near the top, remains of runes over an
oblong square-headed panel, containing the figure of S. John Baptist
bearing the nimbed Agnus Dei. Beneath this panel and over a much
larger central, oblong, circular-headed panel, are two lines of runes,
the upper line beginning with the sign of the cross and reading

[1] p. 39.

Gessus (Jesus), the lower one reading Kristus (Christ). This central panel contains the glorified figure of the great Christ, robed as a priest, bearing in His left hand the sacred roll, His right hand uplifted to bless, treading upon the lion and adder, and His holy head leaning slightly to the right hand surrounded with the circling halo. Below this central figure comes the principal inscription in nine lines of runes. Beneath this, in a wide, circular-headed panel, standing a little sideways, and looking toward the spectator's right hand, is a man holding on his left wrist his hawk, which has flown up from its perch beneath . . . These three figures are the only human representations on the cross. . . .

The details of the *south face* are: at the bottom an intertwined knot-ornament; above this a line of runes beginning with the sign of the cross; above this a very beautiful piece of double-scroll work, consisting of two grape-bearing vines with foliage and clusters, filling an oblong panel. Another line of runes appear above, and a smaller panel of knot-work above this, surmounted again by a panel filled with a single vine-scroll, bearing near the center an early sundial, whose principal time divisions are marked by a cross, and having rich fruit above. Another line of runes separates this panel from a third carving of knot-work, which with some more runes brings us to the top of the cross shaft.

The *north face* has also five panels. The central and largest panel, filled with chequers only, has above and below it and separated by a line of runes, a smaller panel, containing very elegant knot-work presenting elaborate specimens of the sacred sign of the Holy Trinity, the triquetra so constantly used in the early manuscripts. In the lowest compartment on this side are two conventional flower and fruit-bearing vine-scrolls of perfect design and exquisite workmanship, more nobly conceived than perhaps anything of the kind which is known in the land. The uppermost compartment contains a single such scroll. The two divisions—at the top and bottom of this side—containing these three Paradise Trees are separated from the knot-work divisions each by a line of runes. At the very top, preceded by three crosses, is another line of runes— Gessus (Jesus). . . . It will thus be seen that the chief face of the stone bears three sculptured figures, the central one being the Christ; that each of the two parallel sides show three divisions of interlaced work or geometrical design, and three conventional flower and fruit-bearing vines; and that the knot-work displays in various ways the sign of the Trinity.

The *east face* of the cross is filled with one great vine-scroll rising bodily from below and bearing many fruits which are being eaten by beasts and birds. A hound or fox devours a cluster near the ground, further up are two creatures of conventional character, and higher still two birds, hawk or eagle, and raven, while the two topmost fruits are nibbled by two squirrels.

During the eleventh century the interlaced cross declined, and perhaps in the profusion and mixture of all sorts of details in such a cross as described above may be seen the beginnings of the decline. The elaborate interlaced design of Ireland was never executed by Anglo-Saxon artists with the same skill as by the Irish. They were content to give the suggestion of interlacing, without the careful and conscientious carving of the Irish artists. It must be admitted that the Anglo-Saxons appear to have contributed nothing whatever to the development of artistic ornament upon the cross.

(c) The Use of the Monumental Cross

But the question of chief importance, perhaps, in connection with these stone crosses, is the part that they played in the life of the people.

1. *Memorial.* The ancient pagan monoliths that have been described were memorials erected in honor of some departed hero; and in the earliest Christian forms, the pillar-stone, with its cross and circle and simple inscription, served the same purpose. These stones, as already noted, belong to a Celtic area. With the retreat of the British disappeared the custom of erecting a tomb-cross over a grave. In Ireland, according to the *Tripartite Life of St. Patrick,*[1] it seems to have been the custom to raise the cross over the grave of every Christian; but in Anglo-Saxon England the horizontal slab was used instead, and it was not till the tenth century that the headstone cross was employed.[2]

But there were crosses erected to the memory of a saint, friend, or relative, which were not placed at the grave. The cross commemorative of Owen, the shaft of which is now in Ely Cathedral, is an example. It bears the simple inscription, ' *Lucem tuam Ovino da Deus et requiem.*'

[1] p. 325.
[2] Cutts' *Manual for the Study of Sepulchral Slabs,* p. 48.

Of a rather different class of memorial crosses are the following examples. In the life of St. Columba it is related that Ernan, an aged priest, tried to see Columba before he died, but while on his way fell upon the ground, and expired before fulfilling his desire: 'Hence on that spot before the door of the kiln, a cross was raised, and another cross was in like manner put up where the saint resided at the time of his death, which remaineth to this day.'[1]

In the story that Malmesbury tells of the burial of Aldhelm is a similar use. The saint had died at the distance of fifty miles from Glastonbury, and as the funeral procession set out for Glastonbury, where he was to be buried, at each stage of seven miles where the body rested, a cross was afterwards erected. At these crosses the sick were healed, and all seven of them, says the chronicler, were standing in his day, and were called 'bishop stones.'[2]

Simeon of Durham[3] mentions a stone cross erected by Bishop Ethelwold at Lindisfarne in memory of Cuthbert. Its top was broken off by the Danes when they pillaged Lindisfarne, but afterwards the broken part was fastened on with lead, and thereafter the cross was always carried about with the body of Cuthbert whenever it was moved. It came to be venerated by the Northumbrians in memory of Ethelwold and Cuthbert together. The writer says of the cross that 'to this day, standing on high in the cemetery of Durham minster, it shows to all who gaze upon it a memorial of both these pontiffs.'

Crosses were sometimes raised in memory of some great event. After Oswald's victory, the cross of wood remained upright upon the battle-field, and later a stone cross took its place. According to Lingard,[4] after the burning of the Abbey of Medeshamstede (Peterborough) and the massacre of the monks by the Danes, the victims were buried

---

[1] Adamnan, p. 38.
[2] *Gesta Pontif.*, p. 383.
[3] *Opera*, Rolls Series 1.
[4] *Hist. and Antiq.* 2. 234.

in one wide grave; on the surface, a small pyramid of stone was placed, bearing a record of the disaster, and opposite the pyramid, to protect the spot from being profaned, a cross, on which was engraved the image of Christ.

It should be added, however, that many of the crosses which are described as marking the site of a battle, or of a church council, are so described through a local tradition, or more often on pure supposition. Still, while genuine remains are rare, there is no doubt that the custom was known and practised.

2. *Mortuary*. Although the Anglo-Saxons did not place the head-stone cross on the grave till the tenth century, they were accustomed from a much earlier time to erect a cross in the churchyard. This was a custom of Christian Rome,[1] and was doubtless introduced by the Roman missionaries. At the consecration of the cemetery, this cross was erected, together with smaller ones at each of the four corners of the plot, corresponding to the points of the compass, to mark the boundaries. In the consecration service, the bishop began by making the circuit of the grounds with his clergy, chanting the litany. Then he read a portion of the service at the eastern cross, did the same at the southern, western, and northern crosses, and concluded at the cross in the centre.[2]

Although in the earlier period no crosses stood over individual graves, the stone slabs or the stone coffins in which the richer were buried were marked with the emblem of the Christian's hope. There were also small square stones called 'pillow stones,' which lay under the head of the deceased, and bore carved upon their surface the same emblem.[3] Some of these slabs show by their ornament that they are contemporary with the interlaced crosses. Others have no trace of it, and are probably earlier. Many of the interlaced crosses which remain to this day were probably graveyard crosses, as they are often found near the sites of Anglo-Saxon churches.

[1] Schaff-Herzog, 'Kreuz.'
[2] Lingard, *Hist. Antiq.* 2. 252, note.   [3] *Archæologia* 26. 480.

Some miscellaneous crosses connected with burial may be included here. According to Rock,[1] a cross and a book of the Gospels were laid across the body to preserve it from the attack of demons. Frequently buried with the corpse was a cross which, according to the same authority, was "generally of wood, with a sheathing of gilt metal."[2] King Edward the Confessor was buried with a golden crucifix.[3]

I have met but one instance of the so-called 'cross of absolution;' this was found in the tomb of Saint Birinus.[4]

3. *Boundary.* In the crosses of the graveyard, we noted four small crosses marking the limits of the ground. These were 'boundary crosses.' There are references in the terms contained in charters to various boundary crosses, in which they are referred to as a 'gilded cross,' a 'wooden cross,' a 'stone cross,' a 'red cross,' and sometimes merely a 'Christ symbol.'[5] These served to mark the limits of church property.

So the monks of Edmundsbury[6] erected four crosses, one at each extremity of the town, to define the limits of their authority, and Bishop Losinga[7] raised a cross at Norwich to serve as a boundary mark between the land of the church and the borough. St. Guthlac also set up a cross at Croyland as a boundary mark.

There is an Irish canon of the eighth century which directs that a cross should be set up on all consecrated grounds, not only to mark the bounds, but also to sanctify the spot. A few centuries later, in England, a law had to be passed forbidding men to set up a cross falsely upon their lands in order to pass them off as church property, and so evade taxation.[8]

To these boundary stones of the church land, the so-

[1] 2. 312.

[2] Lingard 2. 50.

[3] *Archæol.* 3, 390.

[4] Rock 1. 173, note.

[5] e. g. Earle, *Handbook,* p. 29; *Codex Dipl.* 2. 287.

[6] Dugdale, *Monasticon* 3. 99.

[7] *Ibid.*

[8] Seymour, p. 321.

called ' Rogations ' were made. The Rogation Days were the seventh of the calends of May,[1] and the three days before Ascension Day. In these Rogations, the clergy and all the parish walked in procession with candles and crosses, laid earth and grass upon the boundary stones, and offered prayers to avert pestilence.

4. *Sanctuary*. In the Irish canon quoted above, the cross served not only to mark the boundary but also to consecrate the land. It was so sacred an emblem that none would dare remove it as a landmark, and it made the ground upon which it stood holy. Hence it became a mark of sanctuary. Some churches, out of special reverence for the saints whose bones they possessed, had a peculiar privilege of sanctuary. 'A chair of stone, called the Frid, or Frith stool, was sometimes set near the shrine of certain saints, or the high altar; the churches of York, Hexham, and Beverley enjoyed this privilege, and in the last two these stools are still preserved. The rights of the Frith stool overshadowed the region for the distance of a mile, and guarded to the refugee the widest privilege belonging by charter to this sanctuary, as long as he chose to remain within bounds. Crosses marked the limits of safety. . . . This custom is noticed in the dying wish of St. Cuthbert, who desired to be buried at Farne, lest if buried at Lindisfarne his grave might become a place of refuge for runaways.'[2]

The fugitive who got within the protection of these sanctuary crosses was given a black robe with a yellow cross on his shoulder, in token of the shelter the symbol had given him.[3] The crosses themselves stood very high, so that the fugitive could see them from afar, and be guided to safety.

5. *The Standard Cross*. Probably the earliest use of the monumental cross in Anglo-Saxon England was that as a standard of the faith, and a centre for preaching the Gos-

---

[1] Canons of St. Cuthbert (747 A. D.) at Cloveshoe; q. *ibid*. p. 322.
[2] Rock 3, part 1, p. 365.
[3] Seymour, p. 220.

pel. The custom was practised in the conversion of the Britons, and continued many centuries. When St. Botulf went to found his monastery in the wilderness of Lincolnshire at about the middle of the seventh century, ' he and his companions, before they did anything else, planted the standard of the cross, and set up the ensign of heavenly peace in the cross of Christ.' [1]   In the life of St. Willibald it is written that ' it was the ancient custom of the Saxon nation, on the estate of some of their nobles and great men to erect, not a church, but the sign of the Holy Cross, dedicated to God, beautifully and honorably adorned, and erected on high for the common use of daily prayer.' [2]   Some of the crosses that remain to this day give evidence of serving as a place of general worship, with a bowl hollowed out of a stone upon the base for holding the sacred water, the remainder of the stone serving in all probability for an altar.[3]

This custom of raising the standard cross was doubtless introduced from Rome, and practised by missionaries of the faith generally. For example, Boniface complained of a Gallic bishop, Adalbert, who went about among the Franks, and ' seduced them with divers falsehoods, so that by setting up crosses in the fields and pulpits, he made all the people come together thither and forsake the public churches.' [4] Naturally, in order to attract the most attention and draw the largest crowd, the missionary selected for planting the cross the places of resort and the most conspicuous situations.   So crosses became frequently associated with wells and markets.

These first crosses set up by the missionaries were doubtless crude and frail, but later, especially where there was no church built and the cross had to serve for a place of worship, permanent and highly decorated stones were set up for the purpose.   These early standard crosses served also to consecrate the ground for the site of the church

[1] *Ecclesiologist* 8, 228.   [2] Cutts, *Parish Priests,* p. 24.
[3] *Ibid.*   [4] Boniface, *Opera* I. 117; cf. p. 122.

(according to the custom in the early church of Rome), whenever a church was built beside it to take its place as a centre of worship.

6. *Oratory Crosses.* Nor was the cross merely for public worship and the preaching of the Word; it was also a shrine for private supplication. On the highways and at cross-roads, especially in Cornwall, crosses were erected for the benefit of travelers. Some, evidently, were for the purpose of getting the prayers of wayfarers for the soul of the deceased to whom the cross was erected as a memorial, or for the one who erected the cross himself. For example, one cross is inscribed,

Alcne prepared this cross for his soul.[1]

Other stones served for an entire family; for example,

E. and G. wrought this family stone for Ælfric's soul and for themselves.[2]

These oratory crosses were erected, evidently, as a work of merit.

However, the divisions that we have followed are arbitrary at best. Almost any one of the crosses might have the functions of any or all of the rest, and there is no doubt that many of them served more purposes than one.[3]

The larger of these crosses were generally set up on three steps, symbolical of the Trinity, on which worshipers might kneel. The side of the cross which had the symbol of Christ incised, or bore the image carved, faced the west, with arms pointing north and south. Thus the worshiper turned his face to the east, and the ancient traditions of the position of Christ in the crucifixion were also preserved.

After the Norman conquest these stone crosses were

[1] *Brit. Arch. Journ.* 42. 313.

[2] *Brit. Arch. Journ.* 42. 313.

[3] e. g. the memorial cross of Cuthbert became a graveyard cross at Durham. See above.

broken up and used for building material, whenever they were conveniently to hand. The survivors of this Norman ruthlessness had to suffer, beside the ordinary ravages of time, the iconoclastic zeal of the Puritans, so that it is a marvel that so many beautiful examples of the Anglo-Saxon cross-monument exist to-day.[1]

(d) The Cross in Other Arts

Before concluding this discussion of the cross in Anglo-Saxon art, we should give at least a passing mention to the arts of illumination and of jewelry.

Naturally, the cross was constantly employed as a motive in the designs of the illuminated page. It appears constantly, now conspicuously, now in all sorts of disguises. Sometimes it is used merely in the border of a picture, and again it occupies the full space of the design. Of the latter, a most beautiful example is that given in a facsimile in Plate 12 of Westwood's *Irish and Anglo-Saxon Manuscripts,* a page taken from one of the most beautiful illuminations ever done in England, the Lindisfarne Gospels. It is wholly Celtic in character, and probably was done by Irish artists; at any rate, it came from an ancient seat of Irish culture.

According to the facsimiles which I have examined, the picture of the crucifixion on manuscripts belong to a late period, either the end of the tenth or the eleventh century. An Irish manuscript of the ninth century pictures the Crucified swathed in a conventional garment from head to foot, following the older style of the full tunic, with head erect and arms at right angles to the body.[2] Further, the wound is on the left side.

In the later Anglo-Saxon illuminations, however, a newer style is seen; the head inclines slightly to the right, the body is clothed only in a short tunic extending from the waist to the knee. The wound is on the right side, and the

---

[1] For a list of interlaced stone remains, compiled by J. R. Allen and G. F. Browne, see *Brit. Arch. Journ.* 41. 351.

[2] Westwood, *Irish and A.-S. MSS.*

arms are not stretched in a perfectly straight line from the shoulders. In all of these Christ is alive, though wounded; indeed, the early idea seems to have been that his wound was made before death, and, in fact, was the cause of death.[1] He does not wear a crown of thorns, but has always a halo, which is sometimes cruciform.

The custom of representing the Savior as dead was a later fashion, imported from the East. Kraus[2] cites, as a first example in Europe, a manuscript belonging to the year 1060. But in Westwood's collection[3] is a facsimile of a dead Christ upon the cross in an Anglo-Saxon manuscript attributed by him to the end of the tenth century. However, this custom was not generally followed for some two or three hundred years afterwards, when the transition from symbolism to realism had become complete.

Of the cross in jewelry little need be said. The cross invariably appears on rings with inscriptions, as the cross always accompanied inscriptions. It occurs also on a talismanic ring with a runic charm, perhaps with an added usefulness for good luck. But it was also employed for decorative purposes, notably in the 'Minster Lovell Jewel.'[4] It[5] appeared also on the base of drinking bowls, and the like. The cruciform fibulæ that belong to the Anglo-Saxon period seem to me of no significance in this connection, because the fibulæ of pagan times were often of the same shape.

Although the remains of the Anglo-Saxon goldsmith's art are scanty at best, it is interesting for our purpose to see that, few as they are, they also reflect the veneration for the cross.

[1] Ælfric, *Hom.* I. 216; *Christ* 1447 ff.
[2] *Realencycl. der Christ. Alterth.* p. p. 240.
[3] Plate 43.
[4] For excellent facsimiles of Anglo-Saxon jewelry, see the *Anglo-Saxon Review,* Dec., 1900, p. 170; June, 1900, p. 755.
[5] *Archæologia* 50, pt. 2, p. 406.

V.   LITERARY ASPECTS OF THE CROSS

(a) Theological Mysticism

The custom of searching for allegorical and prophetic types in Scripture was zealously practised by Anglo-Saxon scholars, especially by Bede.   The birth of Eve from the side of the sleeping Adam symbolized the birth of the Bride—*i. e.*, the Church—from the pierced side of Christ as he slept the sleep of death.[1]   Noah's drunkenness, curiously enough, was a prophecy of the crucifixion, and the laughter of Ham prefigured the taunts of the Jews.[2]   Cain, leading Abel out to slay him, was a prophecy of the Jews' leading Christ outside the city, and all the details of the murder of Abel are made to correspond with the details of the crucifixion.[3]   Mount Tabor suggested the cross, because the name is interpreted as ' coming light,' and therefore ' by name and position is pleasing to the mysteries of the life-giving cross.'[4]

Of the direct references to the cross there are a great many;   only a few characteristic ones need be quoted here. First, as to the wood of the cross.   The association of the tree of life with the cross is found all through the Anglo-Saxon literature of the cross, and also in the sacramentaries.   Bede, in his hymn on the passion of St. Andrew, says of his being raised upon the cross: ' Levatur in vitæ arborem.'[5]   In the Benedictional of Ethelwold it is written: ' Deus noster vos perducat ad arborem vitæ, qui eruit de lacu myseriæ, ipse vobis aperiat ianuam paradysi qui congregit portes inferni, Amen.'

But the tree of knowledge of good and evil is also paralleled with the cross.   Bede expounds the words, ' the cool of the day ' (Genesis 3. 8) as follows: ' Doubtless in the same hour in which the first man touched the tree of pre-

---

[1] Bede I. 79.   [2] *Ibid.* 7. 126.   [3] *Ibid.* 7. 75.
    [4] *Ibid.* 8. 22.   [5] *Ibid.* I. 97.

varication, the second man ascended the tree of redemption, and that hour of the day which expelled the prevaricators from Paradise led the Confessor to Paradise.'[1]

The parallelism of the cross on the shoulders of Christ with the fagots borne by Isaac was brought out in the pictures brought by Benedict to adorn his church at Wearmouth.[2] The ark was a favorite type of the cross. The smiting of the rock in the Wilderness signified the Passion, for the rock represented Christ; the rod, the cross; and Moses and Aaron, the chief priests and the doctors of law. David's feigned madness signified the suffering on the cross; his harp was a prophetic type of the cross, and by virtue of that fact was able to drive the evil spirit from Saul. In the words of the Psalmist, ' Take a psalm and bring hither the timbrel' (Ps. 81. 2) ; the timbrel typified the crucifixion because it was a skin stretched upon wood, so also the body of Christ was stretched upon the wood of the cross.[3]

The staff of David,[4] the pomegranate tree under which Saul rested with his army,[5] the pulpit on which Ezra stood to address the people,[6] indeed, any erecting of a pillar or altar, the mention of a tree,[7] or of anything made from a tree, led the exposition directly to the cross.

Secondly, the form of the cross. The marking of blood on the doorposts in the first Passover is frequently referred to as made in the sign of the cross.[8] The four letters of the Hebrew word for God, written on the brow of the priests, signified the four parts of Christ's cross.[9] Whenever the number three hundred appeared it was symbolical of the cross; for example, in the age of Enoch or in the length of the ark.[10] For, according to Bede, following the traditions of the Fathers, ' This number is customarily represented among the Greeks by the letter T. The letter

---

[1] Bede 8. 37. [2] *Ibid.* 4. 376 (*Lives of Holy Abbots*).
[3] *Ibid.* 11. 278. [4] *Ibid.* 8. 100. [5] *Ibid.*
[6] *Ibid.* 9. 15. [7] *Ibid.* 9. 359, 372. [8] Ælfric, *Hom.* 2. 266.
[9] *Ibid.* 7. 324. [10] *Ibid.* 7. 89.

T holds the figure of the cross, lacking only the apex to be the very sign of the cross itself.'[1]

So also all reference to the raising of the hands, and the like, were interpreted as types of the cross. Certainly in many, and probably all of these, Bede, Alcuin, and Ælfric simply followed the exposition of the Fathers.

Thirdly. The explanation of the cross itself. Here also in the explanation of the parts of the cross and the position of the Savior upon the cross the Anglo-Saxon scholar treads carefully in the path of his predecessors. Bede paraphrases the passage from Augustine[2] which interprets the words of the Apostle: ' What is the breadth and length, and height, and depth,' as referring to the dimensions of the cross; and Alcuin[3] copies it word for word. Bede prefaces his discussion with lines from a poem of Sedulius,[4] a fifth century poet,

> Quatuor inde plagos quadrati colligit orbis,
> Splendidus auctoris de vertice fulget eous
> Occiduo sacræ lambuntur sidere plantæ
> Arcton dextra tenet, medium læva erigit axem,
> Cunctaque de membris vivet natura Creantis,
> Et cruce complexum Christus regit undique mundum.

And Alcuin adds to his quotation from Augustine these words which paraphrase Sedulius: ' Indeed as it lay, the cross stretched out toward the four quarters of the world, east and west, north and south, because even so Christ by his passion draws all people to him.'[5] Ælfric, in his sermon on the Passion, repeats the same thought: ' The Lord was fastened with four nails facing the west; his left held the shining south; his right, the north; his head, the east; and he redeemed all the regions of the world hanging thus.'[6]

But a passage attributed to Alcuin echoes Jerome's commentary on Ephesians 3, 18.[7] The writer says: ' More-

---

[1] *Ibid.* p. 173.
[2] Hom. 118, *in S. John,* sec. 5.
[3] 2. 478.
[4] *Carmen Paschale.*
[5] 2. 478.
[6] 2. 254.
[7] Zöckler calls him Pseudo-Alcuin.

5

over, the very cross contains within itself a great mystery, whose position is such that the upper part extends toward Heaven, and the lower part, fixed in the earth, touches the depths of Hell; its breadth stretches out to the regions of the earth.' This grandiose mystical conception of the cross became very popular with later writers, and, according to Bugge,[1] was the idea which gave the Northern mythology its picture of Yggdrasil, the world-tree, whose roots touched Hell, whose top touched Heaven, and whose branches stretched over the earth.

In all this mystical interpretation of the cross and its prophetic types, the work of the Anglo-Saxon theologians seems to have been to reproduce faithfully the conception of the Fathers, with no original contribution of any importance whatever.

(b) *In Poetry*

1. *Latin.*—In the account of the adoration of the cross on Good Friday, there were mentioned the anthems *Ecce lignum crucis, Crucem tuam adoramus, Dum fabricator mundi,* and the famous hymn by Fortunatus, *Pange lingua.* Of the others by Fortunatus, the *Vexilla Regis* is given in full in the Durham Ritual and in the eleventh century Hymnary with its Old English gloss. Alcuin gives the *Crux benedicta nitet,* with the *Pange lingua,* in his Liturgica for Good Friday.[2] Indeed, he appropriates the entire first line of the former for an altar-inscription which he composed, beginning ' Vexillum sublime crucis venerare fidelis.' [3]

In the Old English Hymnary mentioned above there is one other hymn on the cross, which is unglossed, the *Salve Crux, sancta salve mundi gloria,* a hymn by an unknown author—according to Chevalier,[4] probably a Frankish poet of the tenth century.

[1] *Studien über die Entstehung,* etc., p. 468 ff.
[2] 2. 90-91.   [3] 2. 223.
[4] *Repertorium Hymnologicum,* p. 503.

Among the original productions of Anglo-Saxon writers
we find that Bede has a Latin hymn on the birthday of St.
Andrew, in which he puts into the mouth of the saint, as
he sees his cross in the distance, the following salutation:

> Salve, tropæum gloriæ,
> Salve, sacrum victoriæ
> Lignum, Deus quo perditum
> Mundum redemit mortuus.
> O gloriosa fulgidis
> Crux emicas virtutibus,
> Quam Christus ipse proprii
> Membris dicavit corporis.[1]

However, he has written no single poem on the cross.

Alcuin, on the other hand, wrote much verse on the cross.
The following is an inscription for an altar of the cross:

> *Ad aram sanctæ crucis.*
> Aspice, tu lector, nostræ pia signa salutis,
> Ecclesiæ in medio . . . mirabile donum;
> Pro mundi vita, mundi jam vita pependit:
> Pro servis moritur Dominus, quem sancta voluntas,
> Viveret ut servus, semper sit cum sanguine servum.
> Hoc memor esto crucem videasque in lumine stantem,
> Et nox ante Dei faciem feliciter ora.
> Corpore sterne solum, scande sed pectore caelum,
> Proque tuis culpis lacrymas effunde calentes;
> Sit tibi certa salus spei pietate perenni,
> Qui redemit mundum, immaculato sanguine, totum,
> Quique suis famulis clemens peccate remittit.
> Hic quoque sit nobis sacræ spes magna salutis,
> Agmine apostolis quoniam hæc ara refulsit,
> Et simul Helenæ mentis vivacibus almæ,
> Quæ invenisse crucis fertur mirabile lignum,
> In quo Christus honor mundi, laus, vita pependit
> Dum fuit altithronus pro nobis talia passus,
> Quid nos hunc famuli debemus ob ejus amorem
> Jam, nisi nunc illi nosmet quoque tradere totos?
> Sit Deus ille nobis charitas et tota voluntas
> Laus, honor, et virtus, potus, cibus, omnia Christus.[2]

---

[1] *Patrolog. Lat.* 94. 97.

[2] 2. 219.

One other to the cross is as follows:

Ad sanctam crucem.

Vexillum sublime crucis venerare fidelis,
Qua qui se munit, tristia non metuit,
Crux benedicta nitet, Dominus qua carne pependit,
Atque suo clausit funere mentis (F., mortis) iter.
Hic auctor vitæ mortem moriendo peremit,
Vulneribus sanans vulnera nostra suis.[1]

In this, as has been remarked, an entire line has been appropriated from Fortunatus, but in the other, also, are turns of phrase which are echoes of the immensely better work of the older poet. But Alcuin admired and imitated not only the hymns of Fortunatus, but his acrostic verse as well, and in these acrostic poems Alcuin gives a labored, though evidently sincere, tribute to the cross. Some of them are of sufficient importance to quote entire. In his poem *Crux decus es mundi,* he copies the very design of Fortunatus,[2] one which the latter used in his ' Extorquet hoc sorte,' as follows:

In Alcuin's poem the lines of the figure spell:

Crux pia vera salus partes in quattuor orbis,
Surge lavanda tuæ sunt sæcula fonte fidei,
Alma teneto tuam Christo dominante coronam.
Salve sancta rubens fregisti vincula mundi;
Signa valete novis reserate salutibus orbi;
Rector in orbe tuis sanavit sæclas sigillis.

---

[1] *Ibid.*

[2] *Patrolog. Lat.* 5. 88.

A second, which honors the cross only by its figures, is in praise of Charlemagne. The lines run as follows:

Here all the horizontal lines begin, ' Flavius amicus Carlus.'

But these performances of Alcuin fade into insignificance beside the work of his comrade, Josephus Scotus, an Irish scholar, who accompanied him to the court of Charlemagne. His work in this field is much larger in bulk and much more ingenious. An acrostic poem of his on the work of redemption has this design:

and reads:

> Ille pater priscus elidet edendo nepotes.
> Mortis imago fuit mulier poma suasrix.
> Jessus item nobis ieiunans norma salutis.
> Mors fugit vitæ veniens ex virgine radix.

The small cross in the center reads: ' Lege feliciter Carle.'

Another, a sort of epistolary sermon addressed to Charlemagne, has this scheme:

A third, which is a flattering address to the royal patron, makes the cross thus:

And lastly, the most elaborate of all is a long one on the Holy Cross itself, where the cruciform design is as follows:

The lines of the figure read thus:

> Crux mihi certa salus Christi sacrata cruore;
> Crux decus æternum toto venerabile sœclo;
> Crux vita salus credentis Crux mors poena negantis.
> Sancta cruci semper salvit inscriptio corda.

Thus the cruciform acrostic, originated by Fortunatus, was revived by Alcuin, and elaborated still further by his friend Scotus. The tradition was then passed on to Alcuin's pupil, Rabanus Maurus, the great German singer of the cross of the ninth century. His name is the one most commonly associated with this species of literature, and under his hand it far surpassed all preceding efforts in quantity and ingenuity. With him the art may be said to have reached its best, or its worst, according to the point of view.

2. *Old English.*—The Latin hymns and verses on the cross which belong to the Anglo-Saxon period are either the old hymns, especially those of Fortunatus, used in the service of the church, or imitations of his work. But in Old English poetry we find an element that, while founded upon the tradition and rites of the church, is fresh and distinctively

national. The three most important poems for this study
are the *Elene,* the *Dream of the Rood,* and the *Christ.*

At the outset of this chapter we came upon a metrical
homily of Ælfric's on the Exaltation of the Cross—a story
told in verse without ever becoming poetry; and Cynewulf's
Elene, in which the story of the finding of the holy relic is
described with energy and spirit. But at the close of the
Elene, in a little obscure passage of autobiography, Cynewulf says that he was 'guilty of misdeeds, fettered by sins,
tormented with anxieties, bound with bitternesses.' Then
'the mighty King granted me his blameless grace, and shed
it into my mind, . . . unlocked my heart and released the
power of song.' After his conversion he turned to con-
template the cross, the means of his salvation. 'Not once
alone, but many times, I reflected on the tree of glory,
before I had the miracle disclosed concerning the glorious
tree, as in the course of events I found related in books,
in writings, concerning the sign of victory.' This 'miracle'
he has related, evidently as a tribute of love, in the *Elene.*

The authorship of the *Dream of the Rood* is unknown,
but it seems probable that this, too, was written by Cynewulf. It tells of a marvelous vision of the cross. The
opening lines seem to echo the vision of Constantine.

> Hark! of a matchless vision would I speak,
> Which once I dreamed at midnight, when mankind
> At rest were dwelling. Then methought I saw
> A wondrous cross extending up on high,
> With light encircled, tree of trees most bright.
> That beacon all was overlaid with gold;
> And near the earth stood precious stones ablaze,
> While five more sparkled on the shoulder-beam.
>
> No cross was that of wickedness and shame,
> But holy spirits, men on earth, and all
> The glorious creation on it gazed.
> Sublime the tree victorious . . .
>
> .   .   .
>
> Fearful was I before that radiant sight.
> There I beheld that beacon quick to change,

Alter in vesture and in coloring;
Now dewed with moisture, soiled with streaming blood,
And now with gold and glittering gems adorned.
    A long time lying there I sadly looked
Upon the Saviour's cross, until I heard
Resounding there a voice. That wood divine
Then spake. . . .

.   .   .   .   .   .

    I beheld the Master of mankind
Approach with lordly courage as if He
Would mount upon me, and I dared not bow
Nor break, opposing the command of God,
Although I saw earth tremble; all my foes
I might have beaten down, yet I stood fast.
    Then the young Hero laid his garments by,
He that was God Almighty, strong and brave;
And boldly in the sight of all He mounted
The lofty cross, for he would free mankind.
Then, as the Man divine clasped me, I shook;
Yet dared I not bow to the earth nor fall
Upon the ground, but I must needs stand fast.
A cross upraised I lifted a great King,
Lifted the Lord of heaven; and dared not bow.
They pierced me with dark nails, and visible
Upon me still are scars, wide wounds of malice,
Yet might I injure none among them all.
They mocked us both together; then was I
All wet with his blood, which streamed from this man's side
When he at length had breathed the spirit out.

.   .   .   .   .   .

'Now mayest thou know, O hero mine, beloved!
Unutterable sorrows I endured,
Base felons' work. But now hath come the time
When, far and wide, men on the earth, and all
The glorious universe doth honor me,
And to this beacon bow themselves in prayer.
On me a while suffered the Son of God;
Therefore now full of majesty I tower
High under heaven; and I have power to heal
All those who do me reverence.'

.   .   .   .   .   .

    Happy in mind I prayed then to the rood
With great devotion, where I was alone

Without companionship; my soul within
Was quickened to depart, so many years
Of utter weariness had I delayed.
And now my life's great happiness is this,
That to the cross victorious I may come
Alone, above the wont of other men
To worship worthily. . . .
            . . . . and all my help
Must reach me from the rood.

.   .   .   .   .   .

Each day I longing ask:
When will the cross of Christ, which formerly
I here on earth beheld, call me away
From this my transient life, and bring me home
To all delight, the joyous harmonies
Of heaven, where sit at feast the folk of God,
And gladness knows no end.

This is an adoration of the cross that is not ceremonial or conventional, but evidently a genuine expression of personal devotion. It is of especial interest for our purpose, because it expresses and emphasizes ideas found in many stray passages elsewhere.

First, the idea of the brilliant appearance of the cross, shining brightly and adorned with gold and jewels. All through Anglo-Saxon literature the cross is constantly referred to as shining brightly, especially where it figures in visions; [1] this may be due to the famous vision of Constantine, or to the presence of gorgeously adorned crosses in the church, probably both. Then, too, at the last day, the 'red rood was to shine brightly over all the earth,' as we shall see in the *Christ*.

I do not see the necessity of affirming, with Ebert,[2] that the poet must have had in mind a *crux stationalis* or processional cross in writing this poem. The altar-cross was certainly as richly adorned as the processional cross, for that matter, although it seems unnecessary to refer the cross of this vision to any particular cross of the church service.

[1] *Ueber das Angels. Gedicht, Der Traum vom Heiligen Kreuz.*
[2] e. g. *Martyrology*, p. 206.

The reference to the cross being clothed, *wædum geweorðod* (v. 15), may be a recollection of the veiling of the rood on Good Friday in the ceremony already described.

Here, as everywhere else in references to the crucifixion, realism plays but little part. Whenever there do occur touches of realism, they seem evidences only of a keen sympathy on the part of the writer with the sufferings of his Lord; for example, the mention of the ' iron nails ' with which Christ was fastened to the ' hard tree ' in Ælfric,[1] or, in the *Christ,* ' the cruel crown of thorns ' and the ' white hands ' that were pierced.

But the crucifixion to the Anglo-Saxons was first of all an act of free will; Christ mounted the cross as a king would mount his throne, and there he ruled over all the world. The willingness of the sacrifice is repeatedly emphasized, and, further, the crucifixion is represented as an act of triumph, a deed of royal prowess. So in their crucifixes the figure was crowned, not with thorns, but with a diadem.[2]

In endowing the cross with personality, the poet of the *Dream of the Rood* outstrips any other writer. While the cross is never represented as sharing in the guilt of the crucifixion in this poem, it is not merely a helpless instrument but a conscious creature, recognizing its Lord, and suffering, together with him, grief and pain: In this poem the cross is not simply a personality, it is actually deified:

> When will the Cross of Christ, which formerly
> I here on earth beheld, call me away
> From this my transient life, and bring me hence
> To all delights, the joyous harmonies
> Of heaven?

This deification we have already noticed in the charms, where prayers were made to the Holy Rood, and the Holy Rood was expected to bring back strayed or stolen cattle. So also in the conclusion to the charter of Wihtred's that

[1] *Hom.* I. 144. [2] See above, p. 18, note.

was quoted, the curse pronounced upon him who breaks his word is this, that 'the Cross of Christ shall come in vengeance.' Again, in the conclusion to the apostrophe to the Cross that Ælfric puts into the mouth of Heraclius, he says to the Cross, 'Be mindful of this assembly which is here gathered together for the honor of God!'

The *Christ* of Cynewulf we have already quoted from in the discussion of the legends of the Cross. But the chief importance of this poem for our purpose is the description it contains of the apparition of the Cross at the Day of Doom. This was not original with Cynewulf, but is in accordance with an ancient tradition of the church.

An Old English prose account of the various days, with their signs and wonders, leading up to the Great Day, describes the seventh day thus: 'Then shall the Lord reveal the cross on which he suffered, and there shall shine a light over all the world, and he shall show the wound in his side, the wounds of the nails both in his hands and feet, by which he was fastened to the cross, as bloody as they were on the first day.'[1] We find the same idea in liturgy: in the Response at the end of the Third Lesson for the service of the *Invention* is the following: 'Hoc signum crucis erit in caelo cum Dominus ad judicandum venerit.'[2]

In the *Christ* the 'red rood shines brightly,' and it 'blazes upon all peoples.' This idea of its brilliant appearance is also found in Chrysostom, who describes the cross on the last day as 'shining beyond the very sunbeam.'[3]

It is a striking picture that Cynewulf gives of the cross on the Day of Judgment; it is indeed, the poetical apotheosis of the cross, and with it we may conclude this discussion: 'There shall sinful man, sad at heart, behold the greatest affliction. Not for their behoof shall the cross of our Lord, brightest of beacons, stand before all nations, wet with the pure blood of heaven's King, stained with his gore, shining

---

[1] *Das Jüngste Gericht.*   [2] q. Cook, note on *Christ* 192.
[3] *Hom.* 76, on Matt. 24, 16-8; cf. Cook, note on *Christ* 189.

brightly over the vast creation. Shadows shall be put to flight when the resplendent cross shall blaze upon all peoples, . . . when the red rood shall shine brightly over all in the sun's stead.'[1]

Summary

Up to this point we have reviewed the various aspects of the cross in Anglo-Saxon life and literature, section by section. The arrangement into sections is arbitrary, but it serves as well as any other to suggest the diversity of forms in which this symbol appeared, and the many sides of life which it influenced.

The liturgical part of the subject I have not felt competent to discuss in detail, but have left it with references where such detail may be found. I have felt, too, that it had less intimate touch with life and literature than other aspects to which I have devoted more space. However, there has been sufficient material presented to show that the religion of the period was indeed the religion of the cross, from the ceremonial of adoration on Good Friday to the sign of benediction, or the crossing oneself which accompanied every rite of the church. And, as the church of the early Middle Ages touched life on all its sides, this devotion to the cross found expression in matters of every day—in curing sickness, in blessing the tools of trade, in restoring fertility to barren fields, as a charm against misfortune, a solemn form of oath, an inviolable boundary-mark and place of sanctuary, the favorite motive of decoration on manuscript, on jewels, bowls, and on the very coins of commerce. Finally, as a monument, it greeted the eye on every side, on field and highway, in churchyard and market-place. In brief, the old term of mockery, ' worshiper of the cross,' which Aldhelm[2] applied to himself as a synonym for ' Christian,' sums up the story in a word.

The significance of the cross which lay at the foundation

---

[1] ll. 1080-1100. [2] *Patrolog. Lat.* 39. 105.

of all these differing aspects, and unites them all, is stated by a homilist thus:

There is much need for us to bear in mind how the Lord delivered us by his passion from the Devil's power when he ascended the rood-tree and shed his precious blood for our salvation. Wherefore we ought to honor the holy victory-sign of Christ's cross, and follow after it, and pray for the forgiveness of our sins all together, since he suffered for us all on the cross, and endured at the hands of the wicked Jewish people all those reproaches.[1]

Because the True Cross was the instrument by which humanity was ransomed, it was the most precious of earthly possessions, it was wreathed in legends telling of its marvelous odor and life-giving properties, and splinters from it were shrined in precious metals. The representations of the cross standing in the church were adorned with gold, silver, and jewels, because it was the symbol of the Redeemer, and before them the Christian bowed in adoration. He conceived of it even as a divine personality, and invoked it as a saint or a God. And, at last, on the judgment scene of the Great Day, he looked to see it ablaze with ruddy light, towering over all the world.

In the greater part of all the forms of the cross-worship, we have found simply the ideas and practices of the mother church, persisting with little variation on English soil. The rites of the cross in liturgy, the use and significance of the sign of the cross, the vast body of legends of the miracle of the cross, the hymns, the theological literature of the cross—all were transferred from the church of Rome to the church of the Anglo-Saxons. While in these ideas and practices we find no strikingly original elements, they are significant in that they took such deep root in English soil, and overshadowed all classes of society. Even to the semi-pagan, to whom the literature of the Fathers meant nothing, and the ritual in the church little more, the cross was a potent talisman to add to his ancient heathen formulas, and he accepted and trusted it as a ' victory-token.'

[1] *Blickl. Hom.*, p. 96.

It would be difficult to define just the contribution of the Anglo-Saxons to the cult of the cross. Possibly that deification of the cross that we have noticed was first developed on English soil. As far as I can discover, it transcends any veneration of the cross that was known in Rome, and as it is expressed in the *Dream of the Rood* it appears earlier than in any other piece of literature in Europe.

The cross-poetry of the Anglo-Saxons was certainly a contribution to the literature of the cross. It must have been widely known in England, from the testimony of the Ruthwell and Brussels Cross inscriptions, and of its influence abroad we shall have to speak later.

The stone cross with interlaced ornament, while a product of Irish rather than Anglo-Saxon genius, became an important feature of Anglo-Saxon life, and far surpassed the plain monumental cross of the tradition of Rome.

In the sculpture of the cross and the poetry of the cross, the emblem of Christianity reached among the Anglo-Saxons its most devoted and most artistic expression.

Beside the main points noted above, it is necessary to recapitulate two matters of date which were established by the investigation for this chapter, and are important for the discussion in the chapter which follows. First, the stone cross with Celtic ornament, which we have called the interlaced cross, was not known in England before the ninth century. Secondly, the crucifix also was unknown in England before the latter part of the same century, and did not come into general use till the late tenth and eleventh centuries.

CHAPTER II

THE ANGLO-SAXON CROSS IN ITS HISTORICAL SETTING

The great diversity of forms in which the cross manifested itself, and the evident warmth and sincerity of the veneration accorded to it, show how powerful an influence it exerted over the lives and thoughts of this people. We shall try to discover, in this concluding chapter, if there were any events or influences in the Anglo-Saxon period which could have tended to intensify a spirit of devotion to the cross.

The earliest recorded appearance of the cross is that which figured in the procession of Augustine and his monks as they went to meet King Ethelbert. After the king had granted them permission to settle in Canterbury, Bede says that they drew near to the city, also, ' with the holy cross.' The first impression of the cross upon the pagan mind was, therefore, that of a standard of the new Faith. So, too, when the missionaries penetrated farther into heathen territory, they erected crosses as standards and as places of worship and exhortation.

In the next event of importance in the history of the cross in Anglo-Saxon England, this idea of the cross as a standard is strikingly exemplified. It is the victory of Oswald over Cadwalla in 633. To get a picture of the situation of the Angles just before this event, we may turn to the rather florid account of Sharon Turner (1.242-3) :

The Welsh king, Cadwallon, full of projects of revenge against the nations of the Angles, continued his war. Osric rashly ventured to besiege him in a strong town, but an unexpected sally of Cadwallon destroyed the king of Deira. For a year the victor desolated Northumbria : his success struck Eanrid with terror, and his panic hurried him to his fate. He went with twelve soldiers to sue for peace of the Welshman. Notwithstanding the sacred purpose of his visit, he was put to death.

The swords of Cadwallon and his army seemed the agents des-
tined to fulfill their cherished prophecy. The fate of the Anglo-
Saxons was now about to arrive; three of their kings had been
already offered up to the shades of the injured Cymry; an Arthur
had revived in Cadwallon. . . . Triumphant with the fame of four-
teen great battles and sixty skirmishes, Cadwallon despised Oswald,
the brother and successor of Eanfrid, who rallied the Bernician forces
and attempted to become the deliverer of his country.

For the rest of the story, let us listen to Bede:

In the third book of his *Ecclesiastical History*, he tells how
Cadwalla, the king of the Britons, 'for the space of a year reigned
over the provinces of the Northumbrians, not like a victorious
king, but like a rapacious and bloody tyrant,' and how he ended
his series of bloody deeds by treacherously slaying Eanfrid, who
came to him to a parley for terms of peace. 'To this day,' continues
the historian, 'that year is looked upon as unhappy, and hateful to all
good men. . . . Hence it has been agreed by all who have written
about the reigns of the kings to abolish the memory of those
perfidious monarchs, and to assign that year to the reign of the following king, Oswald, a man beloved by God. This last king, after
the death of his brother Eanfrid, advanced with an army, small
indeed in number, but strengthened with the faith of Christ; and
the impious commander of the Britons was slain, though he had
most numerous forces, which he boasted nothing could withstand,
at a place in the English tongue called Denisesburn, that is, Denis'
brook.

'The place is shown to this day, and held in much veneration
where Oswald, being about to engage, erected the sign of the holy
cross, and on his knees prayed to God that he would assist his
worshipers in their great distress. It is further reported that the
cross, being made in haste, and the hole dug in which it was to be
fixed, the king himself, full of faith, laid hold of it and held it
with both hands, till it was set fast by throwing in the earth, and
this done, raising his voice, he cried to his army, " Let us all kneel,
and jointly beseech the true and living God Almighty, in his mercy,
to defend us from the haughty and fierce enemy; for He knows
that we have undertaken a just war for the safety of our nation."
All did as he had commanded, and accordingly, advancing toward
the enemy with the first dawn of day, they obtained the victory as
their faith deserved. In that place of prayer very many miraculous
cures are known to have been performed, as a token and a memorial

[1] Chaps. 1 and 2.

of the king's faith; for even to this day, many are wont to cut off small chips from the wood of the holy cross, which being put into water, men and cattle drinking thereof, or sprinkled with that water, are immediately restored to health.

'The place in the English tongue is called Heavenfield, or the Heavenly Field, which name it formerly received as a presage of what was afterward to happen, denoting that there the heavenly trophy would be erected, the heavenly victory begun, and heavenly miracles be wrought to this day.'

A cruciform church was built on the site of the battle, and the wooden cross that performed so many miracles, and that was still standing in Bede's day, was replaced after its final decay by a cross of stone, to commemorate the event.

King Oswald became both a national hero and a saint, and, after his death in a battle against the Mercians, was regarded as a martyr. Ælfric, for example, devotes a metrical homily to 'St. Oswald, King and Martyr.'

After his death the very ground on which he fell became potent for the healing of the sick. Bede says,[1]

How great his faith was towards God, and how remarkable his devotion, has been made evident by miracles since his death; for in the place where he was killed by the pagans, fighting for his country, infirm men and cattle are healed to this day. Whereupon many took up the very dust of the place where his body fell, and putting it into water, did much good with it to their friends who were sick. This custom came so much into use that, the earth being carried away by degrees, there remained a hole as deep as the height of a man.

Some of these miracles the historian narrates in detail, but he gives much more space to the wondrous miracles effected by the bones of the sainted king. A heavenly light shone all night over his relics, devils were cast out from a man whom the priests had exorcised in vain, a boy was cured of ague, and a man was healed at the point of death.

These tales of miracle show how strong a hold Oswald and his rood had upon the popular imagination. Indeed,

[1] *Eccles. Hist.*, chap. 9.

it is not likely that the influence of this victory upon the national feeling for the cross can be overestimated. The cross had delivered the Angles from their enemies in the hour of greatest need. It was the victory of Constantine repeated in England, and probably the obvious points of similarity in the two stories helped to make the legend of Constantine as popular as it evidently was. This victory of Oswald, as well as that of Constantine, formed the associations with the cross that made appropriate the familiar Old English epithet *sige-bēacn,* the ' banner of victory.'

Alcuin and Ælfric both give accounts of this victory of the rood, both, however, based upon the narrative of Bede. Alcuin's account is contained in his poem *De Pontificibus et Sanctis Ecclesiæ Eboracensis.* In this, the only variation worthy of note is that in the speech that he puts into the mouth of Oswald the army is bidden to bow to the cross:

> Substernite vestros
> Vultus ante crucem.

Accordingly, the entire army, on their knees before the cross, pray to God. Alcuin has inserted an Adoration ceremony into the story.

As we pass from the seventh to the eighth century we find no historical event of significance in connection with the cross, and in literature only the cross-symbolism of Bede. While he frequently repeats, as his life-motto, ' Mihi absit gloria, nisi in cruce Christi Domini nostri,' he gives no evidence of a special feeling of love for the cross; he merely repeats the traditions as he found them in the Fathers, without particular emphasis.

But in the latter part of the eighth century we come upon remarkable poetry of the cross in the work of Cynewulf— and whoever else may have been the poet of the *Dream of the Rood*—in which the adoration of the cross reaches its most ardent expression. Closely following this comes the Latin of Alcuin, who is decidedly a cross-worshiper, though

[1] e. g. *Opera,* ed. Giles, 4. 181; 7. 126.

he was unable to rise to the level of the Old English poetry. He expressed his devotion to the cross chiefly by developing mystical interpretations of its parts, and by reviving and imitating the work of Fortunatus, especially in the cruciform acrostic. In this his colleague, Josephus Scotus, followed his example and surpassed it.

According to the *Chronicle*, in the year 773 ' a fiery Christ-sign appeared in the heavens after sunset,' and in the year 800, ' a cross appeared in the moon on a Wednesday at dawn.' These are the only apparitions of the cross recorded. The first cruciform church of which we have record, after the church of Oswald at Heavenfield, was built in 810.[1] At some time early in the ninth century began the custom of erecting crosses adorned with the famous interlaced ornament. This custom seems to have come from Ireland, but to have spread rapidly over England, Scotland, and Wales. The custom continued in England, at any rate, up to the time of the Norman invasion. Finally, at the battle of Hastings, the army that fought with Harold in the defense of their country shouted the battle-cry, ' The Holy Cross, the Cross of God!'

We find on looking over the course of events in Anglo-Saxon history that, while the cross became almost a national emblem, special interest seems to have been focused upon it during the latter part of the eighth and the first part of the ninth centuries. Of the events in Anglo-Saxon history which we have anything to do with the cross, the victory of Oswald is easily of the first importance. Let us see if the effect of this could have been reinforced by influences from outside of England.

I. THE INFLUENCE OF IRELAND

The art of the Anglo-Saxons was chiefly an imitation of Irish art. It was from Ireland that they learned the arts of illumination, of metal-work, and of carving in stone.

[1] See p. 9.

The types of ornament came also from the same source, notably the famous interlaced patterns that we have already discussed. There were also elements in decoration which came from Frankish artists, and others from Scandinavian, but the basis of all Anglo-Saxon art was the style that came from Ireland, and that reached there the most perfect development.

But this influence may not have been restricted to the style of ornamentation or the shape of the crosses. The monumental cross itself, as we have seen, developed in the British Isles, not from the cross as it was set up in Rome, but from the ancient monoliths of the pagan Celts. We have seen that the huge stone was consecrated to Christian use by the Chi-Rho, or a cross with a circle cut upon its surface; then the stones were roughly hewn into the shape of a cross; finally, a graceful shaft was surmounted by a cross and ring, the whole covered with a wealth of interlaced ornament.

It was natural that the Celtic convert would the more readily erect stone monuments which, as his artistic powers developed, would tend to take the shape of the emblems of his faith. If one may trust the story of the life of St. Patrick, this is strikingly confirmed. In this there is such frequent reference to monumental crosses as to lead one to believe that they must have fairly studded the country-side. The island of Iona, also, a missionary outpost of the Irish church, was famous for its three hundred and sixty crosses. And in the west of Cornwall, where Irish missionaries labored, are a great many remains of ancient stone crosses which precede the time of interlaced ornament.

As in Anglo-Saxon England there were evidently few crosses before the interlaced period, it seems probable that something in the latter eighth century produced a greater devotion toward the cross, which led the Irish artist to devote his painstaking efforts in interlaced design to the stone surface of the cross, and which caused the Anglo-

Saxons to adopt this species of cross for themselves, and to erect great numbers of them.

In the development of the monumental cross we noticed a trace of an ancient pagan custom of the Celts. This is worth inquiring into, to see if there were any elements in Teutonic paganism which contributed to the use of the cross among the Christian Anglo-Saxons.

II. TEUTONIC PAGANISM

According to Grimm,[1] the swastika was a holy sign among the Teutons, and was called by them the *hamars-mark*. This sign was held sacred; they cut it on trees as a boundary-mark, and in blessing the cup the sign of the hammer was made. The significance of blessing, or good luck, seems to have clung to this ancient symbol in all of its world-wide migrations.

According to other authorities, the swastika is not the hammer of Thor at all, and has no connection with the hammer of Thor. 'The best Scandinavian authors,' says Wilson,[2] 'report "Thor hammer" to be the same as the Greek Tau, the same form as the Roman and English capital T.'

If we accept this, we can only recognize an added cross symbol—the tau cross, or Thor's hammer—which had a sacred significance to the pagan. The swastika as the sign of blessing was certainly known and employed. It is found on sepulchral urns, ceintures, brooches, fibulæ, pins, spear-heads, swords, scabbards, etc., in Germany, Bavaria, and Scandinavia.[3]

In these uses—the marking of a boundary, the blessing of the cup, weapons, and utensils, and the sign upon the burial-urn—it is easy to see the likeness to certain Christian uses of the cross, or the sign of the cross. It seems not improbable that such uses, familiar to the pagan, would have made the

[1] *Teutonic Mythology*, Stallybrass, p. 1345.
[2] *The Swastika*, p. 770.   [3] *Ibid.* pp. 862 ff.

same uses of a Christian figure, almost identical, readily accepted.

As a matter of fact, the swastika was known among the Anglo-Saxons,[1] and persisted, at any rate in the ornament of their crosses and coins, after the establishment of Christianity. The illuminations of the Christian Irish show the same device. Wilson[2] mentions the baptismal font of an ancient church in Denmark as decorated with swastikas, showing its use in early Christian times there.

It is evident, then, that the sign was not only not regarded as a device of heathenism, but was accepted by Christians, even, as a form of their cross.

Moreover, both Celtic and Teutonic paganism recognized sacred stones. In Ireland, St. Patrick purified certain of these sacred stones at Mag Selce by inscribing Christian symbols on them. In England, stone-worship had to be forbidden by a special law in King Edgar's time; and the words of Ælfric, ' no Christian man can gain for himself help at any tree or stone save from the holy rood-token,' show that as late as his time the worship of trees and stones still persisted. It is not improbable that the Christian priest was all the more ready to erect the stone cross in order to give the people a stone to which they might bow in worship with propriety.[3]

Of the ancient myths a great deal has been made in regard to their effect upon the ideas of Christian Europe, especially in connection with the conceptions of Christ and the cross. There are, indeed, striking similarities in the Christian and heathen notions. For example, as Christ hung upon the gallows—a common term for the cross—so

---

[1] *Ibid.*, p. 870.   [2] *Ibid.*, p. 867.

[3] It might be added that the idea of bringing the cross into the field of battle, as Oswald did, is not unlike a custom of the pagan Saxons, if we may accept the testimony of Sharon Turner. ' The priests in the hour of battle,' he says, ' took their favorite image from its column and carried it to the field' (Turner, *Hist. A.-S.* 5. 1. 156).

Odin hung upon a tree,[1] which is called a gallows. As Christ, one with God yet the Son of God, offered himself a sacrifice to God in behalf of man, so Odin was a willing sacrifice unto himself.[2] Odin and Christ were both wounded with a spear as they hung, and both cried aloud with anguish.

The resemblance[3] continues also between the mythical treatment of the cross and the myths of the holy tree of the pagans. Odin hung on this tree, and, like Christ, is represented as the fruit of this tree. This world-tree, Yggdrasil, corresponds in many points with the mystical rood-tree of the Christians. It is called the best of trees, the 'tree of life,' and it is described like the tree of life in Paradise—with which the cross was fused—as having a spring of living water at its foot, its top touching the sky, its branches spreading over all the world, and Hell lying beneath its roots.

The relations of Christian and pagan myth in the light of these correspondences has been the subject of much discussion and difference of opinion. Stephens regarded this parallelism as due to pagan influence upon Christians, or the persistence of old traditions among those who were only nominally Christianized. Sophus Bugge just reversed the order, and developed the theory that it was the Christian ideas which affected the neighboring heathen. Müllenhoff, in his *Deutsche Altertumskunde,* contradicts Bugge, and declares again for the native, Germanic origin of the pagan myths. This seems the most natural supposition, and nothing save the scholastic passion for sources need interfere with the opinion that Teutonic mythology and Christian tradition had independent origins. This, however, does not interfere with the possibility that the correspondence of pagan and Christian ideas—as in the swastika noted above

---

[1] *Hovamol,* stanzas 110 ff.   [2] *Ibid.*

[3] For detailed study of correspondences, see Bugge's *Studien über die Entstehung der Nordischen Götter- und Heldensagen.*

—made easier the acceptance of the latter, or a persistence of the one alongside of the other.

The traces of pagan mythology that concern us are found in the pictorial ornament of some of the interlaced crosses. Here the difficulty is that many of the representations may be interpreted as easily in a Christian as a pagan sense. For example, upon some of the crosses (e. g., the Dearham Standing Cross),[1] 'is carved a conventionalized tree. It is customary to interpret this as the heathen world-ash Yggdrasil. It may readily be accounted for by Christian symbolism. The cross was constantly referred to as a tree, and most often as the tree of life. In Fortunatus,[2] the figure is carried out into details of branches, leaves, blossoms, fruit, and seed. What could be more appropriate for a Christian to carve upon the shaft of a cross than the figure of a tree?'

Upon the Gosforth Cross is a figure with arms outstretched, the blood gushing from a wound in the right side; a male figure stands at its right, holding a spear; and on its left, two female figures. Calverley interprets the central figure as Balder, the son of Odin, who was killed by an arrow of mistletoe shot by the evil god Loki. But since it was customary to carve representations of the crucifixion upon crosses of this later style, what more natural than to interpret this as one of them, with Longinus on one side, and Mary with Mary Magdalene on the other? Beneath the foot of one of the women is a serpent, evidently in memory of the prophecy, fulfilled in that scene, that the woman's seed should bruise the head of the serpent.

Again, on the Cross at Kirby Stephen is a rude carving of a male figure bound like a malefactor. The curious part of this is that it has conspicuous *horns*. Calverley and Stephens call it 'Loki bound,' in reference to a myth which we shall meet later. This may be its true explanation, but it is also possible to refer it to Satan, who was to be bound 'a thousand years' and cast into the 'bottomless pit.'[3] I

---

[1] Calverley, p. 515.   [2] *Crux benedicta* and *Pange lingua.*
[3] Rev. 20. 2-3.

know of no tradition that gives Loki horns, though it was a familiar mediæval attribute of Satan.

On the other hand, there are carvings which are un-doubtedly of pagan significance. These pictorial carvings on crosses belong to the period of Scandinavian influence, and were probably executed by Scandinavian artists. As the memories of pagan myth would be fresher among the Danes than among any other Christianized race of the British Isles, it would be surprising if there were no traces of pagan tradition in their art. As a fact, much of this pictorial ornament can be explained only in this way; these are myths, not only of pagan origin, but also bearing no resemblance to Christian doctrines or traditions.[1]

Calverley has pointed out the representations of three heathen monsters in the carving of some of these crosses, and his explanation seems the most reasonable that can be found:

The three monsters whose fathers was Loki, and whose mother was the witch of Jötunhein (the land of giants), were the Fenris-wolf, Jörmungand, the monster of the universe, also called Midgard's Worm,—the huge snake that lay in the great sea coiled around the earth; and a daughter, Hel.

Now when the gods heard that this kindred was being bred up in Jötunheim, and knowing that from such a stock all evil was to be expected on both father's and mother's side, Alfadir bade the children be brought to him, and the worm or snake he cast into the deep sea that lay around all lands, where it grew so that it coiled itself around all the earth and bit its tail with its teeth.[2]

Any one who looks at the huge monster on the top of the Brigham cross-socket, coiled round the hollow, . . . and biting its tail with its teeth, must at once identify the Midgard worm.[3]

' In the Brigham cross-socket,' continues Calverley, ' we have a full representation of the incarnation of Loki, Fenris, the Midgard snake, Hel, and the horse [on which Hel rode[4]], all under bonds. And the cross-head, in similar symbolism, represents the victory over the powers of evil.'

[1] *Gylfaginning,* 34.   [2] Calverley, p. 141.
[3] p. 141.   [4] The brackets are mine.

One of these may serve as a type. On the shortest of the
sculptured sides of the socket is a figure which Calverley
describes as 'composed of a wide distended throat, over
whose cavernous depths fang-like limbs appear to close with
ominous strength.' This is probably Hel, the goddess of
the dead, who lived under the root of the great world-tree,
and devoured those who died of sickness or old age.[1] Grimm
says of her that 'she has gaping yawning jaws ascribed to
her like the wolf; pictures in the MS. of Cædmon represent
her simply by a wide open mouth.' From this comes, of
course, our word 'Hell,' and the mediæval representations
of Hell-mouth in manuscripts, sculpture, and mystery-play.

'In the Danish popular belief,' says Grimm, 'Hel is a
three-legged horse that goes around the country as a harbin-
ger of plague and pestilence. . . . Originally it was no other
than the steed on which the goddess posted over land, pick-
ing up the dead that were her due.'[2]

Curiously enough, three-legged, horse-headed monsters
are not an uncommon feature of much of this late Scandinavian type of ornament.

Let us examine one more instance. It is the picture
of Loki upon the Gosforth Cross. Loki is the Teutonic
Prometheus, and the story of his imprisonment is as follows: 'Skadi took a venomous serpent, and fastened it
upon Loki's face. The venom trickled down from it.
Sigurn, Loki's wife, sat by and held a basin under the
venom; and when the basin was full, carried the poison out.
Meanwhile the venom dropped on Loki, who shrank from
it so violently that the whole earth trembled. This causes
what are now called earthquakes.'[3] The carving on the
cross appears to correspond with this story exactly, showing Loki bound, with a serpent above, and his wife holding
out the cup to catch the venom.

[1] Cf. *Beowulf* 1698; *Teuton. Myth.* I. 312-314.   [2] *Ibid.*
[3] Calverley, p. 142.

These instances are sufficient to show that pagan myths did persist, and appear even upon the ornament of some Christian crosses. We have seen, too, that there were striking correspondences between the mystical conceptions of Christ and the cross, and Odin and the tree. All this, with the use of the swastika, must have contributed a good deal to the reverence of the Anglo-Saxon Christian for the cross. Yet it seems too much to say that the heritage of Teutonic paganism could furnish enough of a spirit for special worship of the cross, or the impulse for erecting the famous stone crosses at any particular period.

It must be borne in mind that the pagan ornament just discussed was a later development in the art of the cross, long after the impulse for erecting the ornamental cross had begun, and, indeed, when the art of the stone cross had already reached its zenith. It belongs to crosses of the tenth or eleventh centuries, belonging to Danish-Saxon territory. We have yet to account for the phenomenon of the special interest in the cross, which, we have found, seemed to be centred in the latter part of the eighth and the beginning of the ninth century.

III. THE ICONOCLASTIC CONTROVERSY

Let us turn to the history of the church. The great question that stirred the Christian church of this period was that of the use of images in worship.

In the history of the cross in art, we saw that the influences that transformed the symbolistic cross with the realistic crucifix came from the image-loving East. The Eastern Christian seems to have inherited from the Greeks a love for all that appealed to the eye; and images of Christ, of Mary, and the saints came to be so numerous, and so commonly worshiped, that the defenders of the Faith had great difficulty in answering the charges of idolatry brought against the Christians by their enemies, the Jews and Mohammedans. A reaction set in, and with Leo III,

Emperor of the East, the Iconoclastic crusade was begun. The history of the long struggle that followed is divided by Schaff [1] into three periods:

1. The war upon images and the abolition of image-worship by the Council of Constantinople, A. D. 726-754. 2. The reaction in favor of image-worship, and its solemn sanction by the second council of Nicea, A. D. 754-787. 3. The renewed conflict of the two parties and the final triumph of image-worship, A. D. 842.

The impulse that set the iconoclastic movement on foot was to destroy the force of the charge of idolatry brought against the Christians by their enemies. The image-worshipers, on the other hand, defended themselves by making a distinction between the quality of the worship accorded to God and that accorded to images, at the same time repudiating the charge of idolatry.

The first attack upon images was an edict issued by the Emperor in 726, which prohibited only the worship of images. In a second edict, four years later, he commanded that all images and pictures should be removed or destroyed. He took down the picture of Christ which stood over the gate of the palace and substituted for it a plain cross, accompanied by an inscription, a part of which is as follows:

'The Emperor can not endure that Christ should be sculptured as a mute and lifeless image graven on earthly materials. But Leo, and his young son Constantine, have at their gates engraven the thrice blessed representation of the cross, the glory of believing monarchs.' [2]

These edicts aroused a storm of opposition, and the servants who took down the picture were killed by a mob. Rebellions burst out in the Greek Archipelago, and Pope Gregory of Rome openly defied the Emperor. However, in his own empire Leo was strong enough to enforce his decrees.

[1] *Hist. Christ. Church* 4. 454.
[2] Walch, *Essay on Ancient Coins*, p. 132.

His son, who succeeded him, was also an iconoclast; he summoned a council in 754 which ' condemned and forbade the public and private worship of sacred images on pain of deposition and excommunication. . . . It denounced all religious representations by painter or sculptor, as presumptuous, pagan, and idolatrous.[1]

Leo IV adhered to the same policy, but after his death his widow, Irene, labored to restore image-worship. She called a council in 787 at Nicæa, which nullified the decree of the previous council of the year 754, and pronounced anathemas upon iconoclasts. After the deposition of Irene, the controversy went on again for thirty-five or forty years. The emperor Theophilus was the last and the most bloody of the iconoclastic emperors, but his widow, like Irene, brought image-worship back again. A final synod in 842 restored to the churches images and the worship of images. It decreed that the event should evermore be celebrated ' by a procession and a renewal of the anathema on the iconoclastic heretics.'

Such, in outline, is the history of the great controversy. The iconoclasts failed of popular support—as all iconoclasts do—because they had nothing to substitute in the place of images. Leo and his followers tried to substitute the cross. Indeed, all those who opposed the worship of images made a notable exception in favor of the cross, attempting to turn the feeling of reverence toward the one visible symbol to which it might properly be offered. But to the Greeks, and to the Church of Rome which had felt much of Greek influence, the cross as a visible image was insufficient.

In the West, however, the feeling was different. The adoration of the cross and the veneration of saints' relics took the place that the worship of images held in the East. The Teutonic tribes did not have the artistic traditions of the Greeks, and apparently did not crave sculptured or painted representations of Christ and the saints as objects of worship.

[1] Schaff 4. 457-8.

For the attitude of the Frankish church in this iconoclastic controversy, I quote once more from Schaff (4.
467):

Charlemagne, with the aid of his chaplains, especially Alcuin,
prepared and published, three years after the Nicene Council, an important work on image-worship under the title *Quatuor Libri Carolini*
(790). He dissents both from the iconoclastic synod of 754 and
the anti-iconoclastic synod of 787, but more from the latter,
which he treats very disrespectfully. He decidedly rejects image-
worship, but allows the use of images for ornament and
devotion, and supports his view with Scripture passages and
patristic quotations. The spirit and aim of the book is almost
Protestant. The chief thoughts are these: God alone is the object
of worship and adoration (*colendus et adorandus*). Saints are
only to be revered (*venerandi*). Images can in no sense be worshiped. To bow or kneel before them, to salute or kiss them, to
strew incense and light candles before them, is idolatrous and super-
stitious. It is far better to search the Scriptures, which know nothing
of such practices. The tales of miracles wrought by images are
inventions of the imagination, or deceptions of the evil spirit. On
the other hand, the iconoclasts, in their honest zeal against idolatry,
went too far in rejecting images altogether. The legitimate and
proper use of images is to adorn the churches and to perpetuate and
popularize the memory of the persons and events which they represent. Yet even this is not necessary; for a Christian should be
able to rise to the contemplation of the virtues of the saints and to
ascend to the fountain of eternal light. . . . The Council of Nicea
committed a great wrong in condemning those who do not worship
images.

The author of the Caroline books, however, falls into the same
inconsistency as the Eastern iconoclasts, by making an exception in
favor of *the sign of the cross* and the relics of the saints. The cross
is called a banner which puts the enemy to flight, and the honoring
of relics is declared to be a great means of promoting piety.

A Synod in Frankfort, A. D. 794, the most important held during
the reign of Charlemagne, and representing the churches of France
and Germany, in the presence of two papal legates . . . endorsed the
doctrine of the *Libri Carolini*, unanimously condemned the worship
of images in any form, and rejected the seventh ecumenical council.
According to an old tradition, the English church agreed with this
decision.

Let us see if anything beside 'an old tradition' points
to the agreement of the English Church. The Frankfort

Synod supported the Caroline Books, which we have seen the Emperor prepared and published 'with the aid of his chaplains, *especially Alcuin.*' Schaff says in his biography of Alcuin (4. 687): 'In 794 he took a prominent part, although simply a deacon, in the council of Frankfort.' Also, in a foot-note to the last sentence of our long quotation, he says: 'This [the agreement of the English Church] rests partly on the probable share which the Anglo-Saxon Alcuin had in the composition of the Caroline Books, partly on the testimony of Simeon of Durham.' Again, in his biography of Alcuin, he says: 'In 792 he sent, in the name of the English bishops, a refutation of image-worship.' This is the 'testimony of Simeon of Durham,' and here, evidently, the historian believes it may be accepted for truth.

But the testimony of the sort we have gained from the investigation of the previous chapter confirms what already seems probable. In all the Anglo-Saxon literature, whether in the vernacular or in Latin, there is not a hint that images were ever used for worship. Lingard, in his discussion of paintings in the Anglo-Saxon church,[1] says, 'Of any species of religious honor paid to the paintings themselves, I do not recollect any instance in the contemporary records. But with respect to the cross it was far otherwise.'

Augustine brought a picture of Christ upon landing in England, and Benedict Biscop in the seventh century brought paintings from Rome. But even such adornment was rare, and, as Lingard says, there is no evidence that these pictures received 'any species of religious honor.'

In the previous chapter we found that the crucifix was apparently unknown in England till the end of the ninth century. This is an important piece of evidence in determining the attitude of the English Church toward image-worship during the great controversy. If even the crucified image was unknown, to say nothing of being worshiped, it is not difficult to guess the position of the English clergy in this quarrel.

[1] *Hist. and Antiq.* 2. 108.

Indeed, all the evidence there is points toward the full sympathy of the English Church with the tenor of the Caroline Books and the Frankfort decrees. Nay, more, these were probably the expression of the English Church itself through Alcuin. Alcuin was not the kind of man to stand apart from the traditions in which he was bred—like Scotus Erigena, for example—but led his age only as the exponent of his age, never as a pioneer. He was just the kind of man to reflect faithfully the traditions of the church in which he was born and bred.

The value of establishing this point about the English Church is this, that it was characteristic of those who opposed image-worship—both the fiercest iconoclasts, like Leo III, for example, and those who took a more moderate position, like Charlemagne—to make a great exception in favor of the cross. The cross was the only image—if so it may be called—to which adoration could properly be paid; and in condemning images, they laid special emphasis upon the cross.

The latter part of the eighth and the beginning of the ninth centuries we have recognized as the period in England when there seemed to be a special impulse toward the honoring of the cross. This period was in the very heart of the iconoclastic war. The theory that this impulse was largely due to the attitude of England in the controversy, the quickening of a regard for the emblem which was already dear to the national heart by the story of Oswald, and already received ' adoration,' to the exclusion of every other object in the church, appears, on the whole, to be the most satisfactory in explaining the facts.

Very likely, beneath the *Elene,* or the *Dream of the Rood,* there was a personal experience of some sort—a dream, for example—in which the cross figured. Yet it would be just this heightened interest in the cross which would account for its being the centre of this religious experience in the mind of the poet, rather than the person of Christ, for example, or Mary, or one of the saints.

We may regard, then, this poetry of the cross in England as perhaps the first fruit of this impetus, giving to it, at the same time, added force by its own warmth, beauty, and sincerity. And it may not be too much to regard the application of the elaborate and minute traceries of Celtic ornament upon stone crosses as the first fruit of this impetus in Ireland, for probably the Irish church was at one with the other churches of the North in regard to the use of images. At all events, as soon as the Irish had developed this style of the cross, the Anglo-Saxons appropriated it for their own, erected it everywhere, and it became the most conspicuous feature of their national art. This impulse found expression, then, in the Old English cross-poetry, the Latin prose and verse of Alcuin, and in the interlaced crosses which came from Ireland.

Finally, let us inquire if this feeling in Anglo-Saxon England had any influence upon the literature of her neighbors on the continent.

'In the ninth century,' says Didron, 'the praises of the cross were sung as men sing those of a god or a hero, and Rhaban Maur, who was archbishop of Mayenne in 847, wrote a poem in honor of the cross.'[1] Rabanus Maurus was undoubtedly the greatest singer of the cross in the ninth century. His effort in verse, *The Praises of the Cross,* finished in 815, has been characterized as 'a monument of misdirected zeal and patience.' In this he develops the cruciform acrostic to a point that is fairly appalling. However, his work became very popular, and was admired as a miracle of ingenuity. It seems to be this, especially, that Didron has in mind.

But the exaltation of the cross 'as a god or a hero' is precisely what we have noted among the Anglo-Saxons. The second book of Rabanus' praises of the cross is an explanation in prose of the figure in his acrostic. The last

[1] I, 371-2.

7

chapter deals with the last figure, representing a monk
adoring a cross, and concludes thus:

O crux alma Dei, usque huc, quantum potui, laudem tuam cecini;
sed quia triumphum perpetem expetis, quem in his mortalibus
pleniter et perfecte non invenis, confer te ad caelestia angelorum
agmina, ibique tibi laus perpetus per cuncta sonabit sæcula.[1]

This is the tone of the *Dream of the Rood*. It would be
interesting to trace a connection between these ideas of
Rabanus and the cross-poetry of the Anglo-Saxons. Alcuin
was called to the court of Charlemagne in the year 752, and
from that time his career is chiefly bound up with the
empire of Charlemagne. His best work, undoubtedly, was
in education; and to his school at Tours were sent young
men of promise from all parts of the realm. One of these
was Rabanus Maurus, and between this brilliant student
and his master there developed a warm and lasting friendship. Naturally in such relations of friend and pupil one
would expect that Rabanus would become throughly imbued
with the traditions of the Church of England. But further
than this, we find that the very poem under discussion was
written by Rabanus at the suggestion of Alcuin.[2]

With this the connection becomes complete. But, unfortunately, the love of the cross in Alcuin found its expression chiefly in the self-imposed penance of the acrostic.
And this was the model that the master set before his pupil,
rather than the *Elene* or the *Dream of the Rood*. So it was
the love of the cross in its scholastic habit that affected
Rabanus, and inspired his *De Laudibus Sanctæ Crucis*.

While Rabanus is by far the most important singer of the
cross of this period in the Frankish empire, two others may
be noticed: Johannes Scotus Erigena, and Otfrid, the
author of the *Evangelienbuch*.

The former was an eccentric Irish scholar who went to
France about the year 843. Among his writings is a poem
to the cross of seventy lines. This has many traces of the

---

[1] I, 294.   [2] Schaff 4. 727.

mysticism of Alcuin, and has also a fine enthusiasm for the cross, which, if he did not get it from Alcuin, he had probably caught in his own country or in England.

The latter, Otfrid, made a rimed paraphrase of the Gospel narrative in the German tongue. In the fifth book of his work, the first three chapters have to do with the cross. These are full of the mystical interpretations of Alcuin, the meaning of the ' heighth and depth,' etc., and the significance of the parts of the cross embracing all the regions of the world. To trace the connection still more clearly to Alcuin, Otfrid was a pupil of Rabanus.

In Chapter 20 of the *Evangelienbuch,* Otfrid describes the Day of Judgment. It would be most interesting if we could discover in this any trace of the *Christ.* The speech of Christ in Otfrid reminds one of the speech of Christ in Cynewulf, but it must be admitted that they are no more similar than would be expected from the fact that both writers used the Gospel narrative. Further, Otfrid omits wholly the most striking feature of the description in the *Christ,* namely, the Apparition of the Rood, a fact that makes it seem clear that the *Christ* was not one of his sources.

We must conclude, then, that the ninth century cross-poetry of France and Germany was inspired largely by the reverence for the cross in Anglo-Saxon England, through the medium, not of the Old English poetry, but of the Latin scholasticism of Alcuin.

BIBLIOGRAPHY

I. GENERAL REFERENCES

Anglo-Saxon Review, a Quarterly Miscellany. London and New York, 1899-1901.

Archæological Societies' Publications:

British Archæological Institute Association Journal. London, 1845.

Cambridge Camden Society. *Ecclesiologist, The.* London, 1841-68.

Royal Archæological Institute of Great Britain and Ireland. *Archæological Journal.* London, 1845.

Society of Antiquaries of London. *Archæologia.* London, 1770. Also, *Vetusta Monumenta, 1747-1895.*

Yorkshire Archæological and Topographical Association Journal. London, 1870. Called since 1893 the *Yorkshire Archæological Society Journal.*

Ashton, John. *The Legendary History of the Cross.* New York, 1887.

Birch, W. De Gray. *Early Drawings and Illuminations.* London, 1879.

Bugge, Sophus. *Studien über die Entstehung der Nordischen Götter- und Heldensagen.* A trans. into German by Oscar Brenner. Munich, 1889.

Calverley, W. S. *Early Sculptured Crosses, Shrines, and Monuments in the Diocese of Carlisle.* Kendall, 1899.

Cook, Albert S. *'Notes on the Ruthwell Cross.'* Publications of the Modern Language Association, Vol. 17, No. 3.

Cutts, E. L. *Parish Priests and their People in the Midd'e Ages in England.* London, 1898.

Didron, A. N. *Manuel d'Iconographie Chrétienne.* Paris, 1845. Translated into English as *Christian Iconography, or the History of Christian Art in the Middle Ages.* London, Vol. I, 1856; Vol. II, 1886.

Ebert, Adolf. *Ueber das Angelsächsische Gedicht Der Traum vom Heiligen Kreuz.* Leipzig, 1884.

Facsimiles of Ancient Charters in the British Museum, 3 parts. London, 1873-7.

Ferguson, J. *Rude Stone Monuments.* London, 1872.

Fosbroke, T. D. *British Monachism.* London, 1817.

Encyclopedia of Antiquities and Elements of A..hæology. 2 vols. London, 1825.

Fulda, Hermann. *Das Kreuz und die Kreuzigung.* Breslau, 1878.

Grimm, J. L. C. *Deutsche Mythologie.* Translated into English by J. S. Stallybrass as *Teutonic Mythology.* 4 vols. London, 1882-88.

Kent, C. W. *Teutonic Antiquities in ' Andreas' and ' Elene.'* Halle 1887.

Kirchenlexikon oder Encyklopädie der Katholischen Theologie und ihrer Hülfswissenschaften. Ed. J. C. Hergenröther and Franz Kaulen. Freiburg, 1886-99.

Lingard, John. *The History and Antiquities of the Anglo-Saxon Church,* etc. 2 vols. London, 1845.

Logeman, H. *L'Inscription Anglo-Saxone au Reliquaire de La Vraie Croix,* etc. Leipzig, etc., 1891.

Martigny, J. A. *Dictionaire des Antiquités Chrétiennes.* Paris, 1877.

Milman, H. H. *History of Latin Christianity.* 9 vols. 1883.

Palæographical Society. *Facsimiles of Manuscripts and Inscriptions.* 1st Series: 3 vols. Ed. E. A. Bond and E. M. Thompson. London, 1873-83. 2nd Series: 2 vols. Ed. E. A. Bond, E. M. Thompson, and G. F. Warner. London, 1889-94.

Pauly, *Real- Encyclopädie der Classischen Altertumswissenschaft.* ed. Georg Wissowa. Stuttgart, 1898-1901.

Ramsay, J. H. *The Foundations of England, or Twelve Centuries of British History.* B. C. 55 A. D. 1154. 2 vols. London, 1898.

Realencyklopädie für Protestantische Theologie und Kirche. Ed. Albert Hauck. Leipzig. 1877-88.

Rimmer, Alfred. *Ancient Stone Crosses of England.* London, 1875.

Rock, Daniel. *The Church of Our Fathers,* etc., 3 vols. in 4 parts. London, 1849-53.

Seymour, W. W. *The Cross in Tradition, History, and Art.* New York and London, 1898.

Schaff, Philip. *History of the Christian Church.* 7 vols. New York, 1882-92.

Schaff-Herzog. *Encyclopædia of Religious Knowledge.* Toronto, New York, and London, 1894.

Stephens, George. *The Old Northern Runic Monuments of Scandinavia and England,* etc. 3 vols. London, 1866-84.

————. *Professor S. Bugge's Studies on Northern Mythology Shortly Examined.* London, 1883.

Turner, Sharon. *The History of the Anglo-Saxons,* etc. 2 vols. Philadelphia, 1841.

Westwood, J. O. *Facsimiles of the Miniatures and Ornaments of Anglo-Saxon and Irish MSS.* London, 1868.

Wilson, Thos. *The Swastika.* London and Washington, 1898.
Vietor, Wilhelm. *Die Northumbrischen Runensteine,* etc. Marburg, 1895.
Zöckler, Otto. *Das Kreuz Christi.* Gütersloh, 1875.

II. LATIN TEXTS

Alcuin. *Alcuini Opera* in *Migne's Patrologia,* 100, 101. Paris, 1851. *Monumenta Germania Historica,* Vol. I. *Poetæ Latini Ævi Carolini,* ed. Louis Traube. Berlin, 1886.
Aldhelm. *Sancti Aldhelmi Opera,* in *Migne's Patrologia,* 89. Paris 1850.
Bede. *Complete Works of Bede,* etc. Ed. J. A. Giles. 12 vols. London, 1843-4.
——. *Venerabilis Bedæ Opera,* in *Migne's Patrologia,* 90-95. Paris 1850-51.
Benedictionale S. Æthelwoldi Episcopi Wintoniensis. Archæologia 24.
Birch, W. de Gray. *Cartularium Saxonicum,* etc. 3 vols. London, 1885-93.
Boniface. *Sancti Bonifacii Opera Omnia,* ed. J. A. Giles. 2 vols. London, 1844.
Columba. *Life of St. Columba, Written by Adamnan,* etc., ed. Wm. Reeves, in *Historians of Scotland,* 7. Edinburgh, 1874.
Dugdale, William. *Monasticon Anglicanum,* ed. John Caley, Henry Ellis, and Buekley Bandinel. 8 vols. London, 1817-30.
Dunstan. *Memorials of St. Dunstan,* ed. Wm. Stubbs. Rolls Series. London, 1874.
Earle, John. *A Handbook to the Land-Charters and Other Saxonic Documents.* Oxford, 1888.
Edmund. *Memorials of St. Edmund's Abbey,* ed. Thos. Arnold. Rolls Series. 3 vols. London, 1890-96.
Edward. *Lives of Edward the Confessor,* ed. H. R. Luard. Rolls Series. London, 1838.
Egbert. *The Pontifical of Egbert, Archbishop of York,* A. D. 732-766, ed. Wm. Greenwell. Surtees Soc. Durham, 1853.
Ethelwold. *Vita S. Æthelwaldi Episcopi Wintoniensis Auctore Ælfrico,* ed. Joseph Stevenson, in *Chronicon Monasterii de Abingdon.* 2. 253-66. Rolls Series. London, 1858.
Fortunatus. *Venantii Fortunati,* etc., *Opera Omnia,* in *Migne's Patrologia* 88. Paris, 1850.
Historia Monasterii S. Augustini Canstuariensis, etc., ed. Charles Hardwick. Rolls Series. London, 1858.

Historians of the Church of York, ed. James Raine. Rolls Series. 3 vols. London, 1879-94.

Kemble, J. M. *Codex Diplomaticus Ævi Saxonici.* Eng. Hist. Soc. 6 vols. London, 1839-48.

Latin Hymns of the Anglo-Saxon Church. Surtees Soc. Vol. 23. Durham, 1851.

Le Livere de Reis de Brittanie e Le Livre de Reis de Engelterre, ed. John Glover. Rolls Series. London, 1865.

Liber Monasterii de Hyda, ed. Edward Edwards. Rolls Series. London, 1866.

Library of the Fathers, translated from the original into English. 39 vols. Oxford, 1845-57.

Oswald. *Vita Oswaldi Archiepiscopi Eboracensis Auctore Anonymo.,* ed. J. Raine. *Historians of Church of York* 1. 399-475. Rolls Series. London, 1879.

Patrick. *The Tripartite Life of Patrick,* ed., with translations, by Whitley Stokes. Rolls Series. 2 vols. London, 1887.

Rabanus. *R. Rabani Mauri,* etc., *Opera Omnia,* in *Migne's Patrologia* 107-117. Paris, 1851-2.

Rituale Ecclesiæ Dunelmensis (Durham Ritual). Surtees Soc. Vol. 10. London, 1840.

Schmid, Reinhold. *Die Gesetze der Angelsachsen.* Leipzig, 1838.

Scotus, Erigena. *Joannis Scoti Opera,* in *Migne's Patrologia* 122.

Scotus, Josephus. *Monumenta Germaniæ Historica,* Vol. 1. *Poetæ Ævi Carolini.*

Simeon of Durham. *Symeonis Monachi Opera Omnia,* ed. Thos. Arnold. Rolls Series. 2 vols. London, 1882.

Thorpe, Benjamin. *Ancient Laws and Institutes of England.* London, 1840.

Vetus Registrum Sarisberiense (The Register of S. Osmund), ed. W. H. R. Jones. Rolls Series. 2 vols. London, 1883.

William of Malmesbury. *Wilhelmi Malmesbirienses De Gestis Pontificum Anglorum,* etc., ed. N. E. S. Hamilton. Rolls Series. London, 1870.

——. *Regum Anglorum,* ed. Wm. Stubbs. Rolls Series. 2 vols. London, 1889.

Wilfrid. *Vita Wilfridi Episcopi Eboracensis.* Auctore Eddio Stephano, in *Historians of Church of York.*

III. OLD ENGLISH TEXTS

Alfred. *Blooms of King Alfred, from the Flores Soliliquorum of S. Augustinus.* Text of W. H. Hulme. *Eng. Stud.* 18. 331-356.

Alfred. *King Alfred's Version of S. Augustine's Soliloquies, with the Latin Original,* ed. H. L. Hargrove, 1902. *Yale Studies in English* XIII.

——. *King Alfred's Old English Version of Boethius de Consolatione Philosophiæ,* ed. W. J. Sedgefield. Oxford, 1899.

——. *King Alfred's Orosius.* Old English text and Latin Original, ed. Henry Sweet. London, 1883. E. E. T. S. 79.

——. *King Alfred's West Saxon Version of Gregory's Pastoral Care, with an English Translation,* ed. Henry Sweet London, 1871. E. E. T. S. 45, 50.

——. *The Old English Version of Bede's Ecclesiastical History.* Part I. Old English text and trans., ed. Thos. Miller. London, 1890. E. E. T. S. 95, 96.

Ælfric. *Homilies of Ælfric,* with an Eng. trans., ed. Benjamin Thorpe. 2 vols. London, 1844-46.

——. *Ælfric's Lives of the Saints,* with an Eng. trans., ed. W. W. Skeat. London. Vol. I. 1881-5. E. E. T. S. 76, 82, parts 3 and 4. vol. 2. Lond. 1890-1900. E. E. T. S. 94, 114.

——. *Supplement to Ælfric's Homilies.* A. Napier. *Herrig's Archiv* 101-2.

——. Ælfric's writings contained in *Ancient Laws and Institutes of England,* ed. B. Thorpe. 1840.

——. *Ælfric de Vetere et de Novo Testamento;* also his *Præfatio Genesis* in *Bibliothek der Angelsächsichen Prosa.,* Bd. I, ed. C. W. M. Grein. Cassel and Göttingen, 1872.

——. Ælfric's writings contained in *Angelsächsische Homilien und Heiligenleben,* ed. B. Assmann. Kassel, 1889.

——. Ælfric's Version of *Alcuin's Interrogationes Sigenulfi in Genesin,* the Anglo-Saxon and the Latin Text, ed. G. E. Maclean. *Anglia* 6, 7.

Altenglische Glossen, ed. A. Napier. *Englishe Studien,* Vol. 11.

Altenglische Glossen. Zeitschrift für Deutsches Alterthum, ed. M. Haupt. Leipzig.

Altenglische Kleinigkeiten, ed. A. Napier. *Anglia* 11.

An Anglo-Saxon Passion of St. George, ed. C. Hardwick. Percy Society, Vol. 28. London, 1850.

Anglo-Saxon and Old English Vocabularies, ed. T. Wright. 2nd ed., R. P. Wülcker. London, 1884.

Anglo-Saxon Version of Apollonius of Tyre, with translation, ed. B. Thorpe. London, 1834.

Angelsächsisches Glossar, ed. H. Leo Halle, 1877.

An Old English Martyrology, ed. G. Herzfeld. London, 1900. E. E. T. S. 116.

Bibliothek der Angelsächsischen Prosa. Bd. 1. C. W. M. Grein,
Cassel and Göttingen, 1872. Bd. 2. Cassel, 1885. Bd. 3.
Cassel, 1889. Bd. 4. Leipzig, 1899. Bd. 5. Leipzig, 1900.
Bibliothek der Angelsächsischen Poesie, ed. C. W. Grein and R. P.
Wülcker. Bd. 1. Kassel, 1883. Bd. 2. Kassel, 1888. Bd.
3. Leipzig, 1897.
Byrhtferth's Handboc, ed. Kluge. *Anglia.* 8.
Blickling Homilies of the Tenth Century, with translation, ed. R.
Morris. London, 1880. E. E. T. S. 58, 63, 72.
Christ of Cynewulf, ed. Albert S. Cook. Boston, 1900.
Das Benedictiner Offizium, ein Altenglisches Brevier aus dem 11.
Jahr., ed. Emil Feiler. Heidelberg, 1901. *Anglistische For-
schungen* 4.
Das Jüngste Gericht. Munich Gelehrte Anzeigen 1.
Die Boulogneser Angelsächsischen Glossen zu Prudentius, ed. A.
Holder. *Germania,* N. S. 11.
De Consuetudine Monachorum, ed. W. S. Logeman. *Anglia* 13.
Domesday, E. E. T. S. 65.
Ein Angelsächsisches Leben des Neot, ed. Wülcker. *Anglia* 3.
Epistola Alexandri, ed. W. M. Baskervill. *Anglia* 4.
Evangelium Nicodemi, in *Heptateuchus Liber Job,* et *Evangelium
Nicodemi Anglo-Saxonice,* ed. Edwardus Thwaites. Ox-
ford, 1698.
Leben des Chad, ed. A. Napier. *Anglia* 10.
Legends of the Holy Rood. R. Morris. E. E. T. S. 46.
Leechdoms, Wortcunning, and Starcraft of Early England, ed. O.
Cockayne. 3 vols. London, 1864-66.
New Aldhelm Glosses, ed. H. Logeman. *Anglia* 13.
Old English Prose Version of the Life of St. Guthlac, ed. Good-
win. London, 1848.
Oldest English Texts, ed. Henry Sweet. E. E. T. S. 83.
Rule of St. Benet, Latin and Anglo-Saxon Interlinear Version, ed.
H. Logeman. London, 1848. E. E. T. S. 90.
*Synoptic Edition of Gospel of St. Matthew; Synoptic Edition of
Gospel of St. Mark; Synoptic Edition of Gospel of St.
Luke; Synoptic Edition of Gospel of St. John,* ed. W. W.
Skeat. Cambridge, Mt., 1887; Mk., 1871; Luke, 1874;
John, 1878.
Two of the Saxon Chronicles Parallel, ed. John Earle. Oxford, 1891.
Introd. notes, etc., 1899.
Wulfstan's Homilies., ed. A. Napier. Weimar, 1882.

———

Otfrid. *Otfrids Evangelienbuch,* ed. Paul Piper. Paderborn, 1878.
Tupper, Frederick. 'The Anglo-Saxon Daegmael,' *Pub. Mod. Lang.
Assoc.* 10. Baltimore, 1895.

PART II

SOME ACCOUNTS
OF THE BEWCASTLE CROSS
Between the years 1607 and 1861

A New Preface

This re-issue of A. S. Cook's collection of *Some Accounts of the Bewcastle Cross* (between the years 1607 and 1861) is intended to make a useful little work generally available once again. Cook provided a brief introduction to the collection, and a series of short notes on the several accounts. It is unfortunate that he confined the excerpts exclusively to the Bewcastle cross, for it is almost impossible to consider that cross without reference to the Ruthwell monument and indeed to the whole corpus of carved crosses which is left to us and to the series of runic inscriptions, on crosses and other objects as well, which have come down to us from the Anglo-Saxon period. In the Preface to this volume, Cook stresses once again his *idée fixe*, with which almost every scholar now disagrees, that Bewcastle and Ruthwell date from the twelfth century. His reasons here adduced are no more convincing than those presented in other publications.[1]

There is a definite stance in Cook's introductory remarks,

---

[1]The major work is, of course, his "The Date of the Ruthwell and Bewcastle Crosses" *Transactions of the Connecticut Academy of Arts and Sciences* 17 (1912), 213–361. See also his review of Bishop G. F. Browne's *The Ancient Cross Shafts at Bewcastle and Ruthwell* (Cambridge University Press, (1916) in *MLN* 32 (1917), 254–66. Of interest also is Cook's paper "The Bewcastel Cross," read before the Modern Language Association of America on 29 December 1909, and printed for him in New Haven in 1913. It is ten pages in length. For representative dissenting views see, for example, A. Campbell's *Old English Grammar*, corrected edition (Oxford, 1964), where *Ruthwell* is seen as the prime example of the "early" Northumbrian dialect, and is (fn. 2) "assigned to the eighth century without hazard." Curiously, Campbell did not mention or discuss the Bewcastle inscription in this context. In recent years art historians and archaeologists have indeed varied the placement of Ruthwell and Bewcastle from the seventh to tenth centuries, but the overwhelming modern consensus for a date *circa* 800 will be discussed below.

and it must be said that he chose to cite, or interpret, previous scholarly opinion to support his notion of a late date.
That two of the earlier commentators Roscarrock and Camden date the Bewcastle monument to the twelfth century is
no firm support, for their reports are brief, somewhat confused and certainly do not deal seriously with the inscription.
Though Haigh and Maughan, those well-known Victorian
antiquaries, both argue for a seventh-century date, they are
dismissed out of hand without evaluation of their work,
because their discussions often include spirited attacks
against one another. To me it seems all the more significant
that earliness of date is one of the few basic points on which
they *do* agree. This brief introduction is no proper place to
enter upon an extended discussion of the development of
scholarly opinion as it has evolved since Cook put his collection together, as only high points and major trends can be
touched upon, but in one major area, that of the inscription, re-reading the commentaries in the light of Dr. Page's
exhaustive study of the Bewcastle runes raises very grave
doubts on the value of the inscription as an indication of
date.[2] As a first point, it should be noted that few early commentators could read the inscriptions at all. Camden's account of 1607 states that the cross is inscribed, but he goes
on to comment "sed litteris ita fugientibus ut legis nequaquam possint." In 1685, Nicholson, on the evidence of the
curate of Bewcastle reported "The characters were so miserably worn out . . . that they were now wholly defaced,
and nothing to be met with worth my while." In his Visita-
tation of 1703, Nicholson described (or perhaps more accurately prefigured) the feeling I have had again and again in
the course of half a dozen visits to Bewcastle, some of several
weeks duration, from 1965 to present: "I try'd to recover the
Runic Inscription on ye West Side of the Cross: But, tho it
looked promising at a distance, we could not accurately
make out even that single line which Sr. H. *Spelman* long

---

[2]See R. Page, "The Bewcastle Cross" *Nottingham Medieval Studies* 4
(1960), 36–57. No reading of the selections presented will be adequate
without a careful reading of Dr. Page's study. See further his *Introduction to English Runes* (London, 1974), especially pp. 134–5, and 147.

since communicated to Ol. *Wormius*." It would seem that Nicholson referred here to the line, or few words, which appeared on the cross *head* of Bewcastle, now lost.[3]

There are clear indications that the cross has suffered from various attempts at "protection," "preservation" and examination during the past four centuries which in most cases did more harm than good. Someone coated it with a "white oyly cement" before Nicholson's visit in 1685; Maughan covered the inscribed parts first of all with soft mud and sods for a few months (*Second Account*, p. 70, n. 21) in order to remove moss and lichen. The desired result of clarification was apparently attained, but this is hardly a practice modern conservators would applaud.[4] Maughan then tried rubbings with lead and grass, then cast the inscribed part in plaster, *then* apparently painted the stone once again. Both he and Haigh, as well as earlier commentators (and doubtless generations of nameless visitors) traced the inscriptions and carvings with their fingers. The most famous and chilling episode records Haigh, in *Maughan's very presence*, finding *CRIS* (CRISTE) by "partly clearing away the moss *with the point of his knife*, and casting a rubbing" (p. 197; italics mine). In the light of all these enthusiastic attempts on the cross, the form of the ante-penultimate letter of the series KYNIBURG found

[3]The head of the cross was discovered in 1615 and lost before Nicholson's visit. Cook rejected this piece (note 3 to p. 3, pp. 128–33), partly on a series of measurements which I cannot follow, even after careful examination of the shaft, partly because the reading ricæs drihtnæs on the cross head would give us two early declensional endings. Cook proposed that the *epistylium crucis* found in 1615 was "the head of an older cross, a cross of quite different shape, fallen, perhaps overthrown and covered with earth, and with some of the letters illegible" (p. 132). Page, quite rightly I think, accepts that the Bewcastle cross head, and the various copies of its runes, are valid evidence; further, he holds that "the last Bewcastle cross-head undoubtedly held the text 'ricæs drihtnæs' while Cotton's comment suggests that there were further, illegible characters" (p. 56). For the various Mss. in which Cotton's comments are found, see Page, "The Bewcastle Cross," pp. 54–6.

[4]Any such drastic change in ambient conditions could well cause the process of deterioration to speed up.
(Keep two lines in proof here for expected communication from **Bob Brill**.)

between the two lowest decorative panels on the north face was carefully studied by Dr. Page. A letter similar to, or identical with this rune-form is found three times in the major inscription-panel. To summarize an extremely detailed investigation, this rune is a modified rune, recorded in early readings as ᚪ, possibly a bind-run ᚢ + ᛖ, but in accounts after 1857 *three* transverse lines across the interior of the rune can be seen.[5] It is thus virtually certain that zealousness of scholars attempting to clarify readings, or their expected versions, or some combination of these conditions has produced an otherwise unknown rune, even on the side of the cross most protected from weather, where we would expect the best conditions of preservation. Therefore, the main inscription on the much more exposed west face is still less to be trusted, and on the evidence of Dr. Page's investigations we may conclude with reasonable certainty that those inscriptions which would tie the cross to Alcfrith and Cyneburg, and thus to the last quarter of the seventh century, are highly suspect. Page's recent work has made it perfectly clear that a firm date for Bewcastle, and perhaps even for Ruthwell and Bewcastle paired, cannot be adduced from runological evidence alone.[6] As a corollary, art historians, therefore, cannot turn to linguists for firm information as to date. The question, therefore, must be put to art historians, historians and archæologists— can recent advances in these fields help provide information here?

First of all, can a case be made for the direct linking of Ruthwell and Bewcastle on art historical grounds? The answer has almost universally been yes, though the question of which monument was earlier, or perhaps even inspired the other, has been interpreted both ways. For reasons I find

[5]See Page, "The Bewcastle Cross," especially Pl. I, fig. 2, and pp. 41–54.

[6]Dr. Page himself concludes that insofar as the letter-forms tell us anything, a date of 750–850 is possible. His extreme caution is well taken, for the corpus of Old English runic inscriptions is so scant. As he points out, "We know so little about the language of western Northumbria in OE times that such a dating must be tentative in the extreme." For more broad-ranging *caveats*, see Page, *Runes*, especially pp. 15–16.

somewhat unclear, many art historians date Bewcastle later than Ruthwell.[7] A notable exception is F. Saxl, who holds that Bewcastle preceded Ruthwell because "The Ruthwell St. John the Baptist shows the southern [Mediterranean] dress more transformed than the corresponding Bewcastle figure," and further suggests that "had the Bewcastle master copied it he would hardly have been able to retranslate it into a more southern stage."[8] As an example of the difficulty of the evidence on which discussion must be based, it is interesting to note that Saxl's view is directly opposed in Ernst Kitzinger's detailed survey of the development of classical draperies in early Northumbrian art in his monograph on the carved figures on the coffin of St. Cuthbert.[9] From a more general perspective, both monuments are approximately the same size; they are both in the border country; both have iconographies which are similar in some respects; both have runic inscriptions of considerable length, though the Bewcastle inscriptions appear to be far less well preserved.

But there are differences as well. The Bewcastle cross is a monolith, while Ruthwell consists of two stones, of slightly different coloration.[10] Ruthwell has its major runic inscrip-

[7]See, for example, M. Schapiro, "The Religious Meaning of the Ruthwell Cross" *Art Bulletin* 26 (1944), 232–45 (hereafter Schapiro). Priority established, p. 243.

[8]F. Saxl, "The Ruthwell Cross," *Journal of the Warburg and Courtauld Institutes* 6 (1943), 1–19 (hereafter Saxl). Quotation, p. 10.

[9]Speaking of the figure on Cuthbert's coffin, his main concern, Kitzinger concludes "All that we can say is that our figures betray the same direct dependence on foreign models which we find in Ruthwell and to a somewhat lesser extent in Bewcastle. They help to clarify the relative positions of these two crosses by showing that the garments worn by the great statuesque figures are meant to be *pallia* and that in this respect the Ruthwell master reproduced Mediterranean prototypes more faithfully than did his colleagues in Cumberland." See Kitzinger's study in *The Relics of St. Cuthbert*, ed. C. F. Battiscombe (Oxford, 1956), pp. 202–304. Quotation, p. 294.

[10]They are generally taken to be the same reddish sandstone, with the color difference due either to the casts of the respective strata from which they were cut, or perhaps the weathering and generally wet condition in which they were kept after the seventeenth-century mutilation.

tion on the borders of the lower stone, which contain vine-scroll decoration, while Bewcastle has an incised banded border on the sole face with figure-sculpture, and the runic inscriptions are confined to the areas above and below the figure-sculpture, and in bands between the two lower deco-rated panels on the north side. Bewcastle is certainly a more eclectic monument, with elements of Celtic orientation, while Ruthwell, with the extremely ambitious iconographi-cal scheme, is more directly "Roman" in orientation.[11] It is certain that Ruthwell and Bewcastle both have Christ stand-ing on the beasts as a figure central to the iconography.[12] On both crosses, John the Baptist holding the *Agnus Dei* stands immediately above Christ on the beasts. There are great problems in interpreting the third, or lowest, figure on

[11]It should be pointed out that at least one Irish high cross, at Moone, rivals Ruthwell in complexity of iconography, and parallels it in impor-tant details. Both have the Crucifixion low on the cross, both have the Flight into Egypt, and Paul and Anthony breaking bread; but the rest of the figure sculpture, and more significantly the relative crudeness of the Irish figures, mark off differences. See further Françoise Henry *Irish Art in the Early Christian Period (to 800 A.D.)*, (London and Ithaca, 1965), pp. 148–51. In this respect it is interesting to note that Professor Rosemary Cramp suggested that while the several Insular traditions are quite independent in their development, "the free-standing *wooden* cross was for the Northern English a gift from the Irish church." *Early Northumbrian Sculpture* (Jarrow Lecture, 1965), p. 5. Italics mine.

[12]In its present placement in the specially-built addition to the church at Ruthwell, the figure that dominates is Christ with Mary Magdalene annointing his feet (Luke VII, 37–8). It is very probable that the place-ment of Bewcastle should be taken as the proper orientation, with Christ on the beasts, as it were, coming out of the East, since it is vir-tually certain that Bewcastle has not been significantly disturbed since its erection. The figure of Christ on the beasts derives from Vulgate Psalm 90. 13, "Super aspidem et basiliscum ambulabis, et conculcabis leonem et draconem." The figure on *Ruthwell* is further identified by the surrounding inscription: IHS XPS : JUDEX AEQUITATIS : BES-TIAE ET DRACONES COGNOUERUNT IN DESERTO SALVA-TOREM MUNDI. Schapiro connects this text with Mark I. 13. His interpretation is the best explication to date of the importance of the figure both on Ruthwell and Bewcastle: "The sculpture represents then Christ with the beasts in the desert, according to Mark, although the pattern of the image is the familiar type of Christ treading on the lion and the dragon. The assimilation is not surprising, since there is an exegetical link between the two subjects. The motif of Christ in the

the Bewcastle cross. It is that of a standing figure, possibly in secular dress, somewhat crowded into its panel, which has a markedly rounded top. It stands in semi-profile, and there is a large bird of prey on the right, which appears to be perched on the figure's left arm, which is extened over a T-shaped perch. The human figure appears to be holding a stick in its right hand.[13] This figure has been interpreted as a secular person, a falconer,[14] and as John the Evangelist with his symbol, the eagle. Saxl argues eloquently for the triad John the Baptist—Christ on the beasts—John the Evangelist on Bewcastle, but while the Ruthwell arrangement of course supports the first two members of the series, it by no means supports the Evangelist figure as part of the series, so the question, at least for the present, must remain open.[15] What we are faced with, then, in the present state

desert belongs to the Temptation, which already in the Gospels is connected with Psalm [90]. In the accounts of the episode in Matthew (IV. 6) and Luke (IV. 10, 11), the devil, in urging Christ to cast himself down from the pinnacle of the temple, quotes Psalm [90]. 11, 12: 'For it is written, he shall give his angels charge concerning thee: and in their hands they shall bear thee up, lest at any time thou dash thy foot against a stone.' Jesus will not tempt the Lord, and the commentators celebrate His victory over the devil by quoting the next verse of Psalm [90], in which the feet of Christ trample on the monsters and wild beasts that symbolize the demon." (Schapiro, p. 233).

[13]Extreme caution is necessary on all of these points, and no more certain description can be given, at least by me, until all of the photographs of the monuments collected by Mr. Ball, Fellow of Lincoln College, Oxford, during an Oxford University trip to the monuments in 1965 in which I took part, and in photographs taken during subsequent visits by Professor Cramp and myself can be studied, and further site-visits made, in the process of a detailed publication of the crosses.

[14]Baldwin-Brown, *Arts in Early England*, V (London, 1921), pp. 282–4, adduces evidence for hawking being practised in England perhaps as early as the seventh century, and cites letters of St. Boniface in the eighth century as proof-positive for the practice of the sport at that time in England.

[15]Saxl states: "The Bewcastle programme is of staggering grandeur and simplicity. As we approach the cross we see first, on a level with ourselves, the huge figure of the Evangelist holding his pen. As in Ruthwell he is shown with his symbol, the Eagle, which soars higher than the other birds. St. John stands as witness to the Christ from the beginning. Above us we see Christ as Victor over the demons, as Judge

of our knowledge, is a pair of monuments which are related in several important respects, though the order in which they were erected, and the date of their production, cannot be set with any certainty on the evidence of the runic inscriptions or the study of the crosses in isolation.

Professor Cramp has surveyed the principal monuments in an important exploratory study, *Early Northumbrian Sculpture*.[16] She deals with the main traditions of the period, working out from major monastic centers such as Hexham, Lindisfarne, and most particularly Monkwearmouth-Jarrow. On the basis of stylistic analysis, particularly of the details on the distinctive inhabited vine-scrolls, she finds important similarities on crosses from Bewcastle, Ruthwell, Jarrow, and Jedburgh, among others:

> If one may summarise the details which distinguish this group of carvings: the tangled ropy vine on both Jarrow vestry and porch fragments is very like Ruthwell, and the spear shaped leaves with knobs on either side where the stem meets the leaf are also distinctively Ruthwell in type—as on the middle section of the east face. The very distinctive flower with petals curled back from central stamens or seed-pods is also only found at Bewcastle, Ruthwell, Jarrow, Jedburgh, in that order of stylisation, although there is from Crayke, Yorkshire, on a fragment of a cross head, a single variant of the flower type, and a similar scroll treatment, but without the distinctive flowers, is known at Norham. On Bewcastle crossed leaves are elegantly used as space-fillers in the

---

of the quick and the dead; and still higher up, the Baptist, holding the sacrificial Lamb, as prophet of the Passion which Christ suffered as *Vere Homo*." (Saxl, p. 8). The crux here is that John the Evangelist appears on the *cross-head* at Ruthwell, shown as a seated figure with symbol, is on a totally different scale than that of the cross-shaft figures, and, as Professor Cramp has shown in a soon-to-be-published study, is almost certainly one of the four evangelists with symbols which originally decorated one side of the cross-head. Thus, Saxl's implicit use of Ruthwell as parallel is not solidly based, and his case not strong.

16 Jarrow Lecture for 1965, cited in note 11 above.

scroll, but on Ruthwell West the leaves have been superseded by fruit and flowers. At Jedburgh there are no real
leaves at all, the veins and lobes having been exaggerated
to such an extent that they have become like fruit. The
Jarrow frieze also shares the same sort of rounded scroll,
the open seed-pod and heavily lobed pointed leaves, and
has in addition a gripping beast as on Ruthwell West,
biting downwards on to the plant stem. This little beast
also appears at Jedburgh, and in a more developed form
at Rothbury. Rothbury also shows the type of sprawling
biped looked at from above which appears on the Ruthwell West scroll.[17]

Further research and excavations, particularly at Jarrow,
have revealed a rich ecclesiastical culture, which could well
have sustained artisans of a very high standard indeed,[18]

[17]Ibid., pp. 10–11.

[18]See further *Proceedings of the Scottish Archæological Forum* 3 (1973),
which centered on problems of Celtic and Northern English monastic
settlements, and in which Professor Cramp surveyed "Anglo-Saxon Monasteries of the North" (pp. 104–24). In her conclusions, she said of
Monkwearmouth-Jarrow "The wealth of these houses, which must have
been considerable, was reflected in their buildings and no doubt also
in their church metalwork and manuscripts. These reflected the aspira-
tion of the community to belong to the antique Christian world. The
small finds from Wearmouth-Jarrow showed a marked lack of personal
possessions. Moreover the food debris is remarkable in contrast with the
late medieval levels—there are very few animal bones—almost all are
fish bones, particularly of local shellfish." (p. 123). Building 'A' at Jarrow
is an example of the splendor of the house: "It is possible in view of
the solid construction of the walls that this was a two-storeyed building.
The structure was faced internally with a creamy plaster, its northern
windows were of stained glass and the southern colourless, its roof was
of small stone roofing-slates and lead flashing and the building was
surrounded by a shallow eavesdrip drain" (p. 121). Since I was privi-
leged to take part in these excavations for various periods over several
seasons, I can only add that certain of the remains, particularly the
stained glass, are of a magnificence that is hard to describe in words.
A new find at the very end of the 1973 season was a large and splendid
building, again with a great deal of stained glass, and with flagged
floors, close to the river on the site. This has yet to be published. For
an account of glass found earlier, see Rosemary Cramp, "Decorated
Window—Glass and Millifiori from Monkwearmouth" *Antiquaries
Journal* 50 (1970), 327–35; the article includes excellent color plates.

who continued the tradition of Roman and Continental
Christianity with remarkable skill.[19]

No account of the crosses, and the milieu in which they
came into being, can close without some brief indication of
recent advances in our knowledge of the richness of the
culture of Northern England in the Early Christian period,
particularly with respect to the widely diverse traditions
which met, fused, and inter-influenced one another in complex ways which we are just beginning to understand. When
Cook wrote, he knew well that there were "Celtic" and
"Roman" strands in Saxon culture; he knew of the Picts; but
recent advances both in archæology, and the re-interpretation
of a whole range of materials indicate clearly how simplifica-
tions will not do. While Ruthwell is perhaps the most
"Roman" of all the famous Northumbrian monuments,
Bewcastle certainly reflects other influences. With respect to
both artifacts and the culture itself, the term Insular has
come to have a more broad meaning over the past quarter
century. Most commonly applied to the script that was wide-
spread throughout English and Irish contexts, the term has
been used (with careful development of the bases for the
application) to refer to a broad cultural milieu, one which
might well have produced both *Beowulf* and Bewcastle.[20]

[19]No more striking evidence of the Continental and Roman traditions
continuing at Monkwearmouth-Jarrow exists than the three pandects of
the Bible made there under the influence of Ceolfrith. Only one of
these survives, now in Florence, and known as the Codex Amiatinus.
Some fragments of the sister volumes remain, one discovered in a Newcastle shop by Canon Greenwell of Durham in 1909. This and similar
leaves are preserved in the British Library; see further E. A. Lowe,
Codices Latines Antiquiores II, p. 177. For an excellent study of Amiatinus, its art, and the tradition it represents, see Rupert Bruce-Mitford's
The Art of the Codex Amiatinus (*Jarrow Lecture*, 1967). (Available also
in *Journal of the British Archæological Association*, 3rd ser. 32 (1969),
1–25). Recent work in history and cultural history has re-stressed the
importance of continued and sustained contact between English and
Continental centers, particularly those in Gaul. See further James
Campbell, "Observations on the Conversion of England" *Ampleforth
Journal* 78 (1973), and Henry Mayr-Harting, *The Coming of Christianity to Anglo-Saxon England* (London, 1972).

[20]See Charles Donahue, "Beowulf and Christian Tradition: A Reconsideration from a Celtic Stance," *Traditio* 21 (1965), 55–116, and his
earlier "Beowulf, Ireland and the Natural Good," *Traditio* 7 (1949–51),
263–77.

Certainly, important manuscripts once considered "Irish" without doubt are now given a different and more "English" placement, speaking from the stance of a modern geography. In his Jarrow Lecture for 1971, Professor Julian Brown viewed not only the Lindisfarne Gospels and other associated manuscripts but also the Book of Kells itself as the product of "a great insular centre . . . subject to Northumbrian influence . . . in eastern Scotland."[21] The discovery of the St. Ninian's Isle treasure, coupled with recent scholarships on the Picts, their language, history, culture and art has shown them to be a far more active contributor to Northumbrian culture than has been suspected. The St. Ninian's Isle treasure is almost certainly a secular hoard—it is certainly a collection of art objects of great beauty and careful design, which may well be representative of changes wrought in the larger Insular context.[22]

We are closer to an understanding of Bewcastle, and of Ruthwell, and the past sixty years have seen the production of vast ranges of evidence undreamed of by A. S. Cook. Most of our new information is the product of archæological discovery, and the study of the culture and art of the period. It now is fairly certain that the Bewcastle inscriptions are of dubious value, and that the best evidence points to the conclusion that both Bewcastle and Ruthwell are to be seen as products of the eighth century, or at any rate sometime between 675–800, rather than the twelfth century. But Professor Cook's work both in this volume and in other publications should not be undervalued. In his resolute tenacity and wide research, and perhaps by his very insistence on the late dating of Ruthwell and Bewcastle, he has undoubtedly caused many scholars to look long and hard at the evidence

[21]Reprinted as "Northumbria and the Book of Kells," *Anglo-Saxon England* 1 (Cambridge, 1972), 219–46. See esp. pp. 234 and 243.

[22]A brief section on the Pictish question has been included in the bibliography. Suffice it to say that the picture we have of this people, their culture and their influence has clarified enormously since F. T. Wainwright in 1955 published a series of essays on the *Problem of the Picts.* For the definitive study of the St. Ninian's Island finds, see Alan Small, Charles Thomas and David Wilson, *St. Ninian's Island and its Treasure,* Aberdeen University Studies 152, 2 vols. (Oxford, 1973).

124   *The Anglo-Saxon Cross*

for the dating of these monuments. Such tenacity, and sheer hard work, must stand as a part of the *lāf* of one of our most distinguished Anglo-Saxonists.

ROBERT T. FARRELL

I General

M. O. Anderson, *Kings and Kingship in Early Scotland* (Rowman and Littlefield, Totowa, New Jersey, 1973).

J. Bannerman *Studies in the History of Dalriada* (Edinburgh, 1974).

M. W. Barley and R. P. C. Hanson, *Christianity in Early Britain 300–700* (Leicester, 1968).

C. F. Battiscombe, ed., *The Relics of St. Cuthbert* (Oxford, 1956).

Baldwin Brown, *The Arts in Early England* (London, 1921).

Julian Brown, "Northumbria and the Book of Kells" *Anglo-Saxon England* 1 (1972), 219–46.

Rupert Bruce-Mitford, *The Art of the Codex Amiatinus* (Jarrow Lecture, 1967), (available also in *Jour. Brit. Arch. Assn.* 3rd ser. 32 (1969), 1–25.

James Campbell "Observations on the Conversion of England," *Ampleforth Journal* 78 (1973), 12–26.

A. S. Cook, "The Date of the Ruthwell and Bewcastle Crosses" *Trans. Conn. Acad. Arts and Sciences* 17 (1912), 213–361.

—— Review of Biship G. F. Browne's *The Ancient Cross Shafts of Bewcastle and Ruthwell* (Cambridge, 1916), *MLN* 32 (1917), 334–66.

—— *The Bewcastle* (New Haven, 1913).

Rosemary Cramp, "The Anglian Sculptured Crosses of Dumfriesshire" *Dumfries and Galloway Antiquarian Society Transcripts* 38 (1959–60), 9–20.

—— *The Monastic Art of Northumbria* (London: Arts Council of Great Britain 1967),

—— *Early Northumbrian Sculpture* (Jarrow Lecture, 1965).

Charles Donahue, "Beowulf and Christian Tradition: A Reconsideration from a Celtic Stance" *Traditio* 21 (1965), 55–116.

Kathleen Hughes, *The Church in Early Irish Society* (London, 1966).

—— *Early Christian Ireland: Introduction to the Sources* (London, 1972).

Sir Thomas D. Kendrick, *Anglo-Saxon Art to 900 A.D.* (London, 1938).

—— et al., *Evangeliorum Quattuor Codex Lindisfarnensis* (Lausanne, 1956).

D. P. Kirby, ed., *St. Wilfrid at Hexham* (Newcastle, 1974).

Françoise Henry, *Irish Art in the Early Christian Period (to 800 A.D.)*, (London and Ithaca, 1965).

Henry Mayr Harting, *The Coming of Christianity to Anglo-Saxon England* (London, 1972).

Eric Mercer, "The Ruthwell and Bewcastle Crosses" *Antiquity* 38 (1964), 268–277.

R. Page, "The Bewcastle Cross" *Nottingham Medieval Studies* 4 (1960), 36–57.

—— *Introduction to English Runes* (London, 1974).

Proceedings of the Scottish Archæological Forum 3 (1973). (Range of papers on problems of Celtic and northern English monastic settlements.)

F. Saxl, "The Ruthwell Cross," *Journal of the Warburg and Courtauld Institutes* (1943), 1–19.

M. Schapiro, "The Religious Meaning of the Ruthwell Cross" *Art Bulletin* 26 (1944), 232–45.

II Pictish Question

Stewart Cruden, *The Early Christian and Pictish Monuments of Scotland* (H.M.S.O. Edinburgh 1964).

A. A. M. Duncan, *Scotland: The Making of the Kingdom* (Edinburgh, 1975).

Isabel Henderson, *The Picts* (London, 1967).

Kathleen Hughes, "Early Christianity in Pictland" (Jarrow Lecture, 1970).

D. P. Kirby, "Bede and the Pictish Church," *Innes Review* 24 (1973), 6–25.

C. Thomas, "An Early Christian Cemetery and Chapel on Ardwall Isle, Kirkudbright" *Medieval Archaeology* 11 (1967), 127–88.

—— *Britain and Ireland in Early Christian Times: A.D. 400–800* (London, 1871).

—— *The Early Christian Archæology of North Britain* (London, 1971).

E. A. Thompson, "The Origin of Christianity in Scotland" *Scottish Historical Review* 37 (1958), 17–22.

F. T. Wainwright, ed., *The Problem of the Picts* (Edinburgh, 1955).

———— *The Northern Isles* (Edinburgh, 1962).

W. J. Watson, *The History of the Celtic Place Names of Scotland* (Edinburgh, 1926).

PREFACE

Since opinion concerning the date of the Bewcastle Cross has varied so widely, I have thought that the considerations brought forward in my monograph, *The Date of the Ruthwell and Bewcastle Crosses* (1912), might fitly be supplemented by such a series of descriptions and opinions as would enable the student who might not have ready access to a large library to trace the history of antiquarian thought on this subject. The present selection will be found, I believe, to contain the most important papers and passages relating to this monument between the year 1607, when Nicholas Roscarrock, a guest of Lord William Howard's at Naworth Castle, touched upon it in a letter to Camden, and 1861, when Father Haigh resumed his earlier study in his *Conquest of Britain*.

I shall not undertake here to deduce all the conclusions which might be drawn from a comparison of these accounts. Some of them will be immediately apparent to the attentive reader ; others will be pointed out in the notes. Three or four facts, however, are sufficiently curious to be remarked. One is that the first two persons that deal with the cross, Roscarrock and Camden, refer it to the twelfth century. Another is that the chequers on the north side, on which they based their opinion, serve now, though for a different reason, to suggest the same general period. A third is that the two persons who are most responsible for creating the popular impression that the cross was erected in the seventh century, Haigh and Maughan, contradict each other and themselves on the most essential points. A fourth is that nothing appears to have been more legible upon the monument two centuries and a quarter ago than at present: *Cynnburug,* for example, is as clear in the most recent photograph as it was to Nicolson in 1685.

The engravings, if compared with the photographs in my recent book, will show how fancy rioted in the earlier delineations, and how inexactly the sculpture was rendered throughout the eighteenth century. With greater accuracy in the representation of the facts, and an exacter science in the interpretation of them, it may be hoped that the cross will soon be assigned to its proper historical place, where, instead of being a stumbling-block and cause of bewilderment, it may serve to illustrate the characteristics of the age to which it belongs.

YALE UNIVERSITY,
        July 9, 1913.

TABLE OF CONTENTS

SOME ACCOUNTS
OF THE BEWCASTLE CROSS

I. ROSCARROCK'S LETTER TO CAMDEN, 1607.

[The first mention of the Bewcastle Cross that I have found is
in the following sentence from a letter by Nicholas Roscarrock, then
residing in the family of Lord William Howard (' Belted Will '),
written to William Camden from ' Nawarde ' (Naworth Castle)
Aug. 7, 1607 (see *Camdeni Epistolæ*, pp. 90—92, and *Surtees Soc. Publ.*
68. 506—7). Roscarrock calls Camden's attention to two errors
in the latter's fifth edition of the *Britannia*, and evidently hopes that
Camden (addressed as Clarenceulx king-of-arms) can utilize his suggestions in the sixth edition, which bears date the same year. On
September 7 Camden had a fall from his horse, and during the con-
finement of nine months which resulted, he put the last hand to
the sixth edition (*Dict. Nat. Biog.*). Accordingly, Roscarrock's
letter must be earlier than Camden's edition of 1607.

For further information concerning Roscarrock, consult *Surtees
Soc. Pub.* 68. 505—9, and *Dict. Nat. Biog.*]

Understanding (good Mr. Clarenceulx) that your
Britayne ys at this present in printinge, and reddy to
come forthe, I thought fitt (in a small showe of our
ancient love) to geve you notice of twoe escapes in
the last edition.

. . . Yf you have any occasion to speak of the
Cross of Buechastell,[1] I assure myselfe the inscription
of one syde ys, *Hubert de Vaux*[2] ; the rather, for that
the checky coate[3] ys above that on the same syde ;
and on the other[4] the name of the Ermyt that made
yt, and I canne in no sorte be brought to thincke it
Eborax,[5] as I perceave you have been advertised.

II. CAMDEN'S ACCOUNT, 1607.

[William Camden's (1551—1623) *Britannia* was first published in 1586. As late as the fifth edition, 1600, there was no mention of the Bewcastle Cross, but in the edition of 1607 (p. 644) the following passage appeared. The first translation below is from Gibson's Camden, 1722 (practically identical with that of 1695), and the second from the second edition of Gough's Camden (1806).]

In cœmiterio Crux in viginti plùs minùs pedes ex vno quadrato saxo graphicè excisa surgit, & inscripta, sed literis ita fugientibus vt legi nequaquam possint. Quod autem ipsa Crux ita interstincta sit, vt clypeus gentilitius familiæ de *Vaulx,* eorum opus fuisse existimare licet.

In the Church-yard, is a Cross, of one entire square stone, about twenty foot high, and curiously wrought. There is an Inscription too, but the letters are so dim that they are not legible. But seeing the Cross is of the same kind, as that in the Arms of the Vaulx,[1] we may suppose that it has been erected by some of that Family.

In the church-yard is a cross near 20 feet high, of one stone, neatly wrought, and having an inscription, but the letters too much consumed by time to be legible. But the cross itself being chequered like the arms of the family of Vaulx makes it probable that it was their work.

III. NICOLSON'S LETTER TO OBADIAH WALKER, 1685.

[William Nicolson (1655—1727) was, when he wrote the subjoined letter, Archdeacon of Carlisle and Rector of Great Salkeld, Cumberland. In 1702 he became Bishop of Carlisle, and in 1718 Bishop of Derry, in Ireland. In 1678 he had visited Leipzig, ' to learn German and the northern languages of Europe ' (*Dict. Nat. Biog.*). He wrote various historical works and antiquarian papers, among the latter being an account of his visit to Ruthwell Cross in 1703, for which see my paper in the *Publications of the Modern Language Association of America* 17. 367—374. The appended letter is from *Philosophical Transactions* 15 (1685). 1287—91.

For Obadiah Walker (1616—1699), Master of University College from 1676 to 1689, see *Dict. Nat. Biog.* He was, with others, author of a Latin version (1678) of John Spelman's life of King Alfred. Nicolson has an entry in his diary under date of Oct. 20, 1684, recording the writing of a letter to Walker about the Bridekirk font, in which he promised ere long a fuller account of that and the ' Pedestal at Bewcastle.']

A Letter from Mr William Nicolson, *to the Reverend* Mr Walker, Master *of* University Coll: *in* Oxford ; *concerning a* Runic Inscription *at* Beaucastle.

'Tis now high time to make good my promise of giving you a more perfect Account of our two *Runic* Inscriptions at *Beau-Castle* and *Bridekirk*. The former is fallen into such an untoward part[1] of our Country, and so far out of the common Road, that I could not much sooner have either an opportunity, or the Courage to look after it. I was assur'd by the Curate[2] of the place, (a Person of good sence & Learning in greater matters,) that the Characters were so miserably worn out since the Lord *William Howard's* time, (by whom they were communicated[3] to Sr *H. Spelman*, & mentioned by *Wormius, Mon. Dan.* p. 161,) that they were now wholly defaced, and nothing to be met

with worth my while. The former part of this Relation I found to be true: for (tho' it appears that the
forementioned Inscription has bin much larger[1] then
Wormius has given it, yet) 'tis at present so far lost,
that, in six or seven lines, none of the Characters are
fairly discernable, save only ⌂ϝ↑ꅺR; and these
too are incoherent, and at great distance from each
other. However, this *Epystilium*[2] *Crucis* (as S[r] *H. Spelman,* in his Letter to *Wormius,* has called it,) is to
this day a noble Monument; and highly merits the
View of a Curious Antiquary. The best account,
S[r], I am able to give you of it, be pleased to take
as follows.

'Tis one entire Free-Stone of about five yards[3] in
height, washed over (as the Font at *Bridekirk,*) with
a white oyly Cement,[4] to preserve it the better from
the injuries [1288] of time and weather. The figure
of it inclines to a square Pyramid; each side whereof
is near two foot[5] broad at the bottom, but upwards
more tapering. On the West side of the Stone, we
have three fair Draughts, which evidently enough
manifest the Monument to be Christian. The Lowest
of these represents the Pourtraicture of a Layman;
with an Hawk, or Eagle, perch'd on his Arm. Over
his head are the forementioned ruines of the Lord
Howard's Inscription. Next to these, the Picture of
some Apostle, Saint, or other Holy man, in a sacerdotal Habit, with a Glory round his Head. On the top
stands the Effigies of the B. V. with the Babe in her
Arms; and both their Heads encircled with Glories
as before.

On the North we have a great deal of Checquer-
work; subscribed with the following Characters,[6] fairly
legible.

Upon the first sight of these Letters, I greedily
ventured to read them *Rynburu* : and was wonderfully
pleased to fancy, that this word thus singly written,
must necessarily betoken the final extirpation and
Burial[1] of the Magical *Runæ* in these parts, reasonably
hoped for, upon the Conversion of the *Danes* to the
Christian Faith. For, that the *Danes* were antiently,
as well as some of the *Laplanders* at present, gross
Idolaters and Sorcerers, is beyond Controversy; and
I could not but remember, that all our Historians tell
us, that they brought their Paganism along with them
into this Kingdome. And therefore 'twas not very
difficult to imagine that they might for some time
practise their *Hocus* tricks here in the North ; where
they were most numerous and least disturbed. This
conceit was the more heightened, by reflecting upon
the natural superstition of our Borderers at this day ;
who are much better acquainted with, and do [1289]
more firmly believe, their old Legendary stories of
Fayries and Witches, then the Articles of their Creed.
And to convince me yet further that they are not
utter strangers to the *Black Arts* of their forefathers,
I accidentally met with a Gentleman in the neighbourhood, who shewed me a Book of Spells and
Magical Receipts, taken (two or three days before)
in the pocket of one of our *Moss-Troopers* : wherein,
among many other conjuring Feats, was prescribed
a certain Remedy for an Ague, by applying a few
barbarous Characters to the Body of the party dis-
tempered. These, methought, were very near akin to
Wormius's RAMRUNER ; which, he says, differed
wholly in figure and shape from the common *Runæ*.
For, though he tells us, that these *Ramruner* were so
called, *Eo quod Molestias, dolores, morbosque hisce in-
fligere inimicis soliti sint Magi* ; yet his great friend

Arng: *Jonas,* more to our purpose, says *that—His etiam usi sunt ad benefaciendum, juvandum, Medicandum tam animi quam Corporis morbis* ; *atque ad ipsos Cacodæmones pellendos & fugandos.* I shall not trouble you with a draught of this Spell ; because I have not yet had an opportunity of learning, whether it may not be an ordinary one, and to be met with (among others of the same nature) in *Paracelsus* or *Cornelius Agrippa.*

If this conjecture be not allowable ; I have, Sr, one more which (it may be) you will think more plausible then the former. For if, instead of making the third and fourth Letters to be two ᚳ. ᚳ. ᛋ. ᛋ. [1] we should suppose them to be ᚾ. ᚾ. E. E. the word will then be *Ryeeburu* ; which I take to signify, in the old *Danish* Language, *Cœmiterium* or *Cadaverum Sepulchrum*. For, tho the true old *Runic* word for *Cadaver* be usually written ᚼRᛅᚾ *Hrae;* yet the *H* may, without any violence to the Orthography of that tongue, be omitted at pleasure; and then the difference of spelling the word, here at *Beaucastle,* and on some of the ragged Monuments in *Denmark,* will not [1290] be great. And for the countenancing of this latter Reading, I think the above mentioned *Checquer work* may be very available: since in that we have a notable Emblem of the *Tumuli,* or burying places of the Antients. (Not to mention the early custome of erecting Crosses and Crucifixes in Church-yards: which perhaps, being well weighed, might prove another encouragement to this second Reading.) I know the Checquer to be the Arms of the *Vaux's,* or *De Vallibus,* the old Proprietours of this part of the North ; but that, I presume, will make nothing for our turn. Because this & the other carved work on the Cross, must of necessity be allow'd, to bear a more antient date [2] then any of the Remains of that Name and Family ; which cannot be run up higher then the Conquest.

On the East we have nothing but a few Flourishes, Draughts of Birds, Grapes and other Fruits : all which I take to be no more then the Statuary's Fancy.

On the South, Flourishes and conceits, as before, and towards the bottom, the following decay'd Inscription.

||ᚢᚠ·ᚾB ⁘⁝ ᚦᚱᛗᛏ⁚||

The Defects in this short piece are sufficient to discourage me from attempting to expound it. But (possibly) it may be read thus.

Gag Ubbo Erlat, i. e.
Latrones Ubbo Vicit.

I confess this has no Affinity (at least, being thus interpreted) with the foregoing Inscription : but may well enough suit with the manners of both antient and modern Inhabitants of this Town and Country.

Upon your pardon and Correction, S[r], of the Impertinencies and Mistakes in this, (which I shall humbly hope [1291] for,) I shall trouble you with my further observations on the Font at *Bridekirk* ; and to all your other Commands shall pay that ready obedience which becomes,

S[r],

Carlile,   *Your most obliged and*
Nov. 2.   *Faithfull Servant*
1685.   WILL. NICOLSON.

ADDITION OF (1695) 1722.

[This letter is reprinted in Gibson's edition of Camden's *Britannia*, 1695 and 1722, omitting the last paragraph, and substituting one based upon Nicolson's (then and ever since) unpublished *History of Northumberland*, Part 6. This runs, in the edition of 1722 (2. 1031) :]

Thus far of that ancient Monument ; besides which, there is a large Inscription on the west ; and on the south side of the Stone, these Letters[1] are fairly discernible,

ᛁᚠᚱᚻᛁᚻᛁᚻᛗᚲᚾ·

IV. NICOLSON'S EPISCOPAL VISITATION OF BEWCASTLE, 1703.

[As stated above, Nicolson became Bishop of Carlisle in 1702. The next year he visited the various churches of his diocese, and noted in what condition they were. The results of the visitations in 1703 and 1704 are embodied in the *Miscellany Accounts of the Diocese of Carlile*, published in 1877 by the Cumberland and Westmoreland Antiquarian and Archæological Society. The subjoined account of Bewcastle is from pp. 56–7.]

BEAUCASTLE. Jul. 30. The Church[1] is built, Chapplewise, all of a heighth, and no Distinction betwixt the Body and the Chancel; onely there's a small Ascent towards the Communion-Table. No Rails. The Children of the parish are taught here by one *John Morley*; who was brought hither by (the present Rector) Mr *Tong*,[2] no such Education haveing been formerly known in these parts. The man has not yet any setled Salary; nor is it probable that he will have any in hast. The pulpit and Reading-Desk are in a tolerable Condition; & so are the Seats, being all lately furnished wth backs, uniformly clumsie. Nothing else is so. There's very little plaister on the Walls; no Appearance of any such thing as ye Queen's Arms or ye Ten Commandments. No Bell, to call them in to Divine Service. The Font wants a pedestal, and looks like a Swine's Trough.

The church-yard is pretty well fenced; and a very small Charge will keep it so. Mr *Benson*[3] and I try'd to recover the Runic Inscription on ye West Side of the cross: But, tho' it looked promiseing at a Distance,[4] we could not assuredly make out even so much as that single line[5] which Sr *H. Spelman* long since Com-

municated to *Ol. Wormius*. That Short one on the
North (which I noted in my Letter to *Ob. Walker*, long
since publish'd in yᵉ Philosophical Transaction, & the
last Edition[1] of *Camden* by Dʳ *Gibson*) is as fair &
legible as it was at first ; and stands exactly thus :[2]

ᚻᚾᛏᛏᛒᚾᚱᚾ ᛝ.

Of which, and the Embroydery that's about it, and
of the Imagery on the other Sides, I have no more
to say than what I have said almost twenty years
agoe ; save that, on the South, there's a many-headed
Thistle,[3] which has not (probably) any Relation to the
Neighboring Kingdom of *Scotland*, any more than the
Vine wᶜʰ is (a little lower) on the same Side.

[57] The Parsonage-House is lately rebuilt by Mʳ
Tong ; who has made it a pretty convenient Dwelling.
Into this, Mʳ *Allen* (the Curate, who also assists Mʳ
Culcheth at *Stapleton*) is now removeing his family.
The Man's a poor ejected Episcopalian of the *Scottish*
Nation. The Men of *Beaucastle* would be well content
with him, if they had him wholly (as in Justice they
ought) to themselves.

V. COX'S *MAGNA BRITANNIA*, 1720.

[In the *Magna Britannia et Hibernia, Antiqua et Nova*, published anonymously in 1720, but edited by Thomas Cox, there is a description (1. 388–9) based upon Nicolson's letter, as republished by Gibson. In the reproduction of the five runes which Nicolson found in the long inscription, the rune for *S* (next to the last) is here replaced by *N*. A novelty is the imaginary representation of the chequered (north) side of the cross, as given below. The inscription at the foot recms to be recut from that in Nicolson's letter. This figure is reproduced in *Gent. Mag.* 12 (1742). 319, opposite one of Smith's plates, and in Hutchinson's *History of Cumberland* 1. 83.]

VI. SMITH'S LETTER TO THE *GENTLEMAN'S MAGAZINE*, 1742.

[For the author, see Maughan's *Memoir*, below, p. 57. As we learn from other letters of his (see, for instance, p. 30 of this same volume), he lived at Boothby, a couple of miles northeast of Brampton. The first plate is from p. 318; the second from p. 529; and the third (p. 15) from p. 132. The description is from pp. 368–9.]

The Explanation of the Runic *Obelisk,*[1] (see p. 318) *by* George Smith, *Esq*;

SIR,

That part of *Cumberland* which lies beyond the Banks of the River *Eden,* Northwards, having been often exposed to the Waste of War, and the People ruined by almost continual Depredations; the Barenness of it seems rather to proceed from the Neglect of Culture than the natural Poverty of the Soil. Within the Embraces of the Frontier Mountains of this Tract lies *Beu-Castle* Church, on a Rivulet called *Kirk-beck,* near an old ruined Castle of the Proprietors of that Part of the Country before the Conquest; and both Church and Castle are built on the Remains of a large *Roman* Fort. Opposite to the Church Porch, at a few Yards Distance, stands the Obelisk, of one entire Stone,[2] 15 Foot and a half high, springing through an Octagon Pedestal, whose Sides were alternately equal. 'Tis nearly the Frustum of a Square Pyramid, each Side being 2 Foot broad[3] at Bottom, and one Foot and a half at Top, wherein a [369] Cross[4] was fixed, which has been demolished long ago, by popular Frenzy and Enthusiasm; and probably its Situation in these unfrequented Desarts has preserved the Remainder from their Fury.

In the Bottom and Top Divisions, of the North Side, (see p. 318) are cut Vine-Trees with Clusters of

The North *and* West *Profpects of the famous* Runic *Obelifk at* Bew-Caftle *in* Cumberland. *Taken by* G. Smith.

A perfpective Vitw Top, wherein the Crofs was fixt, from an Elevation of the ocular Horizon

The Profpects of the South and Eaft Sides will be in our next.

On a Fillet on the North Side.

See the Runic *Infcription on the Weft Side,* p. 132.

Wennock Sc

(Text continued on p. 15.)

The South and East *Prospects of the famous* Runic Obelisk *at* Bew-
Castle *in* Cumberland.   *By* C. Smith, 1741.

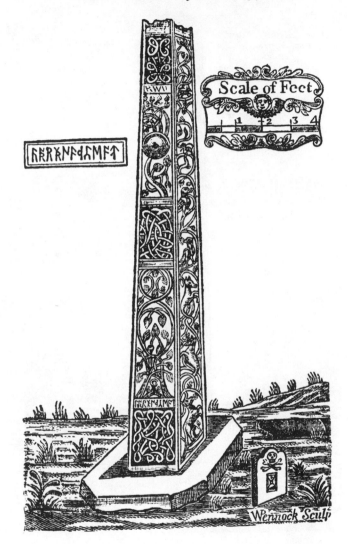

Grapes in Demi-relievo, probably the *Danish* Symbol of Fertility, as *Amathea's* Horn was amongst the *Greeks*.

In a Fillet above the under Vine are these Characters fairly legible [see fillet on the north side, p. 13], which the learned Bishop *Nicolson* expounds RYN-BURU, and thinks that it intimates the Expulsion of the magical *Runæ,* and their Accession to Christianity. But if I may be allowed to dissent from so great a Name, I had rather believe it to be a Sepulchral Monument of one of the *Danish* Kings slain in Battle, and the Reading I think will support my Conjecture.

We infert the following IN-SCRIPTION, not doubting that it will fall into the Hands of fome Gentleman who underftands the Language, and will pleafe to give us the Explication. It is taken from a very curious Obelifk, erected for a Monument in a Churchyard in Cumberland.

For there is no Instance of any Nation using the 1st Character for an R, nor do I remember to have seen it so explained in all the numerous *Runic* Alphabets of *Olaus Wormius,* but the *Danes* about the *Sinus Codanus,*[1] made Use of it for K.[2] Besides the R is *Roman* wherever it occurs, in this and other Inscriptions on this Monument. The 2d is the *Massagetic*[3] U a People about the *Tanais*.[4] The next two Letters are wrong copy'd by the Bishop, the first is a Q, or *Scythian* N, the other an I ; the 4 following are BURU plain ; and the last is

K Final, for the Initial and Final K differing in their Form was common in those Nations, as the Initial and Final M to the *Hebrews.* Upon the whole I read it KUNIBURUK, which in the old *Danish* Language imports *Sepulchrum Regis.* And the checquer Work included

betwixt the two magical Knots (the *Scythian* Method of embellishing Funeral Monuments) very much corroborates my Opinion.

However I so far agree with the Bp that it may also seem to have been designed for a standing Monument of Conversion to Christianity, which might have happen'd on the Loss of their King, and each mutually celebrated by it.

For *Buchanan*[1] tells us, that in the Reign of *Donaldus* (the Sixth[2] of that Name) the *Danes* having wasted *Northumberland,* were met and engag'd by the united Troops of *England* and *Scotland,* with such Uncertainty of Victory, that both Sides were equally glad of Peace, by which the *Danes* obliged themselves to embrace Christianity. This, therefore, was a very proper Monument for so great a Change, and the Figure on the West Side greatly contributes to favour this Conjecture, as I shall shew in my next Dissertation[3] on the three other Sides. This Transaction happened about 850 Years ago, and none believe the Obelisk to be older than 900.[4]

That the Monument is *Danish* appears incontestable from the Characters ; *Scotish* and *Pictish* Monuments having nothing but Hieroglyphick's, and the *Danish* both ; and, excepting *Bride-Kirk*[5] Font, it appears to be the only Monument of that Nation left in *Britain.*

SIR,

Your very humble Servant,

GEO. SMITH.

VII. ARMSTRONG'S PLATE, 1775.

[This plate is found in the *London Magazine* for August, 1775 (44. 388). From references in other places (for example, Gough's edition of Camden's *Britannia*, 1806, 3. 455, note 1), we learn that the plate was furnished by Captain Armstrong, a native of Bewcastle parish, who had served in the army as private, corporal, sergeant, and finally captain, retiring about 1764 (see Hutchinson's *Hist. County Cumberland*, 1794, 1. 80). Whether the accompanying description is by his hand I have no means of knowing. At the bottom of the plate stands: ' Publish'd by R. Baldwin Sep.[r] 1st 1775.']

An Account of a curious OBELISK, *of one Stone, standing in the Church Yard of Bewcastle, in the North East Part of Cumberland, about* 16 *Miles from Carlisle.*

(Illustrated with an elegant Engraving.)

What is here represented is 15 feet high [1]; besides there has been on the top a cross,[2] now broken off, part of which may be seen as a grave stone in the same church yard. The faces of the obelisk are not quite similar, but the 1st and 2d, and the 3d and 4th agree. The figures and carving are very fair, but the inscription which has been on the west face, is not legible. At the top of that face is a figure with a mitre; below that, another in priests habit; then was the inscription, and below that, the figure of a man with a bird, said to be St. Peter and the cock. On the 2d or south face has been a dial,[3] and many other ornaments. The north face has much rich carving, and the chequers seem to point out the arms of some person, and probably to the name of Graham, that being part of their arms, and the present Mr. Graham of Netherby is lord of that manor, and the lawful heir of the last Lord Viscount Preston. On the east face is a running stem of a vine, with foxes [4] or monkeys eating the grapes.

North.   West.   South.   East.

A Curious OBELISK in Bewcastle Church Yard.

(Text continued on p. **19**.)

The whole carving has been done in a masterly manner, and beyond comparison it is the richest ornamented obelisk of one stone now in Britain: but by whom or on what account it was erected, there is not the least to be learned from history.

Cambden, and other historians, mention this stone, though none of them ever saw it. They would gladly have it to be Roman, but the figures and cross plainly speak it to be Christian, and very likely it was erected as a monument near the burial place of the chief man of that place, as the remains of a very large castle are close by it.

VIII. HUTCHINSON'S *HISTORY OF CUMBER-LAND*, 1794.

[The following extract is taken from Hutchinson's *History of the County of Cumberland* 1. 85—87. The plate is much reduced from the original opposite p. 80.]

A friend, at our instance, before we had seen this monument, took some pains to gain the inscription on the north side, in a manner we have often prac-tised with success, by oiling the stone and pressing in wax, and then with printer's ink, taking upon paper the character: it was very confused and imperfect, but ap-peared much in this form,[1] of which, we confess, we are not able to give a probable reading. The ornaments of knots, flowers, and grapes, evidently appear to be the effect of the sculptor's fancy[1]; and we think it would be extending a desire of giving extraordinary import to works of antiquity, to suppose they were intended to carry any emblematical meaning: they are similar to the ornaments of the capitals and fillets in Gothic structures of the eleventh century,[2] or near that time, and no one yet presumed to assert they were to be construed as hieroglyphics. Should we not attempt to object to the readings of the inscription on the north fillet, and admit it might imply that the ground was famous for royal sepulture ; in our apprehension it doth not advance the antiquity of the monument the least. The inscription itself is uncertain; for the prelate and Mr. Smith took it variously, and the wax impression varied from both, and such, we conceive, would be most accurate ; the copies taken by the eye being subject to the effects of light and shade.

Let us examine the work, and perhaps we may draw from thence a more convincing argument. The south front is decorated in the upper compartment with a [86] knot, the next division has something like the figure of a pomegranet,[3] from whence issue branches of fruit and foliage, the third has a knot, the fourth branches of fruit and flowers, beneath which is a fillet with an inscription, copied thus by Mr. Smith, but now appearing irrecoverable by any device: Here is reproduced, but inexactly, the inscription on the left on page 14, above. Beneath this, in the lowest compartment, is a knot. The east front is one entire running branch of foliage flowers and fruit, ornamented with birds and uncouth animals in the old Gothic stile. The crown of the pillar is mortaised to receive the foot of the cross.[4] The north side has, in the upper compartment, foliage and fruit, in the next a knot, in a large space next succeeds the chequy, then a knot, beneath which, is the fillet with the inscription, treated of by the Prelate and Mr. Smith. The west front is the most ornamented, having the following sculptures: in the lowest compartment, well relieved, is the effigies [1] of a person of some dignity, in a long robe to the feet, but without any dress or ornament on the head: it is greatly similar to the chief figure on the north front of Bridekirk font, as to the fashion of the garment; on a pedestal, against which this figure leans, is a bird, which, we conceive, is the raffen, or raven, the ensignia of the Danish standard. This figure seems designed to represent the personage for whom the monument was erected; and though accompanied with the raffen, bears no other marks of royal dignity. Above this figure is a long inscription, which has consisted of nine lines; Mr. Smith delineates the first three letters thus; I H ᴎ. The S, in many old inscriptions, is formed like an inverted Z, and sometimes that letter, in its proper form, is substituted. Late visitors, as well as we, have great doubt whether any such characters were ever legible. Great care was taken to copy the inscription, as it now appears; which may perhaps afford a new construction. Immediately above this inscription is the figure of a religious person, the garments descending to the feet, the head encircled with a nymbus, not now appearing radiated, but merely a circular rise of the stone; the right hand is elevated in a teaching posture, and the other hand holds a roll; a fold of the garment was mistaken by Mr. Armstrong, (who drew the monument, and had it engraved, through regard to the parish where he was born,) for a string of beads. We conceive this figure [that of Christ] to represent St. Cuthbert, to whom the church, as Nicolson and Burn set forth, is dedicated. The upper figures Mr. Armstrong represented like a mitred ecclesiastic ; but in that he was manifestly mistaken, the effigies being that of the holy virgin with the babe.[1] There is no doubt that this was a place of sepulture, for on opening the ground on the east and west sides, above the depth of six feet, human bones were found of a large size, but much broken [87] and disturbed, together with several pieces of rusty iron. The ground had been broken up before, by persons who either searched for treasure, or, like us, laboured with curiosity.

Whether the chequers were designed or not for the arms of the family of Vaux, or de Vallibus, must be a matter of mere conjecture ; we are inclined to think that armorial bearings were not in use at the same time with the Runic characters. . . . The reason given in bishop Nicholson's letter, is applicable to our conjectures on this monument, ' That the Danes were most numerous here, and least disturbed,'[2] which reconciles the mixture of Runic character in an inscription of the eleventh century, as in such desert and little frequented tracks, that the character might remain familiar both to the founder and the sculptor : where the Danes continued longest and least disturbed, their importations would also continue unaffected by other modes, which were gaining acceptation and progress, in more frequented and better peopled situations.

IX. HENRY HOWARD'S ACCOUNT, 1801.

[The volume of *Archæologia* containing this (Vol. 14) was published
in 1803, but the paper, ' Observations on Bridekirk Font and on the
Runic Column at Bewcastle, in Cumberland, by Henry Howard, Esq.
in a Letter to George Nayler, Esq. York Herald, F. A. S.,' was read
May 14, 1801. The paper itself occupies pages 113—118 (our portion
pp. 117—18), and the plate (considerably reduced) follows immediately.

Henry Howard (1757—1842), of Corby Castle, 4½ miles southeast
of Carlisle, spent the most of his life as a country gentleman and
antiquary. The monument to the memory of his first wife (d. 1789),
in Wetheral church, is the theme of two of Wordsworth's sonnets,
Nos. 39 and 40 of the Itinerary Poems of 1833.]

Runic Column at Bewcastle.—Of this celebrated monument I have seen several engravings, none of them
accurate ; but I understand that Mr. de Cardonnel has
published a faithful delineation ; which, however, I
have not had an opportunity of seeing. I send you
the vestiges of the inscriptions, the result of two days
employment on the spot.

The Runic Column, or Obelisk, stands a few feet
from the church, within the precincts of an extensive
Roman station, guarded by a double vallum. In one
angle of this enclosure, a strong oblong building called
Bueth Castle was raised at a later period, probably,
from the form of the stones, out of the ruins of the
Roman fort. The builder availed himself of the ancient foss for two sides of his castle, and cut off the
connexion with the remainder by a new foss. There
is no account of this castle, which is situated in the
wildest part of the borders, having been inhabited
since the reign of Henry the second. The Obelisk
is from the hand of a better artist than the Font at
Bridekirk. It is quadrangular, of one entire grey free
stone, inserted in a larger blue stone, which serves

Fig. 1.

Fig. 2.

Fig. 3.

as its base. The greater base[1] is 22 inches, diminishing to 21; the lesser 16 inches, and 12 only at the top: the shaft 14 feet high. To this a cross[2] appears to have been added, the socket of which is observable. It is unfortunate that the side of the Column containing two figures and the principal inscription, faces to the west, from which quarter the wind and rain are most frequent. The lower figure seems to have been mutilated by accident or intent; but the remainder seems to have suffered only by exposure to the weather. Some parts of [118] the inscription [d], probably owing to the stone being there softer, have been more affected than the rest. The third, fourth, and fifth lines, are the most perfect. Towards the lower part scarce anything is to be made out. On the whole, indeed, little more than the vestiges of this inscription remain; the perpendicular parts of the letters are discernible, and have probably been deepened by the rain, but the horizontal and other parts, are nearly obliterated. In taking the inscription I followed the same plan as at Bridekirk, working[3] the paper in with the finger, and afterwards following the finger at the edges of every part of the letters with the pencil, so that, in the paper I send, you have all that can be either seen or felt of this inscription.

The north inscription of one line only [e], being completely sheltered by the church, has suffered very little injury from time; and, I must say, that the difference observable in the engravings given to the public, must have arisen from want of attention and exactness.

On the south side there is a fillet[4] like that to the north [f], but a few letters only can be made out, the rest are chipped off or worn away.

I request you, my dear Sir, to present to the Society the original tracery of these inscriptions taken by me on the spot.

I have the honour to remain,

Your faithful humble servant,

HENRY HOWARD.

Corby Castle, Carlisle,
   April 16, 1801.

[d] See Pl. XXXIV. fig. 2.   [e] Ibid. fig. 3.   [f] Ibid. fig. 1

X. LYSONS' *MAGNA BRITANNIA*, 1816.

[The account of the Lysons (4. cxcix—cci) reposes largely upon Nicolson. Only a few sentences are here reproduced. The plate occupies two quarto pages, and is accordingly much reduced in our facsimile. The second N of the runic CYNNBURUG, on the north side, is imperfect, and resembles a vertical stroke, with a dot at the right.]

Several very inaccurate figures of it have been published. It is of one stone, 14 feet 6 inches high, 20½ inches in width at the bottom, and 14½ inches at the top on the north and south sides ; and 22 inches at the bottom, and 16 at the top, on the east and west sides. At the top is a socket 8½ by 7½ inches, in which no doubt a cross has formerly been fixed. ... [cc] Over this is another figure sculptured in bas-relief, which, from the *nimbus* round the head, has been supposed to represent some saint ; but as he holds a roll (the sacred *volumen*) in his left hand, and the right hand is elevated in the act of benediction, we should rather suppose it was intended for our Saviour, who is frequently so represented in ancient works of art. Immediately above this figure are some faint traces of another inscription of two lines ; and over this, a third sculpture in bas-relief, which is described by Bishop Nicolson as 'the effigies of the B. V. with the Babe in her arms, and both their heads encircled with glories.' This description, which several succeeding writers appear to have copied, without inspecting the original, is very erroneous. The female figure is so defaced that nothing more than the general outline can be distinguished ; what she holds in her left arm is much better preserved, and is evidently the holy lamb.[1] ... Imme[cci]diately above the lowest knot on the south side was a Runic inscription [2] of one line, now so nearly obliterated, that except in a very favourable light, hardly a stroke can be distinctly made out.

North Side   South Side   East Side   West Side

XI. MAUGHAN'S FIRST ACCOUNT, 1854.

[According to my best information (for which I am indebted to Professor W. G. Collingwood ; Chancellor J. E. Prescott, Canon of Carlisle ; Rev. George Yorke, Rector of Bewcastle ; Rev. T. W. Willis, Vicar of Lanercost ; and Mr. John Maughan, of Maryport, Cumberland, nephew of the antiquary), Rev. John Maughan (pronounced *Mawn*, but locally now and then *Maffan*) was born at Lanercost Abbey Farm, April 18, 1806, and baptized at Lanercost Abbey, January 6, 1807. His grandfather, Nicholas Maughan, born in 1733, came to Lanercost from the County of Durham, and became the tenant of the Abbey Farm. He was married to Elizabeth Bowman, of Nether Denton, was churchwarden in 1789, and died May 14, 1798. He had a son John, the father of the antiquary, who was born at Lanercost in 1770, succeeded to the Abbey Farm, married Mary Moses, and died at Lanercost, April 28, 1830. The Rev. John Maughan, one of a family of thirteen children, was born as stated above, took his degree of B. A. at Trinity College, Dublin, in 1830, was ordained by the Bishop of Chester in 1833, and became Curate of Melling, Liverpool, in the same year. He was Rector of Bewcastle from 1836 to 1873, built the present rectory in 1837, and married Mary Twentyman at Carlisle, July 21, 1840. He died without issue November 13, 1873, and was buried in the graveyard at Lanercost Abbey, next to his wife, who had died at Bewcastle Rectory, January 10, 1872, aged sixty-eight years. Besides his papers on the Maiden Way, from the second of which the following paragraphs are extracted, and the *Memoir* given below, he wrote many papers, chiefly on supposed Roman camps in North Cumberland, for the Cumberland and Westmorland Antiquarian and Archæological Society, between its foundation in 1866 and his death in 1873. Considerable excerpts and adaptations from his *Memoir* were embodied in *The History and Topography of the Counties of Cumberland and Westmorland*, edited by William Whellan, 1860. According to Collingwood, he was ' a qualified medical man, a schoolmaster, magistrate, and farmer.'

Elsewhere Collingwood says, apropos of certain supposed runes near Bewcastle (*Early Sculptured Crosses, Shrines, and Monuments in the Present Diocese of Carlisle*, Kendal, 1899, pp. 52–3): ' Mr. Maughan had been for years the enthusiastic Runologist of the countryside, eagerly expounding the Bewcastle Cross, circulating among his parishioners the story here retold, talking to all and sundry about his theories on Petriana and place-names. In some other antiquarian matters he is known to have been deceived. It was on his authority that the Maiden Way north of Bewcastle was laid down in the Ordnance-map, with many forts, etc., which recent investigation has shown to be imaginary. (Compare his paper on " the Maiden Way," *Archæological Journal*, no. 41, with *Transactions*, C. & W. A. & A. Soc., vol. XV., part II., p. 344, etc.) There is reason to think that he was the victim, especially in his later years, of a series of practical jokes. Old roads, pavements, ruined forts (cottages) were found for him, by the zeal or roguery of his neighbors; and these runes are their creation. They are not the work of a Runic scholar ; they were concocted by a clever Cumbrian who had read the Rector's papers, heard his talk, perhaps used his books, and, like his countrymen, laughed at enthusiasm and loved a joke.'

The following paragraphs are from *Archæological Journal* 11 (1854). 130—4. It is clear that Maughan was at this time inclined to date the cross after the death of Sweyn in 1014.]

In the churchyard the Monolithic Obelisk, or shaft of an ancient cross, is still standing, but remains unexplained. I have recently cleared the inscribed parts from the moss with which they were thickly coated, but have not been able to decypher the characters in a satisfactory manner. The letters appear to be Anglo-Saxon Runes, and much the same as those on the Ruthwell monument in Dumfriesshire. On a fillet on the north side the following letters[1] are very legible. In the year 1685 these characters were somewhat differently read by Bishop Nicholson, and expounded by him to mean, ' Rynburn, the burial of the Runæ,' or ' Ryeburn, Cemeterium, or Cadaverum Sepulchrum.' In the year 1742, an article appeared in the Gentleman's Magazine communicated by Mr. Smith, who read it 'Kuniburuk, Sepulchrum Regis.' As however these interpretations appear to be based on an incorrect copying of the letters, I would suggest another reading. I suppose the second letter to be a Runic Y ; and the penultimate letter to be a compound of OU ; and I would propose to read Kyneburoug. The word Cyne or Kin of the Saxons was synonymous with nation or people ; and the Anglo-Saxon byrig, byrg, burh, burg, buroug, &c., was the generic term for any place, large or small, which was fortified by walls or mounds. The fortifications of the continental Saxons, before their inroads on the Roman Empire, were mere earthworks, for in their half-nomadic state they had neither means nor motive for constructing any other. But their conquest and colonisation of the greater part of Roman Britain put them in possession of a more solid class of fortifications, such as this at Bewcastle. I would suggest, therefore, that these Runes may signify the burgh or fortified town of the nation or people who occupied this district. It is probable that this was in early times a place of some importance. In the reign [131] of Edward I., 1279, John Swinburne obtained a fair and market to be held here.

On a fillet on the south side appear to be the following characters.[1] What the first three may mean is doubtful, but the subsequent letters appear to be the word DANEGELT. This term was first applied to a tribute of 30,000, or according to some writers, 36,000 pounds (A. Sax.), raised in the year 1007 during the reign of Ethelred the Unready, to purchase a precarious peace from the Danes. It was also sometimes used to designate taxes imposed on other extraordinary occasions.

On the western side are three figures, which, as Bishop Nicholson says, ' evidently enough manifest the monument to be Christian.'(3) The highest may be, as the learned prelate suggested, the Blessed Virgin with the Babe in her arms. (4)   The next is that of our Saviour with the glory round his head.   In a compartment underneath this is the principal inscription, consisting of nine lines ; and underneath this is the figure of a man with a bird upon his hand, and in front of him a perch, which, in the absence of a better explanation, may possibly have been intended to represent Odin, or some Danish chieftain, and his dreaded raven : and we may suppose that he was placed at the bottom of the group to typify his conversion and subjection to the Redeemer, who was descended from the Blessed Virgin.   The inscription appears to be as follows, so far as I have been able to trace the letters (see woodcut, p. 132).   The eighth and ninth lines are quite illegible.

In the first line the three characters at the commencement probably form the monogram I H S, and

(3) ' Camden's Britannia,' ed. by Gibson, vol. ii., p. 1028.

(4) It must be admitted that this supposition is somewhat countenanced by the fact that the Church of Bewcastle is dedicated to the Virgin.   The representation, however, of these weather-worn sculptures, given by Lysons in his ' History of Cumberland,' p. cxcix, suggests the notion, that what has been supposed to be the Infant Saviour, may be the Agnus Dei, and it is so described by him. If this be correct, the figure must represent the Baptist,[1] and the two lines of characters, now defaced, under its feet, as shown in Lysons' plate, possibly comprised some mention of St. John. The figure at the base, as some have thought, most probably pourtrayed some person of note by whom this remarkable Christian monument was erected. The bird which he has taken off its perch, appears to be a hawk,[2] introduced, possibly, to mark his noble rank. In examining Lysons' plate, the best representation of the sculptures, hitherto published, attention is arrested by the introduction of a vertical dial [3] on the south side, resembling those at Kirkdale and Bishopstone, described in this volume of the Journal, p. 60, the only examples of so early a date hitherto noticed. — ED.[4]

being placed [132] immediately under the figure of
our Saviour, show that the monument is of a Christian character; the last letter being evidently the
Runic S, and not an inverted Z, as supposed by
Mr. Smith.[1] The third line begins with the letters
PATR: but it appears uncertain whether they are
intended for *pater,*

or part of some such word as *patria,* Patrick, &c.;
or whether the first letter is not W, in which case
the word will probably be WAETRO, the plural of
waeter. In the sixth line we find the word SUENO,
which, taken in connection with the word Danegelt,
on the south side, may indicate the period, as well
as the object, of the erection of the monument. In
the reign of Ethelred the Unready, a terrible deed was
done in England. With a view of providing against
the treachery of those numerous Danish families
(especially such as had been permitted by Alfred the
Great to settle in Northumberland and East Anglia),
who upon any threatened invasion, were ready to

join their countrymen against those among whom they were allowed to reside, Ethelred, with a policy incident to weak princes, adopted the resolution of putting them to the sword throughout his dominions. On the 13th of Nov. 1002, in pursuance of secret instructions sent by the king over the country, the inhabitants of every town and city rose, and murdered all the Danes, who were their neighbours, young and old, men, women, and children. Every Dane was killed, even to [133] Gunilda, the sister of the King of Denmark, who had been married to Earl Paling, a nobleman, and had embraced Christianity: she was first obliged to witness the murder of her husband and child, and then was killed herself. When Sueno, or Sweyn, the King of Denmark, sometimes styled the King of the Sea Kings, heard of this deed of blood, he swore he would have a great revenge. He raised an army and a mightier fleet of ships than ever yet sailed to England, and landing on the western coasts, near Exeter, went forward, laying England waste. Whereso[e]ver the invaders came, they made the Saxons prepare for them great feasts ; and when they had satisfied their appetite, and had drunk a curse to England, with wild rejoicings, they drew their swords, killed their Saxon entertainers, and continued their march. For several years they carried on this war ; burning the crops, farm-houses, barns, mills, granaries, killing the labourers, causing famine and starvation, and leaving heaps of ruin and smoking ashes, where they had found thriving towns, hunting out every corner which had not been previously ransacked. Ethelred overwhelmed with such calamities, at length in the year 1007, agreed to pay the Danegelt to which I have before alluded. In the absence of accurate information, we may not unreasonably suppose this obelisk to have been raised in commemoration of some of the important events of this period. Sweyn was afterwards welcomed by the English people as their Sovereign, but died suddenly in little more than a month after he was proclaimed King of England. Can this have been his burial-place ? (5)

The first letter in the second line is distinctly legible, and undoubtedly U. I sometimes fancy, that by taking the last imperfect letter of the preceding line, we may possibly obtain the word DUNSTANO.[1] Dunstan, however, was dead before the time already mentioned, and though he lived to place the crown upon the head of Ethelred, and may without impropriety be classed among the contemporaries of that period, yet as he died in 988, he cannot have taken any part in the events above mentioned.

[A paragraph here is of the same purport as the second in Note 14, below, p. 52.]

[134] Uncertainty as to the forms of the other letters, prevents me from attempting further explanation of the inscription at present, but I am not without hope that in time I may become better satisfied as to the proper reading.

(5) I may mention that a friend to whom I gave a copy of my reading of the inscription, suggests that in the second line is ' the word *kisle,* one of the cases of *kisil,* gravel.' It is difficult to conceive however, why such an immense stone should be brought from so great a distance and covered with the most elaborate sculpture, for the purpose of making any record about gravel.

XII. HAIGH'S FIRST ACCOUNT, 1857.

[The first part of Haigh's paper was read to the Newcastle Society March 2, 1856, and the second (concluding), April 2; it is clear that his main conclusions lay before Maughan when the latter composed his *Memoir*. Hence, though Haigh's paper was published in the same year as Maughan's, the former is here given precedence.

Daniel Henry Haigh (pronounced *Haig*) was born August 7, 1819. He inherited a considerable fortune, and eventually became a Roman Catholic priest (April 8, 1848).   He lived at Erdington, near Birmingham, from 1848 to 1876, and died at Oscott, May 10, 1879. ' Haigh's varied learning embraced Assyrian and Anglo-Saxon antiquities, numismatics, and Biblical archæology.   He was the chief authority in England on runic literature, and was of much assistance to Professor G. Stephens, who dedicated the English section of his work on " Runic Monuments " to him.   The bulk of his literary work is preserved in the transactions of societies' (*Dict. Nat. Biog.*).

The following paragraphs are taken from ' The Saxon Cross at Bewcastle,' in *Archæologia Æliana*, New Series, I. 149—195.   Much of the article is concerned with such subjects as the Ruthwell and other crosses, other dials than that on the Bewcastle Cross, runic inscriptions on other monuments, Old English proper names, etc. The plate of runes is opposite page 192.

In this same volume (p. vii) is the entry, under January, 1856 :
' Dr. CHARLTON.[1]—On the Bewcastle Cross.']

[151] The monument now stands alone, but once, in all probability, there were two, one at the head, the other at the foot of the grave, as in the example which still remains at Penrith.[2] If so, the other has disappeared, yet it may be still in existence, if the conjecture which will be hazarded in the sequel be considered under all the circumstances probable.

The cross, as we have already observed, is gone, but all record of it has not perished. It appears from a note in the handwriting of Mr. Camden[3] in his own copy of his *Britannia* (now in the Bodleian Library), that Lord William Howard sent it to Lord Arundel,

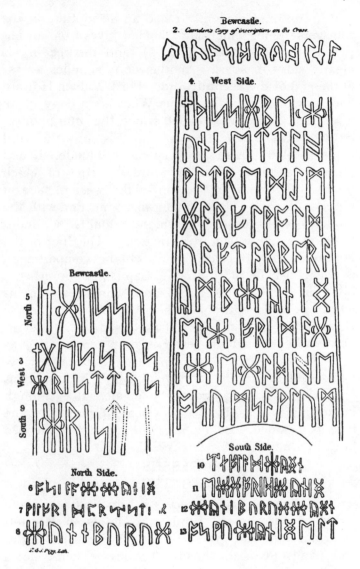

Bewcastle.

2. Camden's Copy of inscription on the Cross.

4. West Side.

Bewcastle.

5 North

3 West

9 South

North Side.

6

7

8

South Side.

10

11

12

13

J. & J. Ray. Lith.

(Text continued on p. 38.)

and he to Mr. Camden. It had an inscription on the
transverse limb, which Mr. Camden gives from an impression he had taken (*Fig.* 2), and the reading is
clearly RICÆS DRIHTNÆ. Another copy supplies an 's'
at the end of the second word. Lord William Howard
had previously sent to Olaus Wormius a copy of an
inscription on this monument, which the latter published in his *Monumenta Danica*.[1] In this copy the word
RICÆS is plain, DRIHTNÆS very much blundered, and
after these, quite plain, the word STICÆTH,[2] of which
traces still remain on the top of the western face of
the monument.[3] These, taken in connection with the
former, give us a meaning which undoubtedly alludes
to the cross, RICÆS DRIHTNÆS STICÆTH. 'The Staff of the
Mighty Lord.' Beneath, in an oblong compartment,
is the effigy of St. John the Baptist, pointing with
his right hand to the Holy Lamb, which rests on his
left arm. This figure had been supposed to be the
Blessed Virgin with the Infant Jesus. Mr. Lysons,
however, corrected this error in part, representing as
a lamb what had been supposed to be the Holy
Child, but the figure [152] which holds it, has in his
engraving the appearance of a female. It is, though
in flowing robes, decidedly a male figure, and the
face is bearded. Below it is an inscription in two
lines of Runes (*Fig.* 3)

✠ GESSUS
CRISTTVS

written above an arched recess in which is a majestic
figure of our Blessed Lord, who holds in His left
hand a scroll, and gives His blessing with His right,
and stands upon the heads of swine. Then follows
the long inscription of nine lines of Runes, commemorating the personage to whom this monument
was erected. (*Fig.* 4)

✖ THISSIGBEC
UNSETTÆH
WÆTREDĒOM
GÆRFLWOLD
UÆFTÆRBARÆ
YMBCYNING
ALCFRIDÆG
ICEGÆDHE
OSVMSAWLVM[1]

Lastly, in another arched recess is a fine figure in profile, holding a hawk in his left hand, above a perch. This doubtless represents the king whose name is mentioned in the inscription above it.

The eastern side of this monument presents a continuous scroll with foliage and fruit, amidst which are a lion, two monsters, two birds and two squirrels feeding on the fruit. Above these doubtless there was an inscription, but the stone is too much broken on this side to show the trace of even a single letter.

On the northern side we read distinctly, in Runic letters nearly six inches long (*Fig.* 5), the Holy Name ✖ GESSU. Below this we have a scroll, then an inscription (*Fig.* 6), OSLAAC CYNING ; then a knot, another inscription (*Fig.* 7), WILFRID [2] PREASTER ; an oblong space filled with chequers, a third inscription, read by the Rev. J. Maughan CYNIWISI or CYNISWID ; a second knot, a fourth inscription (*Fig.* 8), CYNIBURUG [3] ; and lastly, a double scroll.

On the southern side, at the top, are the remains of the name CRISTUS (*Fig.* 9), corresponding to GESSU on the north. Below this is a knot, an inscription (*Fig.* 10), EANFLÆD CYNGN ; a scroll, in the midst of which a dial is introduced, a second inscription (*Fig.* 11), ECGFRID CYNING ; another knot, a third inscription (*Fig.* 12), CYNIBURUG CYNGN ; another scroll, a fourth inscription (*Fig.* 13), ᴏsᴡᴜ ᴄʏɴɪɴ̄ɢᴇʟᴛ, and a third knot.

Such is the Bewcastle monument; a monument interesting in many [153] respects; as one to which we can assign a certain date, and which, therefore, is a material help to us in ascertaining the age of others of the same class, that at Ruthwell in particular; as an evidence of the state of the art of sculpture in the seventh century, the three figures on the west side being equal to any thing we have until the thirteenth[1]; as a monument of our language almost the earliest we have; as belonging to a class of monuments, the memorials of the kings of England before the Conquest, which have almost entirely disappeared; and as such, especially interesting, because the king to whose memory it was raised, played a most important part in the history of his times.

The inscriptions claim our first attention. They are written in the early Saxon dialect of Northumbria, except the names of our Blessed Lord, which have a Latin form, since it was only from missionaries to whom the Latin language was as their mother tongue that our forefathers learned His name; and down to the latest period of their history they followed the same rule, as the Germans do still of adopting, without alteration, into their language, Latin proper names. The spelling of the name ɢᴇssᴜs is particularly interesting, for I believe this is the only monument on which it occurs. Throughout the Durham Ritual and the Northumbrian Gospels, we find instead of it, the word *Hælend* 'Saviour.' The initial ɢ has the power of ʏ, and the double s is probably not a false spelling since it occurs twice.

The long inscription resolves itself into three couplets of alliterative verse; thus,

This sigbecun	This beacon of honour (4)
Settæ Hwætred	set Hwætred
Eom gær f[e]lwoldu	in the year of the great pestilence
Æftær baræ	after the ruler
Ymb cyning Alcfridæ	after King Alcfrid
Gicegæd heosum sawlum	pray for their souls

I have supposed the omission of a letter, *e*, between *f* and *l*. *Fel*, as a prefix, has the sense of 'much' or 'many.' *Woldu* I take to be an adjective, derived, as well as *wól*, a pestilence, from the same root as *weallan* 'to burn or boil,' and *wyllan* 'to make to burn or boil,' (just as *fold*, a flat surface, is derived from *feallan* 'to fall,' and *fyllan* to make to fall), and therefore to have the sense of 'pestilential.' It does not, however, occur in the glossaries, having probably fallen into disuse. The termination in *u* would not have occurred at a later period, but the Durham Ritual shows us that the declension of nouns and adjectives, and the conjugation of verbs, in the early Northumbrian dialect, dif[154]fered in many respects from the later forms of the language on which our modern grammars are founded. This Ritual supplies us with many instances of adjectives ending in *o* (which, as will be seen later, is the equivalent of *u* on these monuments) in the oblique cases ; as, for instance, *in ceastre gihalgado*,[1] 'in civitate sanctificatâ,' *in eco wuldur* 'in æternâ gloriâ.' That there may, however, have been a noun *woldu*,(5) and that this may have been the ancient form of *wól* is not impossible, since from the verb *swelan* 'to burn' we have not

[4] *Sig* implies triumph. In composition it seems to imply special honour. *Beg* is a bracelet, which any one might bear, but *Sigbeg* is a crown.

[5] Still I feel inclined to regard it as originally a participle, even if it did become a noun, just as *fold* and *bold* and other similar words, now nouns, seem to have been past participles.

only *swol* but also *swoluth* and *swoleth,* heat, fever, or
pestilence, and from *stælan*, to place, we have *steald*
as well as *steal,* a station, place or abode. If it were
so, I should read, without any alteration of the sense,
'in the year of the great pestilence.'   I have read
the letters L and W as they are in the rubbing with
which I was furnished by the Rev. J. Maughan. If
I could suppose that marks had been obliterated which
would change these letters into Æ (6) and B, I should
propose another reading, *eom gærfæ boldu* ' also carved
this building,' supposing *gærfæ* the ancient form of
cearf, from *ceorfan* to carve, and *boldu,* a building, the
ancient form of *bold*. Verbs of the strong or complex
order, to which *ceorfan* belongs, did not in later times
add a syllable in the third person singular of the past
tense, but the Durham Ritual gives us an example in
the word *ahofe*[1] '*erexit*' which shows that in early
times they did ; and we have other examples of nouns
ending in *u,* which dropped this syllable in later
times.   The rules of alliteration rendered necessary
the use of *gicegæd* (a word which under a slightly
different form, *gicegath,*[2] occurs in the Durham Ritual)
instead of the more usual *gibiddæd.*   *Heosum* is another
obsolete word,[3] the dative plural regularly formed from
the possessive pronoun ' *heora*,' their.   I can find no
trace of this word elsewhere, the indeclinable *hiora*[4]
invariably occurring in the Durham Ritual ; but as
in modern German the possessive pronouns of the
third person are declinable, equally with those of the
first and second, I think it not improbable that the
same might be the case with the early Saxon language, and that the disuse of the oblique cases might
be the effect of Latin influence. . . .

[6] Mr. Howard's representation of this letter in the Archæologia (Vol. XIV) seems to give this letter Æ.

[162] It is most probable that he [Alcfrid] died in the [163] year 664 ; and in the pestilence of that year, to which so many persons of historical celebrity fell victims, we have the possible cause of his death. This monument marks the place of his burial, and its epitaph confirms the conclusion I had arrived at before I had an opportunity of reading it, and tells us the year of his death. Whilst yet this inscription remained a mystery, the tradition of the country declared that a king was buried at Bewcastle, and the confirmation of this tradition by the inscription (now, it is hoped, correctly read), is a proof, in addition to the many we have from other sources, that the traditions of the people, in remote districts where, without thought of change, the same families continue to occupy the homesteads their fathers did before them, are founded in truth. Alcfrid is the king of whose burial this tradition has preserved the recollection, and he died in the year of the great pestilence, A. D. 664....

CYNIBURUG.—This name occurs upon the north and south sides ; and in the latter instance with the addition of some letters which we have read CYNGN ; but, as the character which stands for NG is very like that for OE, it is possible that these letters may express CUOEN or OWOEN ' queen. ' If, however, they be really as we have read them, we must suppose them an abbreviation of CYNINGIN,[1] i. e. *cyning* with the usual female termination *in,* equivalent to the modern German word *Königinn.* The signification is the same. This illustrious lady, the wife of Alcfrid, has been already mentioned. She was one of the daughters of King Penda, and was united to Alcfrid before the year 653, yet soon after her marriage persuaded him to live in continence with her, as a brother with a sister, being filled with the desire of devoting herself exclusively to a religious life. Whilst her husband lived, her court more resembled a monastery than a palace, for she had collected around her many young females of noble as well as of plebeian rank, who regarded her as their spiritual mother. In the year 664 she and her younger sister Cyniswid appear as witnesses to the foundation charter of Peterborough Minster, along with St. Wilfrid, then on his journey to France for consecration: so that it is probable her husband was already dead. Soon after this she obtained from her brother Wulfhere a grant of land at the place which is now called Caistor, and there she founded a monastery of which she was the first abbess, and her sisters Cyniswid and Cynithryth her successors. The year of her death is not recorded, but the youngest of her sisters, Cynithryth, was abbess in the year of St. Wilfrid's death, A. D. 709. Her character is thus briefly summed up by her biographer: ' She was compassionate to the poor, a tender mother to the afflicted, [164] and was constantly exciting to works of mercy the Kings her brothers,' (*i. e.* Peada, Wulfhere, and Ethelred). I am informed that the Rev. J. Maughan has traced letters on the third slip of the north side, which he thinks may express the name of *Cyniwisi* or *Cyniswid*.[1] I certainly did not observe any letters myself in the place, though I examined it carefully ; but if there be really any traces of such an inscription there, I should think the latter name the more probable reading. . . .

[166] The long inscription, that of two lines above it, the single line on the south side, and another on the north, were all that had hitherto been noticed. A suspicion crossed my mind, whilst engaged in deciphering these, that there must be some letters in the space above the head of St. John the Baptist,

and further, that the reason why the northern and southern sides are broken up into compartments, instead of being filled with a continuous ornament as the eastern side is, must be, that spaces might be left for inscriptions. On this account, and because I felt the great need of scrupulous accuracy in publishing a reading of so important a monument of our language as the long inscription is, I took advantage of an opportunity which a journey into the north afforded me, and extended it to Bewcastle, and the discovery of these inscriptions was the result—a result far exceeding anything I had anticipated.

Thus, as in a Saxon charter after the act of donation we have the names of the witnesses thereto in the order of their rank, so here in the funeral monument of king Alcfrid, after his epitaph, we have the names of those who we may believe assisted at his obsequies, his father Oswiu, his mother-in-law Eanflæd, his widow Cyniburug, and her sister Cyniswid, his uncle Oslaac, his brother Ecgfrid, and his chaplain Wilfrid, bishop elect of York[1]; and above them all the holy name of Jesus. . . .

[173] Fortunately, the history of the period enables us, almost with certainty, to determine the author of this poem [*The Dream of the Rood*], for there was but one person then living to whom it can be ascribed. For reasons which will appear in the sequel, I believe this monument, and that at Bewcastle, to be of the same age, and the work of the same hand, and the latter must have been erected A. D. 664 or 5. Now this was precisely the period at which Cædmon, first of all the English nation, began to compose religious poems, in the monastery of the Abbess Hilda. . . . As then what is related of his inspiration (20) must have

[20] Bede's Eccl. Hist., book iv., cap. 24.

taken place about this time, for the monastery of St. Hilda was founded in the year 655, are we not justified in regarding the lines upon the Ruthwell cross as fragments of a lost poem of his,[1] a poem, however, which a later poet in the tenth century undertook to modernize and adapt to the taste of his own times, as Dryden did with some of the poems of Chaucer? I submit to the judgment of others this conjecture, based upon these grounds, viz. that on this monument, erected about A. D. 665, we have fragments of a religious poem of very high character, and that there was but one man living in England at the time worthy to be named as a religious poet, and that was Cædmon.

In proceeding to notice the sculptured decorations of these two monuments, our attention is first arrested by the mutilated delineation of the crucifixion on that at Ruthwell, and this because M. Didron and others are of opinion that representations of this subject do not, or very rarely, occur before the tenth century.[2] Here, however, we find it on a monument to which we can certainly assign an earlier date, (the seventh century), and there are several other examples on monuments which we have good reason to suppose belong to the seventh or eighth centuries. In the walls of the church of Kirkdale, in Yorkshire, built out of the ruins of St. Gregory's monastery (which I conceive to have been that of Læstingæu) are three crosses, one of which is entirely filled by a very rude crucifixion. On another found at Rothbury, and now in the Museum of the Society, the image of Our Saviour crucified fills the head of the cross, as on the ruder example at Kirkdale. The curious fragments of the cross at Alnwick, (from Woden's Church, Alnmouth), deserve special notice here, because they and the Ruthwell cross mutually illustrate each other. The position of the crucifixion on the cross [174] at Ruthwell shews what was probably the relation of the fragments at Alnwick to the cross of which they formed a part ; and the carving on the latter, being in better preservation than that on the former, shews what was its general design ; viz. Our Saviour extended on the cross, (not depending), the sun and moon above, below apparently the two thieves, and lower still two executioners. Very similar in design to these is the crucifixion represented on one of the crosses at Aycliffe, (of which by the kindness of W. H. D. Longstaffe, Esq., I am enabled to give a representation), where we have the two executioners only, without the thieves. Not to mention other examples on crosses, the west front of the little church of Headbourne Worthy, near Winchester, is nearly filled by a very large crucifix. . . . [175] At Romsey . . . there still remains, quite perfect, a similar crucifix on the external wall of the south transept. . . .

The three figures on the cross at Bewcastle are very superior in dignity and grace to any thing I have ever observed, even of Norman art, and the same may be said of those on the Ruthwell monument.[1] Two of them, St. John the Baptist holding the Holy Lamb, and Our Blessed Saviour trampling on the heads of demons personified by swine, are nearly the same on each monument, the differences of treatment being very slight. . . .

[176] The scroll-work on the eastern side of the Bewcastle monument, and on the two sides of that at Ruthwell, is identical in design, and differs very much from that which is found on other Saxon crosses. In fact I know of nothing like it except small portions on a fragment of a cross in the York Museum, on

another fragment preserved in Jarrow church, and on a cross at Hexham. This resemblance, and that already noticed, in the style of the carving of the imagery, convince me that the two crosses are the work of the same artist or artists, (if we suppose that then, as is the case now-a-days, one who was competent to execute statuary left the carving of flowers and mere ornaments to less skilful hands), and, therefore, that the date of the one cannot be much later than that of the other; nay, I feel inclined to go farther than this, and to hazard the conjecture that the two once formed the same monument, one at the head and the other at the foot[1] of the grave. Believing, as I do, that all these ancient crosses are sepulchral monuments, the absence of an epitaph at Ruthwell, on the lower stone at least, convinces me that something is wanting to make the monument complete. The inscriptions on its fronts are Latin antiphons, allusive to the subjects pourtrayed thereon, and those on its sides English verses descriptive of the Passion. In such a company a memorial inscription would have seemed incongruous. Something seems wanting to the completeness of the monument, and that is supplied by the cross at Bewcastle, where we find an inscription to the memory of king Alcfrid, and the names of other persons of his family. The verification of the Bewcastle traditions disposes me the more readily to credit that which tells us that the Ruthwell cross came thither by sea, and was cast on the shore by shipwreck. If this be really true, whence did it come? Most probably from Cumberland[2]; carried off, perhaps, on account of its beauty, by an army of Danes or Scots, and cast upon the shore of the Solway by a sudden storm.

Before I thought of the connection between these

two crosses, it occurred to me that the reason why
St. John the Baptist was introduced upon that at
Bewcastle might be, that he was the patron saint of
King [177] Alcfrid, and this seemed to clear up a
difficulty which I had felt for some years on another
point of antiquarian research. At Barnack, in Nor-
thamptonshire, three miles from Stamford, there is a
church the tower of which, presenting on three sides
scrolls with birds, and windows filled with tracery of
interlacing knotwork, is certainly a work of the seventh
century, and one which I always regarded as a relic
of the monastery built by St. Wilfrid in this neighbor-
hood on land granted to him by Alcfrid. But we
know that St. Wilfrid's monasteries were all dedicated
to St. Peter and St. Andrew (22) ; and how was the
supposition that Barnack is St. Wilfrid's work to be
reconciled with its dedication to St. John the Baptist ?
Very easily, if St. John the Baptist were indeed the
patron of Alcfrid. And if this were so, then his appearance on the Ruthwell cross adds to the probability that it belonged to the monument erected in
his honour at Bewcastle : and that monument, we may
suppose, consisted of two crosses, one at the head,
the other at the foot of the grave, both presenting
the image of our Blessed Lord, and of Alcfrid's patron
saint ; one devoted to sacred imagery and inscriptions
calculated for the edification of the beholder, the
other presenting his portraiture and an inscription to
his memory. It is even possible that the inscription
upon the upper stone at Ruthwell may have contained
his name. The letters which remain are IDÆ GISCÆ.

---

[22] Eddi, chap. liv., records a vision (A. D. 705), in which St. Wilfrid is reproached for having done this, and having neglected to
build one in honour of the Blessed Virgin, and four years of life
are granted him to supply this omission.

Of these GISCÆ is evidently the beginning of a word such as *gesceapan,* to form or shape, *gesceadan,* to divide or separate, or *gescea,* sobbing, and the rest may be the ending of the word *Alcfridæ.* If any other letters could be traced confirming this conjecture, I should regard this inscription as a sort of postscript to that on the other cross. Nor would such a supposition militate against what I have said above of the incongruity of a memorial inscription with such as the rest of those upon this monument : for the lower stone on which they occur is evidently complete in itself, and as evidently the addition of the upper stone was an afterthought, for which the wish to add such an inscription as this might easily account, and which I cannot but think detracts from the beauty of the monument by destroying its unity.

XIII. MAUGHAN'S SECOND ACCOUNT, 1857.

[This is taken from the rare pamphlet entitled, *A Memoir on the Roman Station and Runic Cross at Bewcastle. with an Appendix on the Roman Inscription on Caeme Craig, and the Runic Inscription in Carlisle Cathedral*, London, Carlisle, Brampton, and Newcastle, 1857. The first of these papers occupies pages 3—9; the first paper in the Appendix, 39—42; the second, referring to the so-called Dolfin runes, 43—44. The essay with which we are concerned falls into two parts—' Runic Cross in Bewcastle Churchyard ' and ' Mr. Haigh's Version '—occupying pages 10—30 and 31—38 respectively. As the footnotes are numbered consecutively throughout the pamphlet, the first one in our part is No. 14.]

RUNIC CROSS IN BEWCASTLE CHURCHYARD.

STONES in the form of a cross, both plain and sculptured, have been reared by our forefathers at different remote periods, and for a variety of purposes,[1] and hence the history of such crosses becomes a subject of investigation replete with the deepest interest. Some of these crosses were simply wayside crosses, being frequently only a small rude square or oblong stone with a small cross cut on the face of it. These, besides being a great resort for beggars, were places where the corpse was allowed to stand for a short period when passing to its last place of rest, in order that a brief prayer might be offered for the soul of the departed. The pious of former days seldom passed these crosses without bowing or kneeling, and offering up their short and devout ejaculations. Crosses were also generally erected wherever a market was held, under the impression, perhaps, as some suppose, that the visible emblem of our redemption might influence the minds of the traders towards honesty and fair dealing, and hence we frequently find the remains of a cross near ancient religious establishments, as for instance at Lanercost, because at such places a market[1] was almost invariably held, often even immediately after the celebration of divine service on the Sabbath. Some of these stones or crosses were erected near the shores, and served as beacons or landmarks ;—others were placed as sentinels or guardians of public springs and wells ; others denoted the place where great battles had been fought and won, and where other important events had occurred, such as the celebrated Percy and Neville crosses ; others denoted a place of sanctuary, where criminals, however guilty, might crave and obtain the protection of the Church ; while others were placed in churchyards to impress the feelings, and increase the ardour of public devotion. The most interesting of this class are those which have been erected to denote the burial-place of some important personage, and of these the cross in the churchyard at Bewcastle may be justly considered as one of the most remarkable specimens.(14)

(14) This pillar, which may be properly classed among the most celebrated of archæological monuments, is nearly the frustum of a square pyramid, measuring 22 inches by 21 at the base, and tapering to 14 inches by 13 at the top of the shaft, being 14½ feet high above its pedestal. The pillar has been fixed with lead in a shallow cavity which has been cut on the crown of a nearly cubical block of stone 4 feet square, and 3 ft. 9 in. high; which stone is now sunk about 3 feet into the ground, and has been tooled off at the upper corners so as to assume the appearance of an unequal-sided octagon. On the top of the pillar was formerly placed a small cross, which has been lost for a considerable period, and hence the pillar is now merely an obelisk.[2]

The traditions of the district say that a king was buried here, and also point out the locality where the shaft of the pillar was

Drawings of the north and west sides of this monument appeared in the 'Gentleman's Magazine' in 1742, p. 317.[1] Captain Armstrong, a surveyor of land, who was born at Lowgrange, about a mile from the monument, is said to [11] have published an engraving[2] of it, out of regard to his native place. A facsimile of the chief inscription[3] was communicated to the Society of Antiquaries in 1801 by the late and very learned Henry Howard, Esq., of Corby Castle, (see Archæologia, vol. 14, p. 118,) and Cardonnell is said

procured; and the traditions are probably correct in both respects. On an extensive, and still unenclosed waste, called White Lyne Common, about five miles from Bewcastle Church, is a long ridge of rocks called the Langbar. About the centre of this ridge a stone is now lying on the surface of the ground, which is nearly fifteen feet in length, and which is the very counterpart of the Bewcastle obelisk in its rude and undressed state. It is evidently the relic of a stone which has been split at some distant period into two equal parts, the marks of the wedges used in the operation being still distinctly traceable, and the side, which, from its present position, may be called the western, apparently much fresher than the other sides, and not covered with so thick a coat of grey moss; as if it had been exposed to the effects of the weather for a shorter period of time. The obelisk is a peculiar species of rock; a very hard, gritty, and durable white freestone, with rather a yellow tinge, thickly covered with spots of a grey hue; precisely such as is found at the Langbar, and the adjacent rocks on the south side of the White Lyne river. A careful comparison of some fragments of the obelisk with other fragments from the Langbar stone, shows them to be unquestionably twins from one and the same parent.

To this supposed and traditional origin of the obelisk it may possibly be objected, that it would be almost impossible to convey such an immense block of stone from such a hilly and now roadless district. This objection, however, is much diminished, if we bear in mind that the old Roman road called the Maiden Way passed near both its present and its supposed original site, which road would probably be in good order at the period when the stone was brought; and that there was an easy and gradual incline across the moor from the Langbar to the Maiden Way; affording facilities for its conveyance to this road.

by Mr. Howard to have published a good representation of the cross.[1] I have not been able to procure
a sight of this representation, but, through the kindness of P. H. Howard, Esq., I have seen a drawing
in water-colours, representing the four sides of the
monument, by Miss Ann Cardonnell, which was sent
to Mr. Howard by her father, and which is far from
accurate. In each of the Histories of Cumberland
published by Hutchinson[2] and Lysons[3], drawings are
also given of this stone; those in Hutchinson bearing
some resemblance to those of Miss Cardonnell. The
best representation which I have seen is that in Lysons,
but in this the figures and some of the so-called
magical knots are not quite correctly delineated, and
the tracings of certain parts of the vines are too thick
to convey a faithful impression of the gracefulness
of the original sculpture. I made a drawing of this
monument some time since, accurate and correct as
possible in all its details, which I presented to Mr. Le
Keux, and he proposed to devote two plates to this
drawing in his valuable work on the Illustration of
Ancient Crosses.

We have no authentic copy or record of the inscriptions on this remarkable monument; or of the
period when they first became illegible; but of this
we may rest assured, that they have not been distinct for more than two centuries. Camden, who died
in 1623, devoted his attention to them, but failed in
deciphering them. In Gibson's edition of Camden's
Britannia, 1695, this monument is thus described[4] :—
'In the churchyard is a cross of one entire square
stone, about twenty foot high, and curiously cut;
there is an inscription, too, but the letters are so dim
that they are not legible. But seeing the cross is of
the same kind as that in the arms of the family of

Vaux, one may conjecture that it has been made by some of that family.' If Camden's measurement be correct, it must comprehend the pedestal, shaft, and the cross on its summit, which cross must consequently have been 21 inches high.[1] From Camden's observations we may naturally infer that the inscription must have been lost long before his day.

Lord William Howard (commonly called Belted Will), who died in the same year as Camden, also attempted to recover the inscription, but without success. In the History of Cumberland, published by Nicholson and Burn,[2] in 1777, we read as follows :—
'The Lord William Howard of Naworth (a lover of antiquities) caused the inscriptions thereon to be carefully copied, and sent them to Sir Henry Spelman to interpret. The task being too hard for Sir Henry, he transmitted the copy to Olaus Wormius, History Professor at Copenhagen, who was then about to publish his Monumenta Danica.'[3]

Sir H. Spelman reads one part of the inscriptions (which is said to have been 'in[4] epistylio crucis,' and which I take to be the bottom line[5] on the south side,) thus[6] :—

i. e., RICES DRYHTNESS[7]: which may be translated, ' of the kingdom of our Lord,' or (the monument) ' of a powerful Lord.'[8] Wanleius, in his Catalogue, p. 248, with a slight variation of the letters, reads this line, 'RYNAS DRYHTNESS,'[9] *i. e.*, 'mysteria Domini,'—'the Runes or mysterious characters of our Lord.'[10] Wanleius took this from the Cottonian Codex in the British Museum. The learned antiquary, Olaus Wormius, in his Monumenta Danica, pp. 162, 168, notices

the inscription sent by Spelman, and prints it exactly
as it was sent to him, but owns at the same time
that he did not know what to make of it. One part
of it, which he[1] says was in[2] epistylio crucis (the bottom line of the south side), supposing the characters
to be Scandinavian Runes, and dividing the line into
eighteen letters,—

he reads thus[3] : *i. e.*, RINO SATU RUNA STINOTH,[4]—' RINO
made these Runic stones.'   Hickes, in his Thesaurus,
Grammatica Anglo-Saxonica, makes some slight deviations from the reading of Spelman, and gives the line
thus,—[12] 'RODEN DRYHTNESS,'[5]—'the cross of our
Lord.'   Bishop Nicholson[6] (formerly Bishop of Carlisle,
who devoted much of his attention to the recovery
of these inscriptions,) says in the year 1685, ' on the
south side, flourishes and conceits as before, and towards the bottom, the following decayed inscription[7] :—

The defects in this short piece are sufficient to discourage me from attempting to expound it ; but possibly it may be read thus :—' GAG UBBO ERLET'[8] :
' Ubbo conquered the robbers.'   I may observe that
the Bishop's copy[9] of these letters is very inaccurate,
and embraces portions of the sculpture, which he has
mistaken for letters.

The late Mr. Kemble, in his memoir,[10] (Archæologia,
vol. xxviii., part 16,) read this line nearly the same
as Spelman—' RICÆS DRYHTNÆS '—' Domini potentis,'
which he said may be part of an inscription—the
first word or words being lost—or the pillar itself
may be taken as part of the sentence, thus, ' Signum

Domini potentis'[1]; which means—'the monument of a powerful lord.' Kemble said[2]—'Whether this inscription (referring to the one read by Grimm) and the stone on which it was cut, stood alone, or whether they formed part of some larger monument, I do not know.'(15)

In the 'Gentleman's Magazine,' 1742, p. 368, is a paper from the pen of Mr. George Smith, who, according to the 'Biographia Cumb.,'[3] was a native of Scotland ; a man of genius and learning ; who lived for some time near Brampton, and was a great contributor to the 'Gentleman's Magazine.' Mr. Smith gives a description of the north side of the monument, but never favoured the public with his promised dissertation on its remaining sides.(16)

(15) Speaking of the present monument, Kemble said—' I beg to refer the reader [4] to the careful copy of this (the inscription) furnished by Mr. Howard of Corby Castle. This plate contains three several portions of the inscription. Of fig. 1 but one letter, an R, is now legible. Fig. 2, which contains indistinct traces of nine lines of Runes, and of which the loss may be said to be irreparable, offers here and there a legible letter or two, but no more. Fig. 3, on the contrary, is still in perfect preservation : unfortunately it supplies us with only one word, and that a proper name—CYNIBURUG or CYNIBURUH, which contains unquestionable evidence of great antiquity. Who this lady was it would be absurd to attempt to guess ; but I think that the fifth line of the inscription in fig. 2 may also possibly have contained her name ; while the second line of the same, commencing with letters which apparently formed the word CRIST, render it likely that this, as well as the Ruthwell pillar, was a Christian work. The most important deduction from the name I have read is, that the inscription was an Anglo-Saxon, not a Norse one.' (Kemble on Anglo-Saxon Runes. Archæologia, vol. 28, p. 346—7.)

(16) In Mr. Smith's paper on the north side it is stated, p. 319, on the authority of the ' Magna Britannia Antiqua et Nova,' that the cross was washed over with a white oily cement.[5] I have noticed several remains of this cement. The letters appear to have been

The late Henry Howard, Esq., of Corby Castle, in
a communication to the Society of Antiquaries in the
year 1801 (see Archæologia, vol. 14, p. 118) says that
he spent two days[1] in an attempt to recover the inscription on this cross.(17)

Although Mr. Howard probably did not actually
succeed in deciphering any part of it, yet, so far as
I know, he was the first person to whose learned researches we are indebted for the very ingenious sug-

filled with it level with the surface of the stone.   It is white, covered
with a thin coat of green, and then with a covering of grey rust of
the exact colour of the stone itself ; so that for a long time it escaped
my observation when embedded in the letters.   It is so hard and
tenacious that it is almost impossible to eradicate it ; the point of a
knife making no impression.   I mention this circumstance because
I have been censured by a Mr. Robert White,[2] of Newcastle, and some
other fastidious antiquarians, for painting the inscribed portions of
the cross—men who had neither the perseverance nor the ability to
recover the lost inscriptions themselves, and who could only snarl at
the attempts and the success of others.   I consider, however, that
I was justified in resorting to every expedient that offered a probability of assistance in tracing the very dubious and worn-out marks,
provided I did no injury to the stone, and I defy the whole body
of these gentlemen to prove that I have injured the cross in the
slightest degree by painting a few portions of it.   I can assure them
that I venerate the cross at Bewcastle as much as if it had been made
from my own bones.

(17) His mode of operation, according to his own account, seems
to have been as follows :—He cut slips of paper of the breadth of the
lines, and took the impression, a few letters at a time, by rubbing
the paper placed thereon with a piece of ivory, working the paper in
as much as possible with the finger, and afterwards following the
finger at the edges of every part of the letters with the pencil.   He
speaks thus of the inscription—' The third, fourth, and fifth lines
are the most perfect.   Towards the lower part scarce anything is to
be made out.   On the whole, indeed, little more than the vestiges
of the inscription remain ; the perpendicular parts of the letters are
discernible, and have probably been deepened by the rain, but the
horizontal and other parts are nearly obliterated.'   He offers no
interpretation of the inscription.

gestion[1] as to Bewcastle being the tomb of King Alfrid. *Although Mr. Howard failed in his attempt to open the lock, yet he was probably the first person to point out the right key.*

[13] In the History of Cumberland published by Hutchinson in 1794 is a long article on this monument, with a copy of the inscription[2] published in the 'Gentleman's Magazine,' which I suspect to have been made first by Lord William Howard, and sent by him to Sir H. Spelman, and afterwards published in the 'Monumenta Danica' of Wormius.[3] The Lysons, in their History of Cumberland, have also favoured this cross with a passing notice. Many antiquarians have visited it at different periods, but I am not aware that any one has published any account or explanation of it, besides the parties already mentioned. I shall now venture to offer a detailed account of it.

THE CROSS.

On the crown of the pillar is a cavity $7\frac{1}{2}$ inches deep and $8\frac{1}{2}$ inches square, designed to hold the foot of the small cross which formerly surmounted the shaft; the loss of which is much to be regretted. Mr. Smith, in his dissertation already mentioned, says that it was demolished long ago by popular frenzy and enthusiasm. The tradition of the district says that it was broken off by an ill-aimed cannon ball when Cromwell destroyed the castle. But both of these statements are probably incorrect. From Gough's edition of Camden we find that a slip of paper had been found in *Camden's own copy* of his 'Britannia' (Ed. 1607, in the Bodleian Library), accompanied by the following note[4]—'I received this morning a ston from my Lord of Arundel, sent him from my Lord William. It was the head of a cross at Bucastle.'

Now Camden died in 1623, and as Cromwell did not visit these parts till about 20 years afterwards (if he ever visited them at all), it is very evident from this fact, and from this statement of Camden, that the disappearance of this cross may be more justly attributed to the antiquarian propensities of Belted Will, than to any of the errant balls of Cromwell's artillery.

East Side.

A vine springing from the bottom of the pillar, and highly relieved, is represented as gracefully winding up the East side in serpentine undulations, with numerous branches starting from it, covered with foliage and bunches of grapes. This side of the monument bears a considerable resemblance to two sides of the Runic monument at Ruthwell, near Dumfries, which is said to be the only stone[1] hitherto discovered in Scotland with a Runic inscription : no Runes having yet been found even in the Orkney or Shetland Isles, where they might have been expected in abundance.

In each of the regular and flowing curves of the vine an animal, or a bird, is artfully sculptured (in alto relievo) in what is considered by some people as the old Gothic style, and is in the act of feeding on the fruit. In the lowest curve is a quadruped somewhat resembling a fox-hound. In each of the next two curves is the representation of an imaginary biped, having the head and shoulders of an animal, while the body tapers away into a long, flexible, and curled tail, with an enlarged point, curiously entwined round the stem and branches, the lower biped bearing some resemblance to one on the cross at Ruthwell. In the curve above this is a bird like a hawk or an eagle ; and in the next curve is a bird like a raven ; these two birds being nearly the same in figure, but considerably larger than two similar birds at Ruthwell. In each of the two succeeding curves is a sculptured squirrel, the Ruthwell Cross differing from this at Bewcastle in having more birds, and only one squirrel. The vine, gradually growing more slender, winds again into two elegant curves, and appears to terminate with clusters of grapes.

The sculpture on this side of the cross has suffered very little damage from the corroding effects of the weather. The buds, blossoms, and fruit have been so carefully and exquisitely delineated by the chisel of the workman, and are still so faithfully preserved, that they seem as if they were things only just starting into life.(18) There [14] is no inscription now on the east side. It is probable however that there have been some letters near the top of the shaft on a part which has been broken off.

West Side.

The west side is the most important on account of its ornaments, and also its inscriptions. On a plain surface (about nine inches deep, near the top of the cross) which appears to have surmounted the dec-

(18) Bishop Nicholson looks upon these flourishes and conceits as nothing more ' than the statuary's fancy '; and Mr. Hutchinson thinks ' it would be extending a desire of giving extraordinary import to works of antiquity to suppose they were intended to carry any emblematical meaning : they are similar to the ornaments of the capitals and fillets in Gothic structures of the eleventh century, or near about that time, and no one ever yet presumed to assert they were to be construed as hieroglyphics.' According to Boece,[1] the hieroglyphic figures on ancient crosses were borrowed from the Egyptians, and were used by the natives in place of letters ; and both he and subsequent historians have assigned a Danish origin to many of them—an idea which is quite repudiated by the present race of Danish antiquarians.

orated parts on each of the four sides, are the following remains of Runic letters.

They are apparently fragments of the letters K, S,
and S, in the word KRISTUS, which occurs again a
little lower down on this side : the lower part of the
letter K, the middle and lower part of the first S, and
the termination of the last S, being all that now remains of the word. It will appear from the succeeding pages of this Treatise why I suppose these fragments to be constituent parts of the word KRISTTUS.
    Bishop Nicholson says—' On the west side of the
stone we have three fair draughts, which evidently
enough manifest the monument to be Christian. . . .
On the top stands the effigies of the B. V. with the
Babe in her arms and both their heads encircled with
glories.' Mr. Hutchinson coincides with the prelate
as to this figure, and Mr. Armstrong represents it like
a mitred ecclesiastic. The Lysons say of this sculpture—' The female figure is so defaced that nothing
more than a general outline can be distinguished ;
what she holds in her left arm is much better preserved, and is the holy lamb.' On carefully remov-
ing the moss from the stone I ascertained that the
Lysons were correct as to the ' Agnus Dei,' but not
as to the figure of a female, for the beard itself, if
there were no other marks, affords sufficient proof
that it must be the representation of St. John the
Baptist, and not of the Blessed Virgin. The head of
the ' Agnus Dei ' has been encircled with a small
, nimbus ' or ' glory,' but there is no trace of one

surrounding the head of the Apostle. There is a similar figure on the Ruthwell Cross, although it has evidently not been sculptured from the same design. Dr. Duncan, in his illustrations of the Ruthwell monument, describes this image as representing ' the Father standing on two globes or worlds (indicating probably the world which now is and that which is to come) with the Agnus Dei in his bosom.'

Immediately below this figure are two lines of Runic letters to which my attention was at first drawn by the very imperfect representation of them in the plates in Lysons. On divesting these letters of their mossy covering, and obtaining a mould in plaster of Paris from this part of the stone, I found that although extremely dim, the letters were still perfect and legible. This short inscription is in the Latin language, while the other inscriptions on the monument are in the Anglo-Saxon, thus rendering the monument one of the bi-lingual order. The inscription, when rendered into the English language, is simply ' Jesus Christ ' ; and undoubtedly refers to the figure of our Saviour immediately below it, thus limiting the period of the erection of the monument to the Christian era. It may be read thus[1] in Runic and Roman characters :—

+ GESSUS
KRISTTUS.

Mr. Smith says—' That the monument is Danish appears incontestible from the characters : Scottish and Pictish monuments having nothing but hieroglyphics, and the Danish both.' Mr. Hutchinson thinks that 'his assertion was hasty of the Scottish and Pictish monuments'—but he also appears to consider the monument Danish. These letters, however, are undoubtedly Anglo-Saxon Runes, and they, as well as the others found on this cross, generally agree with those found [15] in the Codex Exoniensis published by Hickes, thus proving the monument to be of Anglo-Saxon construction ; and hence arises one of the most important subjects of inquiry connected with this memorial, to which I now beg to draw the reader's special notice for a few moments.

It has been a question much debated amongst our learned Antiquarians whether the Anglo-Saxons had any system of writing peculiar to themselves, or whether they used entirely the Roman characters of Augustine. This stone, however, seems to set the matter quite at rest,[1] and a doubt can no longer be entertained on this point. Hence it becomes a monument of the greatest historical interest and importance, and goes far to prove that *the earliest Anglo-Saxon colonists* were acquainted with the use of letters ; for assuredly if they were first taught to read and write by St. Augustine in the Roman characters, we cannot believe that Runic characters would be introduced at any subsequent period. The Roman characters would be much more easily learned and used ; and hence their general adoption in preference to the rude forms of the Anglo-Saxon letters, which in all probability were little known by the mass of the people.

It ought, however, to be carefully borne in mind that before the coming of Augustine into this country, in the year 597, we have scarcely a single trustworthy record of any one event in the history of our country. When Augustine and his companions introduced their system of Christian observances into this island, there can be little doubt but that they introduced at the same time a *system of writing and the keeping of annals;* and hence the few documents of this early period bear the marks of their Roman as well as ecclesiastical origin. It is very remarkable that the Charters, and other important documents of that early period, are all in the Latin language. Although in the early ages of the Christian Church many prelates as well as princes were unable to write even their own names, yet it is probable that the order of the clergy, as a body, occupied a much better position, so far as this goes, than the laity ; and hence the clergy became at that early period the tabelliones, *i. e.*, the draughtsmen and engrossers of these instruments, and remained such for many succeeding centuries. Hence also arose the prevalence of the Latin language. It is not unreasonable to suppose, however, that some of the Anglo Saxons, especially those of the ecclesiastical order, were acquainted with a system of writing different from the Roman, although we cannot believe that there was any wide dispersion of such a power of recording the events of the time.(19)

(19) The letters of the alphabet have always been called ' Runes,' *i. e.*, secret letters (' run ' signifying a secret or mystery), probably because known only to very few persons ; and hence the letters on this cross may be properly designated Anglo-Saxon Runes. Such Runes were only fitted for short inscriptions, and consequently we generally find them on stones or blocks of wood, and probably they might, as has been generally supposed, be used for little else than auguries, divinations, and witchcraft. They were not at all adapted for continuous writing, and there is perhaps little probability of their having ever been put to any such use. Modern researches have gone far to prove that the Runic alphabet and characters of the Germans, Anglo-Saxons, and Dano-Saxons, were not a corruption of a more perfect alphabet, but that they possessed an undeniably primitive stamp, which bears a certain degree of resemblance to the alphabets of almost all the early inhabitants of Europe—such as the

We may now return from our digression and proceed with the further examination of the inscription. The first thing that arrests our attention is the mark of the Cross which precedes this inscription, and also some of the other inscriptions on this monument. This use of the holy emblem as a prefix is full of interest.(20)   The mode of [16] spelling the names of our Redeemer is also interesting, as it shows the

Etruscans, the Turditanians, the Celtiberians, &c., but more especially a decided affinity to the Ionic, *i. e.*, the most ancient of the Greek alphabets; which circumstance is considered by some as pointing to the east as the source of Runic civilization.   Bosworth, in his Saxon Grammar, page 27, says—' Fortunatus, indeed, in the sixth century, mentions the rude Runes of the Gothic hordes of Italy. But Hickes cannot produce a single instance of Runic alphabetical writing older than the eleventh century, when Runes, which were only Talismanic figures, were first applied to alphabetical use, by expressing sounds instead of representing things.'   Several Anglo-Saxon Runic inscriptions have, however, been discovered and deciphered, which are undoubtedly connected with a period long anterior to the eleventh century; and the Bewcastle pillar is, I believe, at present the earliest known specimen of Anglo-Saxon Runic writing.

(20) Professor Wilson, in his Prehistoric Annals of Scotland, elucidates the Runic inscriptions on the crosses in the Isle of Man, and infers from the mark of the cross which occurs on one of them, that such a mark was used to show that the inscription was the work of an Ecclesiastic.   We must not, however, draw any such general inference from the use of this mark on this cross.   It is not necessary to suppose that the occurrence of the mark of the cross generally denotes anything of the kind : and more especially so on this Bewcastle monument.   Mosheim tells us (even as early as the third century) that the cross was supposed to administer a victorious power over all sorts of trials and calamities, and that no Christian undertook anything of moment without arming himself with the influence of this triumphant sign.   The use of the cross as a symbol appears to have been very prevalent among our Anglo-Saxon forefathers. On nearly every one of their coins the legends, or inscriptions, have the cross prefixed.   Again, if we look into Anglo-Saxon Charters of an early period, and other documents, we find these marks of the crosses by dozens, as prefixes to the signatures of each of the parties.

method in use among our Anglo-Saxon forefathers in the 7th century.[1] We may presume that the Italian mode of spelling the word ' Gessus ' with a G was in use from an early period ; and it appears to be still continued in that language, for in a legal document in Italian, dated at Leghorn in Tuscany in the last century, I find the word ' Gessus ' commencing

In short, the universality of the sign of the cross is recognized in the earliest Italian as well as Anglo-Saxon documents. It seems also to have been prevalent as a prefix to the Roman inscriptions after a certain period. In a thick Italian quarto volume, ' Roma Sotteranea,' published at Rome in 1650 by Antonius Bossius, an Ecclesiastical antiquarian, which contains a copious history of those wonderful burial-places at Rome called the Catacombs, we find facsimiles of a large number of the inscriptions which are to be met with there, and we also find the cross attached to a very considerable part of these inscriptions. In fact, the cross appears to have been the almost universally adopted symbol of our redemption by every nation which embraced Christianity. Besides the numerous instances of its appearance on the gravestones of the primitive Christians in the Catacombs we know that the earliest Christians gloried in its use. The banners of the Emperor Constantine were, by directions from heaven, as has been stated, blazoned with this representation of Christ crucified, ' in hoc signo vinces.' Among Christians in the east, even to this day, it is the usual sign of recognition ; and in the Greek Churches this emblem is everywhere to be found. Long before material crosses were in use, Tertullian tells us that ' upon every motion, at their going out or coming in, at dressing, at their going to the bath, or at meals, or to bed, or whatever their employments or occasions called them to, the primitive Christians were wont to mark their foreheads with the sign of the cross,' adding that ' this was a practice which tradition had introduced, custom had confirmed, and which the present generation received upon the credit of that which went before them.' It is probable, however, that the cross was only an adopted symbol, and that it was by no means confined to Christians, and to Christian monuments. The Egyptians regarded it as the emblem of reproduction and resurrection. It is more than probable that a heathen feeling lurked under this symbol, and that it was held binding, even before the introduction of Christianity. The hammer of the heathen god Thunor (Thor) was at one

with the letter G. I have carefully examined the in-scriptions given in the 'Roma Sotteranea,' but have found no trace of these names so spelt there. In fact the word 'Jesus' scarcely ever occurs in the very long list of inscriptions given by Bossius. I find the expressions 'domino Zesu,' and 'pie Zesus'; and these are the nearest approaches to the orthography of the Bewcastle Monument.

The letter K and the double letter T in the word 'Kristtus' also merit a passing notice. The letter K for C is sometimes found in Roman inscriptions. Horsley mentions an altar found at Stanwix, near Carlisle, afterwards placed at Drawdykes Castle, in which K is used for C; thus, 'conjux Karissima' instead of 'conjux carissima.' The letter K for C also appears in other inscriptions of an older date than any in Britain. The doubling of the letter T is said by some Saxon grammarians to be characteristic of Dano-Saxon usage, but its appearance on the Bew-castle Monument shows it to have been so used long before the Danes visited this country. A character similar to the second letter in the first line is given

time the symbol in all contracts, and that hammer was literally and really the representation of a cross.   In the ' Runographia Scandica ' of Olaus Verellus[1] twelve illustrations of stones with Scandinavian Runic inscriptions are given in which the cross is conspicuous.   This emblem on these stones cannot be supposed to have any connection with Christianity, for Odin was the god to whom the Scandinavians paid their homage.   In the first of these illustrations on which the cross appears, the inscription is as follows:—'Jubern Ukvi has inscribed this stone to the memory of his father Irbern, and has dedicated these sepulchral Runes to the god Odin.'   It is also worth observing that this mark or sign seems to have been appropriated from the very beginning to some great mystery, for we read in the Book of Exodus that the Israelites could overcome the Amalekites no longer than Moses, by stretching out his arms, continued in the form of a cross.

as the letter O in the Exeter manuscript published by Hickes ; and the use of the dipthong Œ instead of the vowel E is by no means contrary to Saxon usage. In the Mœso-Gothic language the word 'Jesus' was written with the dipthong AI—thus, IAISUS. Hence I was for a long time in doubt whether these two lines ought to be read 'Iœssus Kristtus,' or 'Gessus Kristtus' with a cross prefixed. Having, however, obtained a very good rubbing of the lines, and having found the cross prefixed in so many other parts of the monument, I am now of opinion that the latter reading is probably the correct one.

I believe I am right in asserting that [17] these two lines form the *first portion of the inscriptions of the Bewcastle monument which have been correctly deciphered by any one.* After considerable trouble and research I succeeded in recovering them in the summer of 1854, and I made a communication to that effect soon afterwards to Mr. Way, one of the Secretaries of the Archæological Institute. I also mentioned my reading of these two lines to several other persons who saw the monument, and pointed out to them the variety in the reading.

Below the two lines of Runes above-mentioned is a figure which Bishop Nicholson conjectures to be 'the picture of some Apostle, Saint, or other holy man, in a sacerdotal habit, with a glory round his head.' Mr. Hutchinson describes it as 'the figure of a religious person, the garments descending to his feet, the head encircled with a nimbus, not now appearing radiated, but merely a circular rise of the stone ; the right hand is elevated in a teaching posture, and the other hand holds a roll : a fold of the garment was mistaken by Mr. Armstrong for a string of beads. We conceive this figure to represent St. Cuthbert, to whom the Church, as set forth by Nicholson and Burn, is dedicated.' The Lysons say—'As he holds a roll (the sacred volumen) in his left hand, and the right hand is elevated in the act of benediction, we should rather suppose it was intended for our Saviour, who is frequently so represented in ancient works of art.' The two Runic lines above the figure now show that the Lysons were correct in their conjectures. The figure appears to be nearly an accurate fac-simile of the representation of our Saviour on the Ruthwell Cross. On the Bewcastle pillar each of the feet of our Saviour is represented as placed upon a pedestal which is no longer distinct. On the Ruthwell Cross each of these pedestals is more perfect, and represents the head of a pig,[1] and they are undoubtedly intended for the same objects on the Bewcastle monument, probably having an allusion to the miracle of the devils cast into the herd of swine.

Under this figure of our Redeemer we find the remains of an inscription of nine lines, of which Camden said, 'the letters are so dim that they are not legible,' and which were considered so decayed in the time of Bishop Nicholson that he described them as 'the forementioned ruins of Lord Howard's inscription'; and declined even attempting to make out any part of it.(21)

(21) During the last few years my attention has been specially directed from time to time to the recovery of this long-lost inscription. I covered the inscribed parts first of all with soft mud and sods for a few months, which process entirely removed the thick coat of moss and lichens with which the letters were so thickly covered, without doing any injury to the stone. I then tried to obtain dry rubbings with lead, and grass, but from the defaced state of the letters, these rubbings were very imperfect and unsatisfactory. I next obtained a mould and cast of the inscribed part in plaster of Paris, but without any great result. I then gave these parts a coat of paint which ren-

The following wood-cut shows the inscription in its Runic characters,[1] and beneath is the inscription in Roman letters, the letters in brackets denoting compound Runes. The Roman letters, of course, are not on the stone.

RUNIC.

ROMAN.

+ [TH]ISSIGB[EA]CN
[THU]NSETT[ON]H
W[AET]REDW[AETH]
GARALWFWOL
[THU]AFTALCFRI
[THU]EAN KYNI[ING]
EAC OSWIU[ING]
+ GEBID HE
OSINNASAW[HU]LA.[2]

dered the letters more distinct than the cast. I afterwards tried some rubbings after the following method which was partly recommend-

[18] I read the inscription thus—
+ THISSIG BEACN THUN SETTON HWAETRED
WAETHGAR ALWFWOLTHU AFT ALCFRITHU
EAN KYNIING EAC OSWIUING. + GEBID HEO
SINNA SAWHULA—
and it may be thus translated : + *Hwætred, Wæthgar,*
and *Alwfwold* (the names of three persons)—setton—
set up—thissig thun beacn—*this slender pillar*—aft
Alcfrithu—*in memory of Alcfrid*—ean Kyniing—*ane
King*—eac Oswiuing—*and son of Oswy.* + Gebid—
pray thou—heo—*for them*—sinna—*their sins*—sawhula
—*their souls.*

In this inscription the first character or mark is, I
now believe, that of a cross, although it is not very
distinct. I was for a long time[1] inclined to adopt the
idea of Bishop Nicholson[2] that the inscription commenced with the monogram IHS for ' Jesus hominum
Salvator,' *i. e.,* Jesus the Saviour of men. Good
rubbings, however, and repeated examinations of the
stone, and the frequent occurrence of this emblem
on other parts of the cross, lead me to the conclusion

ed by Mr. Way in March, 1854, and which was more successful than
the other processes : I cut slips of white paper, such as is generally
used by printers, rather broader than the length of the letters; a
separate slip for each line. I fastened these slips, one at a time, to
the stone with strings to prevent them from slipping, having previously pricked them well with a pin to allow the air to escape through
them. With a large sponge I then saturated them well with water,
and pressed them to the stone till they adhered closely to it. After
allowing them time to dry, and while still sticking to the stone, I
gave them a careful rubbing with a black-lead rubber. By this
process I succeeded in getting some good rubbings; and from these
rubbings, combined with the previous processes, and a repeated
dwelling of the eye upon the letters, and countless tracings of the
depressions and marks with the point of the finger, I have succeeded
in gaining such knowledge of the almost worn-out characters, that
I now venture to offer a version of this interesting inscription.

that it has commenced with a cross. The word 'thissig' is not an unusual form of the pronoun 'this,' such a termination being often[1] affixed to adjectives and pronouns. The word 'beacn' is variously written 'beacen, beacn, bocn, bycn, becen, and becn,' and denotes 'a beacon, sign, or token.'(22)

The word 'thun'[2] means thin or slender, and has probably some reference to the size and shape of the monument. The first letter in the word 'thun' is a Trirunor, or compound Rune, being composed of the letters 'TH'— þ —and the letter U— ᚾ —and hence by combination we have the Trirunor THU— ᚦ (23)

The word 'setton' is the third person plural of the perfect tense of the verb 'settan'—*to set or place*, and agrees with the three nominative cases Hwætred, Wæthgar, and Alwfwolthu.(24)

(22) These two words may possibly be read thus : ' this sigbeacn ' —sigbeacn being a compound word derived from ' sige '—*victory, triumph :* and hence the word ' sigbeacn ' means *a token of triumph or victory*. But as we have no record of any triumph or victory gained by Alcfrid for which the monument was reared, this part of the inscription may perhaps be more correctly rendered thus, ' thissig beacn.'

(23) The cross-bars in this letter were for a long time a complete puzzle to me, having been noticed by me from the first. At last it was suggested that it might possibly be the compound Runic character ' THU,' and from that time I experienced no further insurmountable difficulty in reading the inscription. From Mr. Howard's plate of the inscription it is evident that he had noticed these cross-bars. The same character appears in the words Alwfwolthu, Alcfrithu, and Ecgfrithu.

(24) An old schoolfellow, the Rev. Thos. Calvert, of Norwich, visited Bewcastle for the purpose of inspecting the Monument, but had not an opportunity of seeing the inscription, as it was at that time covered with sods. He very shrewdly suggested that I might probably find the words ' beacon ' and ' setta ' upon it, as, in

'Aft' is the preposition, *after or in memory of*, and governs the word [19] Alcfrithu, to whom the monument was erected. The word 'ean'[1]—*one*—is very similar to our provincial word 'ane,' which is still in use in this district.(25)

The word 'Gebid'[2] stands for 'bid,' and is the second person singular of the imperative mood of the verb 'biddan'—*to pray, to bid, or require.*[3] The syllable 'ge' is simply an expletive or augment, such an expletive being in common use.(26)

The word 'heo' is not an unusual form of the pronoun. 'Sinna' is the plural form of 'sin' or

addition to the host of ingenious speculations already advanced as to the object of its erection, he thought it might have been a beacon or boundary cross set up to mark the extent of the fifteen miles around Carlisle granted by King Egfrid to the religious establishments at that city. After the monument was cleaned I sent him a copy of the inscribed part so far as I was then able to trace it. In letters which I afterwards received from him he favoured me with the following acute observations. ' If the second word could be read *sigbeakn* it might mean *a sign of victory* '——' Can the first part of the second line be ' *upsetta,*' i. e., set up." He also suggested that ' Hwætred ' might be an appellative, ' brave in council '; and stated that it occurred in the Codex Exoniensis; and that it might also be a Saxon proper name; that ' thun ' might be for ' thegn or then,' *a thane*; that the first word might be ' thissig,' an old form of ' this,' analogous to ' ænig,' *one*; and that it might perhaps be read thus: ' thissig bealtun[4] setta,' *set up this funeral monument.* This latter suggestion, however, (although a very ingenious one) would destroy the alliteration of the verse, and does not occupy all the traces on the stone.

(25) In Scott's ' Border Exploits ' we find a plate of a gravestone with the following inscription—' HEIR LYES ANE WORTHIE PERSON CALIT WILLIAM ARMSTRONG OF SARK WHO DIED THE 10 DAY OF JUNE 1658 ÆTATIS SUÆ 56.'

(26) Bosworth, in his Anglo Saxon Dictionary, on the word ' ge ' says—'In verbs it seems sometimes to be a mere augment . . . it often changes the signification from literal to figurative; as . . . biddan *to bid, require*; gebiddan *to pray.*'

'syn,' and signifies *sins*. 'Sawhula' is the plural formation of the word 'sawl,' also written 'sawol' and 'sawul,' the letter 'h' being also introduced according to a very common Anglo-Saxon usage.[1]

The inscription seems to consist of a few couplets of the alliterative versification of Anglo-Saxon poetry. Hence it becomes very important, and takes us far in advance of many of the preconceived opinions respecting our Anglo-Saxon forefathers.(27)

It may be read in four couplets,[2] thus—

1. + Thissig beacn
   Thun setton
2.   Hwætred Wæthgar Alwfwolthu
   Aft Alcfrithu
3.   Ean Kyniing
   Eac Oswiuing
4. + Gebid heo sinna
   Sawhula.

In the first couplet we have the compound letters TH as the alliterating letters : in the second couplet the letters A : in the third the letters E : and in the

(27) Olaus Wormius, in the appendix to his Treatise de Literatura Runica, has given a particular account of the Gothic poetry, commonly called Runic. He informs us that there were no fewer than 136 different kinds of measure or verse used in the *Vyses*. He says that the Runic harmony did not depend either upon rhyme, or upon metrical feet, or quantity of syllables, but chiefly upon the number of syllables, and *the disposition of the letters*. In each distich, or couple of lines, it was requisite that three words should begin with the same letter : two of the corresponding words being placed in the first line of the distich, and the third in the second line, frequent inversions and transpositions being permitted in this poetry. The curious in this subject may consult likewise Dr. Hickes's Thesaurus Linguarum Septentrionalium ; particularly the 23rd chapter of his Grammatica Anglo-Saxonica et Mœso-Gothica. It appears that the Anglo-Saxons admired, and, in some measure, followed the northern *Scaldi or Runæ* in forming the structure of their verse by a period-

fourth the letters S. It is remarkable that these couplets rhyme with each other, and thus establish a probability (or perhaps something more) that both alliteration and rhyme have been made use of by the Anglo-Saxons from a very early period. Although we cannot actually produce any Anglo-Saxon poem in rhyme of that era, yet the Anglo-Saxon poets Aldhelm, A.D. 709—Boniface, A.D. 754—the Venerable Bede, A.D. 735 —Alcuin, and others—have left behind them Latin Poems in rhyme, which pre-supposes that this species of versification was anterior to, and commonly known in their time.

A very interesting question arises, whether this Bewcastle specimen of Anglo-Saxon poetry is not the oldest on record, being nearly 1200 years old. My own impression is that no earlier example has been discovered. This circumstance considerably enhances the value and importance of this ancient cross. The only specimen of Anglo-Saxon poetry which can be supposed to compete with this is a fragment of a song

ical repetition of similar letters, or by alliteration, *and disregarded a fixed and determinate number* of syllables. Rask, in his Anglo-Saxon Grammar, page 108, gives more specific rules for alliteration. Mr. Rask says—' The Saxon alliteration is thus constructed : in two adjacent and connected lines of verse there must be three words which begin with one and the same letter, so that the third or last alliterative word stands the first word in the second line, and the first two words are both introduced in the first line. The initial letters in these three words are called alliterative. The alliterative letter in the second line is called *the chief letter*, and the other two are called *assistant letters* . . . . If the chief letter be a vowel, the assistants must be vowels, but they need not be the same. *In short verses only one assistant letter is occasionally found.* In Anglo-Saxon poetry the words followed each other in continued succession, as in prose, and were not written in lines and verses as in our modern poetry. The division into verses was made by the regular succession of the alliterating letters.

which was written by Cædmon, a monk who accustomed himself late in life to write religious poetry ;
and who died A.D. 680. His song was inserted by
King Alfred in his Translation of Bede's Ecclesiastical
History. In this brief fragment two of the couplets
appear as rhyming with each other. This inscription
also appears to upset some of the statements and
theories of our best Anglo-Saxon grammarians with
respect to what are called Dano-Saxon idioms and
dialects, [20] throwing all their conjectures as to peculiarities introduced by the Danes topsy-turvy, and
proving these supposed peculiarities to have belonged
from the first to the Anglo-Saxon language.

No doubt much ignorance prevails generally regarding the habits of our Anglo-Saxon ancestors, for
both public and private documents are only few and
scanty which give us any insight into the general
polity and social history of these our forefathers ; and
yet there are certain salient points in them which
may be interesting to a majority of readers. In this
memoir I shall, therefore, endeavour to give a brief
philological examination of the words, as well as a
biographical sketch (so far as history supplies us
with the necessary data) of the persons whose names
occur on this monument ; from which the reader will
be able to draw his own inferences as to the state
and grade of morals and civilization twelve hundred
years ago, when the institutions of the Britons were
probably in a progress of perishing through their
own corruption, and received fresh life and vigour re-
infused into them through the sanctity of the more
lofty morality of the Christian dispensation.

Oswy.

I shall commence my biographical sketch with Oswy,
(as being the head of the family) whom I find de-

scribed in the ' Britannia Sancta' as a religious prince
who omitted no opportunity of exhorting his friends
to embrace the true way of salvation, and inducing
them to submit to the sweet yoke of the faith and
law of Christ. I find the name occurring as 'Oswiu,'
which is simply an abbreviation[1] of the Latin termination 'Oswius.' I also find the word written 'Osuiu,'
and Nennius calls him 'Osguid.' The termination
'ing' after a proper name, according to Anglo-Saxon
usage, denoted 'the son of such a person'; hence
the word 'Oswiuing' means 'the son of Oswy.'

By the Anglo-Saxon Kingdom of Northhumbria we
generally understand all the counties in England north
of the river Humber, and the southern counties of
Scotland nearly as far as Edinburgh. In the year 633,
or, according to some historians, 644, after the death
of King Edwin, it was divided into two parts, namely,
the Kingdom of Deira under Osric, which comprehended (nearly) the counties of York, Durham, Lan-
cashire, Westmorland, and Cumberland ; and the Kingdom of Bernicia under Eanfrid, which contained the
county of Northumberland and the southern counties
of Scotland. Higden (Lib. 1, De Regnis Regnorum-
que Limitibus) says that the Tyne divided the Kingdoms of Deira and Bernicia.(28)

These two kings, Osric and Eanfrid, being soon
afterwards slain by Cadwalla, King of the Britons,

(28) The following extract is from Sir F. Palgrave's interesting
little book, History of the Anglo-Saxons :—' The British kingdoms
of Defyr and Bryneich—Latinised into Deira and Bernicia'—extending from the Humber to the Firth of Forth, were divided from
each other by a forest, occupying a tract between the Tyne and
the Tees ; and which, unreclaimed by man, was abandoned to wild
deer. Properly speaking, this border land does not seem to have
originally belonged to either kingdom ; but, in subsequent times, the
boundary between Deira and Bernicia was usually fixed at the Tyne.'

the Kingdom of Northhumbria came to Oswald, who is said to have held it nine years. In the year 642, Oswy, son of Ethelfrid, succeeded to the Kingdom of Northhumbria, on the death of Oswald, who was slain by Penda, King of the Mercians. Oswy reigned 28 years, and Henry of Huntingdon (Lib. 2.) tells us that he subdued a great part of the nations of the Picts and Scots, and made them tributary. He also enjoyed the title of Bretwalda, which gave him an authority over all the other Anglo-Saxon kings.

Oswy, during the early part of his reign, had a partner in the royal dignity called Oswin, of the race of King Edwin, a man of wonderful piety and devotion, who governed the province of the Deiri seven years in very great prosperity, and was himself beloved by all men. But Oswy could not live at peace with him. Oswin, perceiving that he could not maintain a war against one who had more auxiliaries than himself, took refuge in the house of Earl Hunwald, in Yorkshire, where he was betrayed by him, and slain in a cruel and detestable manner by the orders of Oswy, in the year 650. After the death of Oswin the kingdom of Deira probably devolved upon Alcfrid, the son of Oswy ; his father retaining the northern portion of the kingdom of Northhumbria. Notwithstanding this outrage, Oswy appears to have been a man zealous in the maintenance of the Christian faith, for when [21] Prince Peada, son of Penda, King of Mercia, came to Oswy in the year 653 requesting to have his daughter Elfleda given to him in marriage, he could not obtain Oswy's sanction unless he would first embrace the faith of Christ, and be baptized, with the nation which he governed.

Oswy continued firm to the religious professions of his youth, probably influenced by the persuasions of his Queen Eanfleda, the daughter of Eadwin, King of Deira, who had been driven from her native Northumbria in her infancy, and, after an education among her maternal relatives in Kent, returned into Northumbria as the wife of Oswy, inheriting (it is said) all the religious constancy of her mother and her grandmother.(29)

Alfrid or Alcfrid.

The peculiar way in which the word ' Alcfrithu ' is spelt may seem somewhat objectionable,[1] but we ought to bear in mind that orthography has been very capricious, and at all periods has assumed the features of a constant tendency to change. In fact, it would now be quite impossible to settle the orthography which was prevalent at any given former period, or to reduce the various modes of spelling names, which we find in ancient charters and other documents, to any consistent form. The Latin termination of proper names in ' thus ' (and its abbreviation ' thu ') instead of ' dus,' appears to have been quite common. As a proof of the numerous and irregular modes of spelling names among the Anglo-Saxons we may adduce the following instances. We find Ethelbirthum, Egelbrictum, and Egelbrightum (the h before the t) for Ethelbert : Oidilvaldo for Ethelwald : Edbrithum, Egbrithro, Egbirtho, Egberthus, Edbriht, Edbrit, and Edbrichtus for Egbert : and many others. In a charter of Coenulf, or Cynulf, King of the Saxons (A.D. 808, Ms. C. C., Cantab., cxi. f., 77) we find the signature ' Alhfrithi.'[2] In the Anglo-Saxon charters we also find the signatures Egfrido, Ecgfrith,

(29) In Gale's Appendix 1 to our old British historian Nennius we read that Osguid (Oswy) had two wives—the one called Nemmedt the daughter of Roith the son of Rum, and the other called Eanfled. His first wife Nemmedt was also called Ricmmelth[3] in Nennius.

Egfrid, Ecgfrithi, Ecgfridus, Ecgferth, for Egfrid, the brother of the Alcfrid whose name is recorded on this monument; and we also find the signatures Wilfridus, Wilfrith, Wilfrid, Wilfrithus, for Wilfrid, a bishop, and friend of Alcfrid. Numerous other instances might be easily adduced.

Cases, however, do sometimes occur where the variation of a single letter in the mode of spelling what is apparently the same name makes a very wide and important difference. We may take the word 'Alfrid,' as an example. Oswy had two sons, each of them a king, but at different periods, who in our English translations of Venerable Bede's Ecclesiastical History are generally called 'Alfrid.' On referring, however, to Stephenson's[1] Latin edition of Bede,[2] we find a small but an essential distinction. The name of the first 'Alfrid,' who is the person to whom this pillar was erected, is in that edition written thus, 'Alchfrido.' (Bk. 3, ch. 14.) And a note upon this place says :—'*Ealhfrith, Saxon version. This individual has frequently been confounded with Aldfrid, a natural son of Oswy, who succeeded his father in* 685. *Upon this subject a note in Lappenberg, Gesch. v., England* 1, 180, *may be consulted with advantage.*(30) Bede in other passages calls the first Alcfrid, and the second

(30) Bede, in his Life of St. Cuthbert, ch. 24, states that Aldfrid was the illegitimate brother of Egfrid ; and that he subjected himself to voluntary exile in Ireland, during which he devoted himself to the study of the scriptures. It appears (from the Britannia Sancta) to have been customary for many of the English to leave their native country and retire into Ireland, either for the sake of improving themselves in divine learning, or to embrace there a more holy and continent life; the Irish most willingly receiving them, and furnishing them with their daily sustenance, and supplying them with books, and teaching them gratis. In the library of the Dean and Chapter of Durham is preserved an ancient Ritual which is said to have belonged to Aldfrid.[3] Asser, in his Annals (anno 705), describes him

Aldfrid. In the Ang. Sax. Chron. the latter is styled
'Aldfrith,' and 'Ealdferth.' This Aldfrid succeeded
his brother Egfrid in the kingdom of Northhumbria
in the year 685, and died in 705. In Stephenson's
edition of Bede we find the words Alchfrido, [22] Alch-
fridi, and Alchfrid, for the first king ; and Aldfridi,
Aldfrido, Aldfrid, and Alfrid, for the second king.
In the Life of Wilfrid by Eddie, who flourished about
50 years after the erection of the monument, we find
the name of the first Alfrid mentioned eight times,
and it is remarkable that it is spelt in six different
ways, none of them agreeing with the orthography
of Bede ; thus, Aluchfrido, Ealfridus, Alucfridus, Al-
fridus, Ahlfridus, Alhfridum. In the same work we
also find the second Alfrid mentioned, and spelt
thus—Alfridum, Alfredo, Aldfridum (with a note Ald-
frithum).

We may now pass on to a biographical sketch of
the Alfrid, or Alcfrid, for whom this cross was erected.[1]
History gives us very little intimation of the various
rulers who within their petty territories assumed the
names of kings, and exercised the regal power ; and
just about as little of the extent and the nature of
the authority and powers often claimed and exercised
by the sons and brothers of the ruling sovereigns.
Perhaps in the early periods of Anglo-Saxon history
the very name of king 'Kyniing,' may have been

as a monk when he died. He is also mentioned in Fordun, bk. 3,
ch. 43. Alcwin, who, according to Gale, flourished about the year
780, calls him 'Altfrido '—(*De Pontificibus,* line 843)—and says
that he was devoted to sacred studies from his early youth. In
another passage (line 1080) he calls him 'Aldfridum.' According
to Camden he was buried at Driffield, in Yorkshire. In the Saxon
version of Bede he is called ' Ealdfrith.' This Aldfrid is also
mentioned in the Chronicle of Holyrood, as succeeding to the kingdom A. D. 685, and dying A. D. 705.

assumed by the sons of sovereigns whether they exercised the sovereign rights or not. The word 'kyning' or 'cyniing' was derived from 'kyn' or 'cyn,' which signified 'a nation or people,' and sometimes 'the head of the nation or people'; the termination 'ing' at the end of proper nouns denoted 'the son of such a person,' and hence the word 'Kyniing' would mean simply 'the son of the head of the nation.' It is somewhat strange that scarcely any charters belonging to the kingdom of Northhumbria have survived to the present day, and hence from such documents we can form no idea whatever of the style adopted by the kings of that country. It is very probable, however, that they carefully maintained the distinction between Deira and Bernicia, which has been overlooked by many historians of Anglo-Saxon England. Hence in the case of Alcfrid we have every reason to suppose that he was really and virtually king over Deira, and exercised all the rights and jurisdictions, and had all the appanages of an independent sovereign.

According to the Ecclesiastical History of the Venerable Bede, from whom, of course, I derive the chief part of this biography, Alfrid was one of the sons of Oswy, and, according to Eddie, reigned along with his father.(31)

Of the early life of Alfrid little is recorded, except that 'he was instructed in Christianity by Wilfrid, a most learned man, who had first gone to Rome to learn the ecclesia[s]tical doctrine.' Eddie informs us that he entreated Wilfrid to reside with him, and

(31) He could not be the son of Eanfleda, for we find him mentioned in the year 642,[1] nine years before the marriage of Oswy and Eanfleda, and yet he appears to have been warmly attached to his mother-in-law, and influenced by her Christian principles.

preach the Word of God to him and his people, and that Wilfrid complied with his affectionate request, and that they became attached to each other, even as the souls of David and Jonathan. Hence Alcfrid became attached to the customs of Rome, and thought that Wilfrid's doctrine ought to be preferred before all the traditions of the Scottish or native priests. Alcfrid probably became King of Deira about the year 650,[1] when his father Oswy slew Oswin, who was at that time king of that province. Of such a fact, however, we have no record, nor is there any record of the time and place of his death. So far as can be ascertained he disappears from history about the year 665,[2] *i. e.,* nearly 1,200 years from this time. In the year 642 we find Alcfrid in rebellion[3] against his father. Oswy, having succeeded to the kingdom of Northhumbria, was (as Bede informs us, Lib. 3, ch. 14) harassed by Penda the Pagan King of Mercia, and by the Pagan nation of the Mercians, that had slain his brother, as also by his son Alcfrid, and by Ethelwald, the son of his brother who resigned[4] before him.(32)

Alcfrid appears to have been firmly attached to Wilfrid, an able Englishman of the Roman party, whose attainments had been matured in southern Europe. He gave him a monastery of forty families at a place called Rhypum (Ripon) according to Bede (Lib. 3, ch. 25) ; which place he had not long before

(32) Geoffrey of Monmouth (book 2, ch. 11) calls this Alfrid the brother of Oswy. As Geoffrey, however, did not write before the twelfth century (a few hundred years after Bede and the events narrated) we may presume that the statement of Bede is the more correct. From the narrative of Geoffrey we learn that this insurrection was commenced in consequence of Oswy making large presents of gold and silver to Cadwalla, who was at that time possessed of the government of all Britain, and because Oswy had made peace with, and submission to him.

given to those that followed the [23] system of the Scots for a monastery ; but forasmuch as they afterwards, being left to their choice, prepared to quit the place rather than alter their religious opinions, he gave the place to Wilfrid.(33) From Bede's History of the Abbots of Weremouth we learn that Alchfrid was desirous to make a pilgrimage to the shrines of the Apostles at Rome, and had engaged Biscop to accompany him on his journey, who had just returned from that place ; but the King (Oswy) prevented his son's journey. At the request of Alcfrid, Agilbert (bishop of the West Saxons, who was on a visit to Oswy and Alcfrid in the province of the Northhumbrians) made Wilfrid a priest in his monastery at Dorchester, near Oxford. So says Bede, but Eddie[1] informs us that he ordained him priest at Ripon according to the King's command. Among the Bernicians was the episcopal seat of Hagustaldum, or

(33) In reference to this monastery we find the following statement in Bede's Life of St. Cuthbert (sect. 12)—' And when some years after it pleased King Alcfrid, for the redemption of his soul, to give to the Abbot Eata a certain dominion in his kingdom called ' In Hrypum,' there to construct a monastery, the same Abbot taking some of the brethren along with him, amongst whom Cudberct was one, he founded the required monastery, and in it he instituted the same monastic discipline which he had previously established at Melrose.' Bede, in his history of the Abbots of Weremouth also says—' Alchfrid gave Rippon to Eata, Abbot of Melross, to build a monastery there ; he afterwards gave this monastery to Wilfrid, and Eata with his monks returned to Mailros.' These statements are partly confirmed by Eddie in his Life of Wilfrid, who says—(ch. 8,) that ' Alcfrid's love for Wilfrid increased from day to day, and that he gave him the land of ten tributary families at Eastanford, and a short time afterwards the monastery In HRypis, with the land of 30 families, for the safety of his soul, and appointed him Abbot, and that all the people (noble and ignoble) looked upon him as a prophet of God.'

Hexham, which was bestowed by King Alcfrid[1] upon
St. Cuthbert, which Malmesbury (somewhat mistaken
in the scale of miles) placed but 50 miles from Yorke,
and commendeth for 'beauty of structure before any
building on this side the Alps.' In this church sat
nine bishops, among whom the learned John of
Beverley was advanced to that dignity by King Alcfrid,[2] and then swayed the pastoral staff, till he was
translated to Yorke. About the year 652 (according
to some authorities 644) we find Alcfrid and Oswy
jointly presiding over a religious controversy[3] respecting the observance of Easter.(34)

(34) Bede, in his account of this controversy, is considered by
some to have been a zealous adversary of the Scottish and ancient
British observance of Easter, and to have shewn at all points a leaning
towards the church of Rome. Oswy, who had been instructed and
baptized by the Scots or native priests, and was very perfectly skilled
in their language, thought nothing better than what they taught,
and kept the Easter festival according to the primitive British
customs. His wife Eanfleda, however, who had been brought up
in the Court of Kent, which had been converted to Christianity by
missionaries from Rome, would not abandon the Kentish usages for
those of Northhumbria, being in this probably supported by Alcfrid
and his partizans. Hence Easter was celebrated at the Court of
Oswy on different days; one party enjoying its festivities, while the
other placed in strong contrast with them the austerities of Lent.
At length Oswy consented to purchase domestic peace by hearing
a solemn argument in the monastery which he had recently founded
at Whitby. The cause was conducted on the part of the British by
Colman, then bishop of Northhumbria or Lindisfarne, assisted by
Chad, bishop of Essex. On the part of Rome, or the Kentish usages,
Agilbert was the principal, but he devolved the advocacy of his
cause upon Wilfrid, on account of his own imperfect acquaintance
with the Anglo-Saxon language. The British, or national divines,
insisted chiefly upon a tradition, originating, as alleged, in St. John,
our Lord's beloved disciple. The foreign party traced the Roman
tradition to St. Peter, who was, as they said, intrusted by Christ
with the keys of Heaven. 'Were they really intrusted to him?'
asked Oswy. 'Undoubtedly so,' he was answered. 'And can

Bede informs us that the Middle Angles were converted to Christianity through the instrumentality of
Alcfrid. Peada, their king, came to Oswy, requesting
his daughter for a wife. Oswy refused to comply
unless he [24] would embrace the faith of Christ.
When he heard the preaching of truth, the promise
of the heavenly kingdom, and the hope of resurrec-

you allege the grant of any such privilege to an authority of yours ? '
Oswy then demanded. ' We cannot,' Colman replied. ' I must
leave your party then,' said Oswy, ' for I should not choose to
disoblige him who keeps the keys of Heaven. It might be found
impossible to get the door open when I seek admittance.' Thus
Oswy decided in favour of the Roman party in a way which reminds
us of the language of one of Cooper's braves of the wigwam, and his
decision was generally applauded. The result of this controversy
was that the ancient usages of Britain were formally renounced as
to the time of observing Easter. Colman and many of his adherents
were disgusted, and retired to their brethren in Scotland.[1] Eddie
gives a brief account of this Paschal controversy in the 10th chapter.
It may be observed, however, that this triumph of the Roman party
involved little or no change in articles of belief. We have no evidence that any papal peculiarities of doctrine were then established.
Mosheim (century 7, ch. 3) says:—' In Britain warm controversies
concerning baptism, the tonsure, and particularly the famous dispute
concerning the time of celebrating the Easter festival, were carried
on between the ancient Britons and the new converts to Christianity which Augustine had made among the Anglo-Saxons. The
fundamental doctrines of Christianity were not at all affected by
these controversies, which, on that account, were more innocent and
less important than they otherwise would have been. Besides, they
were entirely terminated in the 8th century, in favour of the Anglo-
Saxons, by the Benedictine Monks. It should also be noted that
although Wilfrid appealed to the authority of the Roman See, as
deserving respectful attention, yet he did not claim for it any right
of deciding the controversy. In the opin[i]on of some the Roman
party might have prevailed before had it not been for the uncommon
merits of Aidan and Finian, and that its prevalence on this occasion
arose from Colman being not equal to his predecessors. A principal
reason, however, may have been the influence which Eanfleda
exercised over the compliant mind of her husband Oswy.'

tion and future immortality, he declared that he would willingly become a Christian, even though he should be refused the virgin ; being chiefly prevailed on to receive the faith by King Oswy's son Alcfrid, who was his relation and friend, and had married his sister Cyneburga, the daughter of King Penda. Accordingly he was baptized with all his earls and soldiers.

In the year 665 Alcfrid sent Wilfrid with a great multitude of men and much money to the King of France, to be consecrated bishop over him (Alcfrid) and his people. In Wilfrid, however, real excellencies appear to have been alloyed by levity and ostentation. He did not hasten to return after his consecration, but thoughtlessly displayed his new dignity amidst the tempting hospitalities of Gaul. Alcfrid,[1] his royal patron, became disgusted by this delay, and conferred the Northhumbrian bishopric upon another.[2](35)

From Bede, and others of our old British Chroniclers, we find Alcfrid, in the year 655, fighting on the side of his father Oswy against his father-in-law Penda, the King of Mercia.

Although the Pagans had three times the number of men, yet King Oswy, and his son Alcfrid, met them with a very small army, confiding, it is said, in the conduct of Christ, Oswy having previously vowed that, if he should come off victorious, he would dedicate his daughter to our Lord in holy virginity, and give twelve farms to build monasteries. The engagement beginning, the Pagans were defeated, the thirty commanders, and those who had come to the assistance of Penda, were put to flight, and almost all of them slain. The battle was fought near the river Vinwed (Winwidfield), near Leeds, which then, with

(35) Bede, Lib. 3, ch. 28.— Soames, p. 66.— William of Malmesbury, Lib. 3.— Henry of Huntingdon, Lib. 3.

the great rains, had not only filled its channel, but overflowed its banks, so that many more were drowned in flight than destroyed by the sword.(36)

Such is the history of Alcfrid as it has been handed down to us by our British historians. We may now take a passing glance at his supposed death. Bede (Lib. 3, ch. 27,) tells us that in the year 644[1] a sudden pestilence (called by some the yellow plague) depopulated the southern coasts of Britain, and, extending into the province of the Northhumbrians, ravaged the country far and near, and destroyed a great multitude of men. The pestilence did no less harm in Ireland. This plague is also mentioned in the Anglo-Saxon Chronicle *under the same date ;* in one of the manuscripts of Nennius ; and in Henry of Huntingdon (Lib. 3). It has been presumed that Alcfrid fell a victim to this plague. If so, it is not unreasonable to suppose that he breathed his last in his Saxon city of Bewcastle, and that he was buried here. Against this supposed cause of his death, however, we must bear in mind that, in the year 665,[2] *i. e.*, the year after the plague, Bede informs us that Alcfrid sent Wilfrid to France for consecration, and a similar statement had been previously made by Eddie.(37)

(36) Henry of Huntingdon (Lib. 3), speaking of this battle, says that ' the Almighty God was present with His people, and dissolved the fortitude of King Penda, and took away from his arms the usual strength of his nerves, and ordered his brave heart to pine with grief, so that he neither recognized himself in his blows, nor was he impenetrable to the arms of his enemies : and he was amazed that his enemies were such as he used to be to his enemies, while on the other hand he was such as they used to be. He, who therefore had always shed the blood of others, now experienced what he himself had done, while he tinged the earth with his own blood, and covered it with his brains.'

(37) Henry of Huntingdon (Lib. 3), and Bede, both relate that Tuda, *the Bishop of* Northumbria, fell a victim to its ravages, but

[25] *Hwætred.*

The preceding sketch embraces every thing which I can find recorded in history respecting Alcfrid. Besides the names of Oswy and Alcfrid, the words Hwætred, Wæthgar, and Alwfwolthu seem to require a slight notice, as they resemble Anglo-Saxon names which we find recorded in history.

The word Hwætred is compounded of 'hwæt, wit, with, or wiht'—'quick or sharp;'—and of 'red, rede, rad, or rod,' (differing only in dialect), signifying 'counsel.' Hence Hwætred means 'quick in counsel.' The word 'Hwætred' occurs in the Codex Exoniensis, 477, 5, in a poem called 'The Ruin.' Thorpe translates it as an adjective. Ethmüller,[1] in his Dictionary, gives the word as a proper name. A person named Withred, or Wihtred, is mentioned by Henry of Huntingdon (Lib. 4), and by the Anglo-Saxon Chronicle, as King of Kent in the year 692. Higden mentions him as King in the year 686, and neither of them state that such was the death of *King Alcfrid*; a strong presumption that the king did not perish in this plague. St. Chad is also said to have been taken with the contagion while on a visit to his beloved solitude of Lestingau, which put an end to his mortal life. Bede, in his life of St. Cuthbert, tells us that 'this great pestilence, which made such havoc in Britain and Ireland, visited also the monastery of Mailros, where St. Cuthbert was seized with it. All the brethren passed the night in prayer for him, as looking upon the life of so holy a man most necessary for the edification of their community. In the morning they told him what they had been doing : at which, rising up, he called for his shoes and his staff, saying—' Why do I lie here any longer ; God will certainly hear the prayers of so many holy men.' And so it was ; for he quickly recovered.' It is also said that Boisil had foretold this plague three years before, and that he himself should die of it, which came to pass. (Ibid.) It seems strange, therefore, that so many deaths should be detailed, and yet that there should be no record of the death of King Alcfrid, *if he perished in this plague.*

calls him 'Whitred,' the legitimate son of Egbert. This person may possibly be the party whose name is here recorded. At all events he appears to have entertained religious views and aspirations similar to those of Alcfrid. Queen Eanfleda had been brought up at the Court of Kent, and was sent for by Oswy in the year 651,[1] and became his wife. This Witred, who might at that time be one of the young princes[2] at that Court, may have attended her on her marriage journey to Northhumbria, or may have visited the Northumbrian Court at some subsequent period, and thus have formed an attachment to Alcfrid, and afterwards erected this Cross to his memory.

Wæthgar.

This word is derived from 'with,'—'quick or sharp' —and 'gar or gær'—'a spear': hence it signifies 'quick or expert in the use of the spear.' It may be also a proper name. A person named 'Wihtgar' (the h before the t) is mentioned in the Anglo-Saxon Chronicle, anno 514, as Lord of the Isle of Wight. He was the first to establish an Anglo-Saxon colony there. He also was the founder of Carisbrooke Castle. Camden (p. 130,) says that it was called 'Whitgara-burgh,' from him, and now by contraction 'Cares-brook.' Of course he cannot be the person whose name is recorded on this monument, but we may draw an inference that such a name was in use among the Anglo-Saxons.

Alfwold.

'Aelf,' which, according to various dialects, as Camden says, is pronounced 'ulf, wolph, hulph, hilp, helfe, or helpe,' implies 'assistance.' 'Wold or wald' means 'a ruler or governor.' Hence the word

Alfwold means 'an auxiliary governor.' But it may also be a proper noun, occurring under a variety of modes of spelling.(38) William of Malmesbury mentions a King of the East Angles named 'Elwold' soon after the time of Alcfrid, who might possibly be the person mentioned here.[1] Bede says that Sigebert, the King of the East Angles, often visited the Court of Northhumbria, and was converted to the Christian faith in A.D. 653, through the persuasion of Oswy. This Elwold may have attended Sigebert on some of these occasions, and thus have become acquainted with, and attached to Alcfrid, and hence from motives of friendship and regard he may have aided in erecting this pillar to his memory.

We may now return to a further examination of the Cross. Below the chief inscription is a figure, which, as Bishop Nicholson says, 'represents the portraiture of a layman with a hawk or eagle perched

(38) In Ingram's Anglo-Saxon Chronicle, A. D. 778, we find 'Alfwold' mentioned as a King of Northhumbria, and a note upon this passage says '*Alfold. Cot.*' Again in A. D. 780, we find him called 'Alwold,' and a note says, '*Aelfwold Lands.*' In 789 he died and was buried at Hexham. Higden says that he was slain by his own people. The Anglo-Saxon Chronicle also mentions a person of the name of 'Alfwold' as bishop of Dorset, who died in A. D. 978. Henry of Huntingdon mentions one 'Owlfhold' about A. D. 910. A King of the East Angles is mentioned by Roger de Hoveden as dying A. D. 749, whom he calls 'Elfwald.' He also uses the word 'Elwald,' 'Alfwald,' and 'Elfwold.' In the Anglo-Saxon Charters we find this name with the Latin terminations 'dus' and 'thus,' and their several inflections. Hence we have Alwfwolthu as an Anglo-Saxon corruption of Alwfwolthus or Alwfwolthum. We often find the Latin termination dropped entirely, and the word ending in 'wald or wold.' The first syllable occurs in the Anglo-Saxon Charters under various modes of spelling. We find 'Alf, Elf, Olf, Ælf;' and in a charter[2] of Eadwig (A. D. 956, Ms. Lands. 417, fol. 11, b.) we have the name 'Alwlf,' which has a great resemblance to the orthography of the Bewcastle Cross.

on his arm.' [26] Hutchinson describes it as 'the effigies of a person of some dignity, in a long robe to the feet, but without any dress or ornament on the head : on a pedestal against which this figure leans is a bird, which, we conceive, is a raffen, or raven, the insignia of the Danish standard. This figure seems designed to represent the personage for whom the monument was erected, and though accompanied with the raven, bears no other marks of royal dignity.' In Lysons it is thus spoken of : 'At the bottom on the west side is sculptured, in bas-relief, the figure of a man bareheaded, habited in a gown which reaches to the middle of his legs, holding a bird (most probably a hawk) on his hand, just above its perch.' To these nearly correct observations of the Lysons I would only add that the figure is not bare headed, but appears to be covered with something resembling a close hood.

South Side.

The sculpture on the south side is divided into five compartments. In the bottom, central, and top divisions are magical knots. In the second are two vines intersecting each other, and in the fourth is another vine, in one of the curves of which a vertical sundial has been placed, somewhat resembling the dial placed over the Saxon porch on the south side of Bishopstone Church, in Sussex, and also resembling the Saxon dial placed over the south porch of Kirkdale Church, in the North Riding of Yorkshire : a short description of each of which may be found at page 60 of the eleventh volume of the Archæological Journal. In the Bewcastle Dial the principal divisions are marked by crosses, as on the fore-mentioned dials, which are considered examples of a very early date,

the Kirkdale Dials having been made, as it is supposed, between the years 1056 and 1065.

On the plain surface near the top of the Cross we
have the following characters :—

L I C E

The word 'lic' or 'lice' is very distinct, but of
the remaining letters we have only the lower part.
On the east side of the Cross, where the sentence
has probably been continued and completed, this plain
surface is totally gone so as to leave no traces whatever, so that this part of the inscription may be considered as irreparably lost. The word 'lic,' or 'lice,'
may perhaps be intended to express something respecting 'a dead body.' In the Dream of the Holy
Rood (Archæologia, vol. 30, p. 31,) the word 'lices'
occurs, and signifies the corpse of our Saviour. The
word 'lice' may also be part of the word 'liceman'[1]
—a body.

Between the highest and the next compartment are
traces of letters which I read thus :—

E C G F R I [THU]

i. e.,' of Ecgfrid.' Ecgfrid was the son of Oswy, and
brother of Alchfrid, and succeeded his father in the
kingdom of Northhumbria in the year 670, according
to the Ang. Sax. Chronicle. Eddie (ch. 20) speaks
of him as king of both Deira and Bernicia. In the
year 660 he married Etheldrida, the daughter of Anna,

king of the East Angles, who lived with him 12 years, and at last retired as a nun into the monastery of the Abbess Edda (the aunt of Ecgfrid) at Coludi (Coldingham), Berwickshire. Egfrid afterwards married Ermenburga. Eddie says that while Etheldrida lived with him he was triumphant everywhere, but after the separation he ceased to be victorious.

Egfrid appears to have been instrumental in founding the monasteries at Wearmouth and Jarrow. (39)

In 685 Egfrid rashly led his army to ravage the province of the Picts, much [27] against the advice of his friends, and particularly of Cuthbert, who had lately been appointed Bishop of Hexham by him. The enemy made show as if they fled, and the king was drawn into the straits of inaccessible mountains and slain, with the greatest part of his forces. Egfrid is said to have carried his conquests to the western ocean, and held Cumberland as a tributary province of his kingdom.

Between the second and third divisions (from the top) of the decorated parts of the Cross we find traces of Runes, which I venture to read thus :—

R I C E S [TH] Æ S :

(39) Bede, in his history of the Abbots of Weremouth, says that he bestowed on Biscop, of his own possessions, as much land as might maintain 70 families, ordering him to build thereon a monastery, which was accordingly performed. This monastery was built at the mouth of the river Were (thence called Weremouth) in the year 674. The king was so well pleased with the zeal and industry of Biscop, and with the fruits which began plentifully to spring from this pious foundation, that he afterwards added to his former donation a second gift of lands, on which Biscop built another monastery on the opposite side of the same river. This was the monastery of Jarrow. These monasteries were destroyed by the Danes, but a small priory was afterwards established at Jarrow.

i. e., ' of this kingdom,'—the kingdom of Northhumbria.

Between the third and fourth divisions we also find traces of characters :

thus—KYNINGES,[1] *i. e.,* 'King.'

Between the lowest and second compartment is another line of Runes which has been noticed by Spelman and others as previously described. I would suggest that the line may be read thus :—

+ F R U [MA]N GEAR,[2]

i. e., 'in the first year.' The four lines on this side of the Cross are evidently connected with each other, and are to be read thus :—'fruman gear Ecgfrithu kyninges rices thæs,'—*in the first year (of the reign) of Egfrid, king of this kingdom of Northhumbria,*[3] *i. e.,* A.D. 670, in which year we may conclude that this monument was erected.

The form of date used on this monument may be considered rather peculiar. Some are of opinion (perhaps without sound grounds) that the era of the Incarnation was not introduced into England till the time of Bede, *i. e.,* about a century after the erection of this pillar. It is a remarkable fact that we have only two original charters of the seventh century, and that the date of the Incarnation does not appear in either of these documents. We cannot infer, however, from this fact that such a mode of dating was then unknown. This would be pushing an argument to an unjust conclusion. Such an inference would be an abuse of the rules of logic. It may be re-marked, however, that the mode of dating by the regnal years of the kings was frequently adopted, as must be well known to every one conversant in Anglo-Saxon diplomacy ; and I think there can be little question but such a mode has been adopted on this monument.

North Side.

On the north side are also five compartments oc-cupied by sculpture. In the highest and lowest divis-ions we find vines with foliage and fruit. Mr. Smith considers them 'as probably the Danish symbols of fertility, as Amalthea's horn was among the Greeks.' In the second and fourth divisions are two curiously devised, and intricately twisted knots, often called 'magical knots,' and by some considered the 'knot-work of Scottish and Irish sculptors.' The third di-vision is filled with a quantity of chequerwork.(40)

(40) This chequerwork is pronounced by Mr. Smith to be 'a Scythian method of embellishing funeral ornaments'; and is regarded by Bishop Nicholson 'as a notable emblem of the tumuli or burying places of the Ancients.' Camden says—'Seeing the cross is chequered like the arms of Vaux, we may suppose that it has been erected by some of them.' Hutchinson[1] thinks that 'the cross must of necessity be allowed to bear a more ancient date than any of the remains of that name; which cannot be run up higher than the Conquest.' He also thinks that 'armorial bearings were not in use at the same time as the Runic characters.' It is probable, however, that this chequerwork had no reference to the family of Vaux or De Vallibus, as they were not really and legally possessed of the Lordship of Bewcastle until the reign of Henry the Second, or about the middle of the 12th century, which is too late a period for the decoration of this monument. The late ingenious Mr. Howard suggested that 'very possibly the family of De Vallibus took their arms from this column, being one of the most remarkable things in the barony.' The cheque appears to have been a device used by the Gauls and Britons long before the erection of this cross. The Gaulic manufactory of woollen cloth spoken of by Diodorus (Lib. 5),

[28] Immediately above the lowest compartment is one line of Runic characters of which Bishop Nicholson in his letter to Mr. Walker says, 'Upon first sight of these letters I greedily ventured to read them 'Rynburn'[1]; and I was wonderfully pleased to fancy that this word thus singly written must necessarily betoken the final extirpation, and burial of the magical Runæ, in these parts, reasonably hoped on the conversion of the Danes to the Christian faith.' The learned prelate also conjectured that the word might be 'Ryeeburn,'[1] which he takes in the old Danish language to signify 'a burial place of the dead.' The representation of these Runes given by the Bishop is inaccurate, and he has evidently comprehended in it some of the flutings of the pillar. It is difficult to imagine how the Bishop could fall into such an error, for the letters on this side of the monument are still perfect and legible, having been fortunately preserved

and in Pliny's Natural History (Lib. 8, ch. 48), was woven chequerwise, of which our Scottish plaids are perfect remains. Bishop Anselm's[2] Book concerning 'Virginity,' written about the year 680—the era of the cross nearly—when the art of weaving in this country was probably in a comparatively rude state, contains a distinct indication that chequered robes were then in fashion; and many of the figures in Rosselini's Egyptian work are dressed in chequered cloths. The cheques are still retained in common use to this day among the inhabitants of Wales, the descendants of the ancient Britons: and so great is their veneration for their ancient emblem that whenever a Welchman leaves his native mountains to reside in an English town, he is sure to carry this symbol along with him. Shops with the sign of the chequers were common even among the Romans, as is evident from the views of Pompeii presented by Sir W. Hamilton to the Antiquarian Society. A human figure in a chequered robe is sculptured on the side of an altar which was found in digging a cellar for the Grapes Inn, on the site of the Roman Station at Carlisle, thus establishing the probability that the cheque was used among the Romans in Britain. We read also of nets of chequer-work in the days of King Solomon, 1 Kings, vii., 17.

from the effects of the weather by their proximity to the Church, which has afforded them its friendly shelter ;[1] and in the manuscript journal which the Bishop kept of his visitation in 1703 the Runes are more correctly traced by him.[2]

Mr. Smith dissents from the reading of the Bishop, and rather thinks it to be a sepulchral monument of the Danish kings. He reads it 'Kuniburuk,' which, he says, in the old Danish language, imports 'the burial place of a king.' Mr. Smith, however, agrees with the Bishop that it may also have been designed for a standing monument of conversion to Christianity which might have happened on the loss of their king, and each be mutually celebrated by it. But from the inscription on the west side it does not appear to have been intended for anything more than a memorial cross.

Mr. Kemble, with Mr. Howard's plate as a guide,[3] who traced it thus,

pronounced the word to be 'CYNIBURUG' or 'CYNIBURUK,'[4] the proper name of a lady ; and he attached some value to it as proving the inscription Anglo-Saxon—not Norse.[5]

After repeated and careful examinations the letters appear to me to be—

KYNNBUR(THU)G,

the name of the wife of Alchfrid. Eddie, who wrote about fifty years after the erection of the cross, does not mention the name of Alcfrid's queen; but in Stephenson's edition of Bede[6] (who probably wrote his history about 100 years [1] after the erection of the monument) we read of a lady whom he calls ' Cyneburga,' the daughter of Penda, King of Mercia, and the wife of Alcfrid. This is undoubtedly the same person, the name having somewhat changed in a century. In Ingram's edition of the Anglo-Saxon Chronicle, in the year 656, we read of ' Kyneburg' and 'Kynesuuith,' the daughters of King Penda, and the sisters of Wulfhere who in that year is said to have succeeded his brother Peada in the kingdom of the Mercians. These ladies appear to have counselled their brother Wulfhere to endow and dignify the monastery at Medehamstede,(41) which in the year 963 was named Peterborough, and in that year we read in the above-named chronicle that Elfsy, who was then Abbot, took up the bodies of St. Kyneburh and St. Kyneswith, who lay at Castor, and brought them to Peterborough.(42)

(41) It may appear strange that Wulfhere should have adopted the counsel of his sisters, but it must be borne in mind that the ladies were very important personages in the days of our Anglo-Saxon forefathers. Gurdon, in his Antiquities of Parliament, says—' The ladies of birth and quality sat in council with the Saxon Witas.' The abbess Hilda, says Bede, presided in an ecclesiastical Synod. In Wighfred's great council at Becconceld, A. D. 694, the abbesses sat and deliberated ; and five of them signed decrees of the council.

(42) William of Malmesbury (Lib. 1, ch. 4) tells us that Cyneberg retired to the monastery which her brothers Wulfhere and Ethelred had built, and that she and her sister Kyneswith were superior to others of their sex for the piety and chastity of their lives. Henry of Huntingdon (Lib. 3) calls this lady Chineburgam, and her sister Cinewissem. Ingulph of Croyland calls her Kynenburgam, and says that she and her sister were ' ambas sanctâ continentiâ præcellentes.' Kyneburg appears to have made large presents to the monastery at Medehamstede, for when it was destroyed by the Danes, A. D. 870, Ingulph says that ' the precious gifts ' of the holy virgins Kineburgæ and Kinespitæ were trodden under foot ; and in another passage he calls these gifts ' sacredrelics,' and says that the Abbot took them

[29] In the 'Britannia Sancta' Cyneburg is spoken of as a devout and fervent Christian, whose heart was much more set on the kingdom of heaven than on her earthly diadem : insomuch that she had an impatient desire to quit the world and all its vanities, and to consecrate herself, body and soul, to Jesus Christ. By her means, in a short time, King Alchfrid's Court was converted in a manner into a monastery, or school of regular discipline and Christian perfection. After her release from the matrimonial bond by the death of her husband she returned into her native country of Mercia, and there chose for the place of her retreat a town then called Dormundcaster, afterwards from her Kyneburgcastor—now Castor or Caistor. Here she built, or (as others say) found already built by her brother Wulfhere, a monastery for sacred virgins, over whom she became mother and abbess. To this monastery, as we learn from the author of her life in Capgrave, many virgins of all ranks and degrees resorted, to be instructed by her in rules and exercises of a religious life ; and whilst the daughters of princes reverenced her as a mistress, the poor were admitted to regard her as a companion : and both the one and the other honoured her as a parent. She was, says this author, a mirror of all sanctity. She had a wonderful compassion and charity for the poor, exhorting kings and princes to almsgiving and works of mercy. Henschenius is positive that she died before the year 680, but Higden says that she was appointed over the Monastery of Glovernia in 681.

away with him in his flight. Ranulph Higden (Lib. 5, Anno 681) says that Osric, King of the Mercians, built a monastery de Glovernia,[1] over which he appointed his sister Kineburgam.

Kyneswitha.

Between the second and third compartments (from the bottom) is another very indistinct line of Runes which I venture to read thus—

KYNESWI[TH]A[1]

This was the name of the mother as well as a sister[2] of Cyneburg. Of the mother, nothing of note is recorded. From the two sisters being so frequently mentioned together, and from the similarity of their religious views and feelings, we may presume that they were strongly attached to each other, and that the sister's name is recorded here. William of Malmesbury (Lib. 4) says that she was dedicated to God from her infancy, and that she kept her glorious resolution to her old age. Not content with saving herself alone, she prevailed also with King Offa, to whom she had (against her will) been promised in marriage, to devote himself to a single life. She afterwards retired to the Monastery of Dormundcaster, where she died, 'after having lived a pattern of all virtues for many years.'

Wulfhere.

Between the third and fourth compartments is another line of Runes which, though indistinct, appears to be—

MYRCNA KYNG,[3]

i. e., King of the Mercians.

The above line of Runes appears to be connected with another line between the fourth and fifth divisions, which may be read thus—

WULFHERE,[1]

who was a son of Penda, brother of Cyneburg, and King of the Mercians. He succeeded his brother Peada in the year 657, according to the Anglo-Saxon Chronicle.(43)

[30] Eddie calls him Wlfarius, and says that he frequently invited Wilfrid (while Abbot at Ripon) to go into Mercia, and exercise the office of bishop there, and that he made many grants of lands, for the salvation of his soul, where he presently appointed monasteries. In the year 661 we find him instrumental in converting the people of the Isle of Wight : and in the year 665 he was a means of the reconversion of the East Saxons, who had begun to restore the temples that had been abandoned, and to adore idols,

(43) He is respresented by Malmesbury as a man of great strength of mind and body, and although a zealous Christian yet his reputation was sullied by an act of simony, being the first of the kings of the Angles who sold the bishopric of London. In the year 657 we find him engaged in the foundation and endowment of the monastery of Medehamstede. He is said to have granted large tracts of lands and fens to this monastery. From the Life of his Queen Ermenilda in Capgrave, we learn that he was induced, through her influence, to root out of his dominions, the worship of idols, and all heathenish superstitions ; and to stock his kingdom with priests and churches for the worship of the true and living God. He is also said to have contributed liberally towards the foundation of a monastery for religious virgins at Wenlock in Shropshire. He also by his bounty enabled Bishop Chadd to found a monastery at a place called Barrow, in the province of Lindsey.

as if they might by those means be protected against the mortality, *i. e.,* the yellow plague. According to the Anglo-Saxon Chronicle in the year 675, Wulfhere and Escwin fought at Beadanhead ; and the same year Wulfhere died.

On the plain surface near the top of the Cross are the following characters :

The three Crosses may be emblematical of the crucifixion, the central one appearing rather higher than the others.   The word ' GESSUS ' is very plain, all the letters being quite distinct except the G, and the part where the U and the S approach each other, which appears to have experienced some injury.(44)

The word ' Gessus' is evidently connected with the fragments of the word ' Kristtus ' on the west side ; and has probably formed part of a sentence which has been completed on the two other sides, but of which only a small portion now remains.

Having made this minute and, I fear, tedious attempt to explain the inscriptions on this cross, I may now leave the subject in the hands of those who are more versed in such recondite researches, hoping that if there be another and a better solution of the enigma, it may be found.

(44) The letter S has a little peculiarity in its form, the last stroke being carried up nearly to the same height as the top of the other letters.   The letter S in the word ' Oswiuing ' appears to have the same form ; as also some others on this monument ; and there is one somewhat similar to it on the Ruthwell pillar.   There is also an S of a similar form in the Runic inscription in Carlisle Cathedral.

[31] MR. HAIGH'S VERSION.

It is now my painful duty to make a few observations on a different version of these inscriptions, which
has been offered by the Rev. D. H. Haigh, of Erdington, near Birmingham, read before the Society of
Antiquarians of Newcastle-upon-Tyne, and since published in their transactions. I feel extreme reluctance
in entering upon this course, but I also feel that I have
been driven into it through the officiousness of certain
parties, the patrons of Mr. Haigh's version. Mr. Robert
White,[1] to whom I have already alluded, in a letter to
the Gateshead Observer, dated Oct. 29, 1856, after
acknowledging his own ignorance of Runes, throws out
an insinuation that I am equally ignorant of the language
and its characters. In a paper on Runes, read at the
January meeting, 1856, of the Antiquarian Society, at
Newcastle, Dr. Charlton introduced Mr. Haigh's version,
and then alluded to one which had been suggested by
myself, and although Dr. Charlton had never seen the
Bewcastle pillar, and consequently could have had no
opportunity of comparing either version with the original,
yet he expressed an opinion that the version of Mr.
Haigh was 'the more probable of the two, and nearer
the truth.'[2] Other insinuations have been made against
my version by parties who know nothing of the Runic
language. I feel, therefore, called upon to enter into
a minute detail, and to adopt a course which I should
not have thought of adopting under other circumstances.

My first acquaintance with Mr. Haigh arose from a
letter which I received from him, in which he requested
me to send him a rubbing of the chief inscription. In
this letter, amongst other things, he stated that he
had a 'suspicion that the long inscription, and one
of the others, present us with the name of a king of

Northumberland,' *without however mentioning his name.*
In my reply, promising him a rubbing, I asked him
whether Alfrid was the Northumberland king to whom
he alluded ; my attention having from an early period
been directed to Alfrid, from the suggestion made by
Mr. Howard[1] to the Antiquarian Society, and from a
communication I received from another party in 1852
respecting Cyneburg, and also from Kemble's observations on this name.

In reply, he stated that he expected to find the
name of Alcfrid, and also the name of Sighard, or
Sigfrid, in the chief inscription. In another letter he
said that he also expected to find the name of Alfrid
in the bottom line on the south side, but before he
came to the end of this letter he stated that a *new
suspicion had come across his mind, that the bottom line
of the south*[2] *was more probably* ' Oswiu Kyningk.' He
had not then seen any rubbing of this line, and consequently his reading was merely guessing.

I made a rubbing of the chief inscription, partly
according to the process already described, except
that (according to his instruction) *it was made with
two sheets of brown paper, placed one above the other,*
instead of one of thin white. The paper was thus too
thick for such shallow letters and marks, and the
rubbing was very confused, unintelligible, and illegible
even by myself when standing by it, and making it,
and having a tolerable idea of the letters beforehand.
Having a lurking suspicion that his intentions were
not altogether of a pure and disinterested character,
I took special care that the rubbing should not be
perfect and satisfactory in those parts where I had
not decided as to the correct reading.

In acknowledging the receipt of this rubbing of the
chief inscription, he said—' *all traces of impressions*

are effaced.' He felt satisfied however 'that perfect impressions would enable him to read every letter'—'that he should have no difficulty in reading the whole if he could once get good impressions.' But then here was the principal difficulty which every person has hitherto experienced who has made the slightest attempt to decipher these inscriptions.

Mr. Haigh stated in direct terms that '*all traces of impressions were effaced.*' After such a plain statement few persons would suppose that he would ever [32] attempt to impose a version of this inscription (from such a rubbing) either upon the Society of Antiquarians at Newcastle, or at any other place. Few persons, however, it would seem have any idea how sanguine some antiquarians become, and what confidence they assume in their own powers of success. *In a few days he did actually give, and without the least hesitation, a version of this long-lost inscription.*

Within a fortnight after he had stated that *all impressions were effaced,* I received a letter from him saying *that he could read the whole of them; that he felt quite sure of most of them, and that the name of Roetbert was most interesting, because the monumental inscription to his memory had been found at Falstone, not far from Bewcastle.* This, however, of course proved nothing. There might have been fifty stones found with the name of Roetbert inscribed upon them, and yet it would not follow that the fifty-first would necessarily have the same name upon it. In his letter, he gave me a part of his version, which commenced with the words 'thæs sigbecun.' I wrote to him by return of post stating that I had sometimes thought that the inscription might commence with 'a cross' and the word 'this,' and stated some reasons both for and against it. I also stated some objections to the latter part of his word 'sigbecun'; more especially the letter C, inasmuch as I could not find that his traces of this letter corresponded with the marks now remaining on the stone. A reading somewhat similar had been proposed long before I knew of the existence of such a person as Mr. Haigh.

In a few days I received another letter from him, which I thought to be of a somewhat snappish character. He said 'the last letter of the first line is *certainly* ✦✦ *i. e.,* C or K [1].' This word 'certainly' shows at least great confidence in his own power of reading the rubbings, especially when we recollect that he had so shortly before stated that 'all traces of impressions were effaced.' He said the letter C or K, of the form given by him, was found also on the Ruthwell pillar, which, however, I do not look upon as any proof that this form of the letter should occur on the Bewcastle pillar also. *I have since very carefully examined the Ruthwell pillar, and I can find no letter upon it of the form given by him.* There is no such letter given in the accurate drawings of the Ruthwell pillar by Dr. Duncan, and I have no hesitation in stating that when Mr. Haigh said that the letter C or K, of the form given by him, was found on the Ruthwell pillar, *he was speaking without due caution. I now assert, without the least fear of contradiction, that no such letter occurs either on the Ruthwell, or the Bewcastle pillar.*

He also sent me in another letter his reading of another rubbing which I had sent him. The bottom line of the south side, which I read + FRU(MA)NGEAR is read by him OSWU CYN(ING) ELT, *i. e.,* Oswy King the elder—'elt' perhaps for 'aelter,' the elder or head of the family.

He says that he was puzzled with this line at first, *the rubbing was so black, but when he looked at the back of the rubbing he could read the impression of the letters distinctly.* He had in fact (as appeared from one of his former letters) formed his own convictions as to this reading by anticipation, *i. e.,* before he had seen the rubbing of it ; and rather than acknowledge himself either beaten or in error, *he professes to read it by the back of the paper where there never was any rubbing at all.* It is evident that by such a mode any person would be capable of reading anything, or everything, just as his fancy might suggest. The first two letters of this line (the F and the R) are perfect ; as well marked as any letters on the stone. They are letters about which I never experienced any doubt or difficulty, being distinctly visible at a considerable distance as soon as the moss was removed. He converts

the letter 𝕽—F—into an ᛡ—S—thus rejecting marks

which are quite plain, and substituting marks where none are visible : and by rejecting the tail of the

letter ᚱ—R—he contrives to convert it into the

letter ᚹ—W. Some of the other letters in this line

are not so plain and distinctly legible.

[33] The following was his version of the long inscription. I shall place mine by its side. The latter part of the woodcut represents his improved reading.

MAUGHAN'S.   HAIGH'S.

+ [TH]ISSIG : B[EA]CN :   + [TH]IS : SIGBEC
[THU]N : SETTON : H   UN : SETTÆ : H
W[ÆT]RED : W[ÆTH]   WÆTRED : WIT
GAR : ALWFWOL   GÆR : FLWOLD
[THU] : AFT : ALCFRI   U : ROETB[ER]T :
[THU] : EAN : CYNI[ING] :   UMÆ : CYN[ING] ;
EAC : OSWIU[ING] :   ALCFRI[TH]Æ : G
+ GEBID : HE   EGIDÆD :
O : SINNA : SAW[HU]LA.   HISSUM : SAULE.[1]

He says—'If we find two false spellings in this inscription—Flwold for Felwold, and Gegidæd, for Gebidæd, I can only say that from my experience of
other inscriptions I only wonder there are not more.
We have even in this monument three other inscriptions, and every line of them is blundered.' Thus
it appears every thing must succumb to his conceptions of right and wrong. He even professes to know
better how things should have been 1200 years ago
than the person who wrote the inscriptions, who, according to the general opinion as to the origin of

such Runic inscriptions, would be one of the learned ecclesiastics of that day. His version thus comprehends *two false spellings and three other blundered inscriptions,* while my version requires nothing of the kind. His reading was as follows :— + This sigbecun settæ Hwætred Witgær Flwoldu Roetbert umæ Cyning Alcfrithæ. Gegidæd hissum saule, *i. e.,* 'Hwætred, Witgær, Felwold, and Roetbert set up this beacon of victory in memory of Alcfrid. Pray for his soul.'

Soon after he sent me his reading, [34] he wrote to me again, requesting me to enter upon all the trouble of making another set of rubbings for him at the inclement season of the new year—rubbings not only of the same parts which I had done before for him—but of some other parts—with fresh instructions as to the mode of proceeding, stating at the same time that his reading would be found to be correct. Before he could receive any answer from me, he arrived at Bewcastle. He *immediately commenced* making rubbings for himself, but after attempting in two or three places he gave it up—on what grounds he did not state. He then began to examine the stone with his eye and his finger. I shall now present the reader with a short review of his readings, *and his own exposition of them,* taken from a memorandum made as soon as he left.

As to the word 'sigbecun' he said that the letter C was made thus— —, and showed me where the tracings of the letter had been, of which, however, I could not see the least relic now, and which did not at all correspond with the traces which were actually to be seen on the stone. The lower side —mark of my compound letter —EA—before my letter C, which is one of the best and deepest marks on the stone, which has evidently a connection with the letter E before it, but no visible connection with the letter C following it—this mark he said was the angular loop of his letter C. Being anxious to hear his opinions and explanations of the other parts of the stone, I did not venture to make any observations of an opposing nature, judging it most prudent to allow him to proceed when he was in a communicative humour. I merely observed, however, as it were casually, that there was a good trace of the side stroke of the letter 𝖪 —C—rather different from what he read it. He said peremptorily—'*it was a blot.*' He thus rejects the two perpendicular strokes of my letters C and N, which are very perfectly defined, and which have no break in the middle, as his letter C would require, and adopts a letter of which I cannot see full and satisfactory traces. He stated that my letter 𝖪 —C—was not in use at the time when this Cross was erected, but that the character as given by him was always used for a C. Where he gets this information from I know not—neither can I conceive how he can speak with authority on such a matter, when it has been hitherto a very doubtful and disputed point whether there were any Anglo-Saxon Runes at all at that period. Besides this word 'beacn' I find the letter 𝖪 —for a C—in the words '*Alcfrithu, eac, myrcna, lice, Ecgfrithu, and rices.*' In the words '*Kynnburthug, Kyneswitha,—Kyng, Kristtus, Kyniing, and Kyninges.*' I find a character rather similar to the form of the C as given by Mr. Haigh, but not exactly like it. In every instance where this character ᛣ —K—occurs on this monument, the lower part of it has always a flat top, no appearance of side-loops, and merely two dots above the side strokes. It certainly is not used as he shapes it. If it occurred in his word 'sigbecun' as he shapes it, then the two upright strokes of my letters C and N would want about a third of their form in the middle of each of them, but no such want can be seen on the stone. The strokes are perfect and visible enough from top to bottom.

I then directed his attention to the appearance of marks across the letter ᚻ at the commencement of the second line, which, I thought, formed the trirunor, or compound Rune—THU—several instances of compound Runes appearing on the stone. He said *'they were merely accidental marks, and of no consequence at all.'*

The two following words, 'settæ' and 'Hwætred' are the only words in which our versions approach to the character of being 'identical.' I deciphered this part of the inscriptions a long time before Mr. Haigh made any attempt to do so.

Mr. Haigh next turned his attention to my word 'Wæthgar,' which he said *was or ought to be Witgær*. I pointed out the marks of the angle on the side of the last perpendicular stroke, which made it the compound letter TH, thus ᛗᚦ (ÆTH.) He said 'they were faults, *and ought not to have been there.* Although he spoke so positively [35] at that time as to the word 'Witgær,' yet he has since changed it into the words 'eom gær.'

As to the word 'Flwoldu,' he assured me he was quite correct about it. He showed me his tracings of the word, evidently adopting the slightest weather mark or injury to the stone where it suited him, and pronouncing the deepest and best-defined cuttings to be *blots, faults, or accidents,* when they did not suit him. *This he did throughout all the inscriptions.* Although he was so positive as to the word Flwoldu being the name of a person, he has since converted it into a common substantive, signifying 'pestilence.'

He now came to the word 'Roetbert,' which made him stare at first, but he soon saw his way through it, rejecting several of the existing marks, and placing marks where there were none.

On my observing that one of the letters had a very good upright stroke, and a good side stroke, diverging so as to resemble the letter Λ —C—he again told me that such a letter was not then in use, and that it was introduced into the Runic alphabet at a sub-sequent period. But he reads this letter C as a B, *and in order to effect this, he gives it a side-loop at the top, of which there is no decisive trace, and he carries the bottom of the under side-loop down through the half-inch space between the lines of the inscription into the space between the letters Y and N of the line below. He said that such faults were quite common,* but how he contrives to make them quite common I know not, for the Bewcastle inscription is probably the only one of that early period, and this will be the only instance on this monument where the letter B is so formed—*if it is formed thus*......Although he stated so dogmatically that Roetbert was the name of one of the parties who erected this monument, he has since changed his mind on this point, and now asserts that the monument was erected to him jointly with Alcfrid.

In the 6th line he found the word 'umæ,' which he translated 'in memory of.' I know of no Anglo-Saxon Dictionary or even Glossary where such a word occurs. He has since changed his word 'umæ' into ' ymb.'

In the 7th line he gets his word ' Alcfrithæ.' To the first upright stroke he attaches an under side-mark, so as to form the letter A. Of this mark I can see no visible trace—no depression, such as might have been expected, if ever a mark had been cut here, and a part of the stone cut away. He reads the second upright stroke as the letter L. At the third letter C he requires too much space. Between the F and the R there is also rather too much space. His next two letters are so close together that the letter I is act-ually placed upon the side marks of his preceding letter R. An objection may also be raised against his word ' Alcfrithæ,' as applied to a person of the male sex. Proper names ending in ' tha' generally denote a female. In Anglo-Saxon charters it is invariably so. We find *Kynigitha* and *Kynigithe,* Queen of Kent, mentioned in the same charter of her husband in 694. We also find *Mildrythæ,* Abbess of the Mon-astery in Thanet ; *Frithogitha,* Queen of the West-Saxons ; *Kyneswitha,* Queen of Offa, King of Mercia ; also *Ælfrythæ,* another Queen of Mercia. We also find the names *Kynedritha, Etheldritha, Ælswytha,* and many others, but in no instance do we find a man's name ending in ' tha' or ' thæ.' Higden (p. 251) men-tions one Alfritha, the Queen of Kenulphus. Camden, speaking of Stonehenge, tells us that Alfritha, wife of King Edgar, built and endowed a stately nunnery that she might expiate her crime in killing her son-in-law, King Edward, by penance and good works. This is another instance of the word being applied to a female. Hence we have fair grounds for rejecting this word as the name of King Alcfrid.

In the word ' Gegidæd,' the letter Ⲙ —E has only
one upright stroke visible on the stone, and how he
forms the remainder of this word I can scarcely comprehend. He altered his words ' hissum saule' into
' heosum [1] saulum' ; *passing through the space between the
ines again to get the top of the first letter* U *in ' heosum,'
rejecting the cross bar of the* H *altogether in ' sawhula,'*
and attaching a side-mark to the top of one of its
uprights so as to get his letter L.

Such are the two versions of this inscription. With
the exception of a few friendly suggestions, I am only
indebted for my version to my own time, my own la-
bour, my own perseverance, and most especially to
my own residence on the [36] spot, which has enabled
me to examine and re-examine, to correct and re-cor-
rect, not only my own frequent errors, but also the
errors of others.

In another paper read before the Society of Antiquaries at Newcastle Mr. Haigh has made some alterations of which I have only seen a translation in Roman
letters ; but not a copy of the Runic characters. In
this paper he reads the chief inscription thus—' This
sigbecun sættæ Hwætred eom gaer flwoldu Roetbert
ymb Alcfridæ. Gicegæd heosum saulum.'—' This
memorial set Hwætred in the great pestilence year to
Roetbert to King Alcfride. Pray for their souls.' On
these alterations I shall now make a few remarks.

His first alteration occurs in his word ' Witgær,'
which he changes into the two words 'eom gaer.'
The word ' eom' appears to be open to a few objections. The letters in this word require five perpendicular or full upright strokes, while on the stone
there are only three. Besides, in the Anglo-Saxon
language, the word ' eom' is either a pronoun, mean-

ing 'to them'—'eom' for 'heom,' and that for the dative plural 'him' : or else it is the indicative mood of the defective verb 'wesan'—'to be,' and signifies, in plain English, 'I am.' I know of no instance where 'eom' occurs for the preposition 'in.'

An objection may also be raised against the word 'gaer.' In Anglo-Saxon we have the word 'gear,' signifying 'a year,' but not the word 'gaer.' The Runic characters on the stone may be read 'gar' or 'gaer,' but not 'gear'; and hence, probably, he takes the liberty of transposing the vowels E and A, but we may question whether the liberty is not an unwarrantable one. I find a trace of every mark necessary for the word 'Wæthgar'; but I feel bound to say that 'eom gaer' appears a very doubtful reading. It also appears very doubtful whether Alfrid did die in the great pestilence year, for, according to Bede, he was alive in the following year.

In the first reading he introduced Roetbert as one of the party who erected the monument to Alcfrid, but in his second reading he supposes the monument to be raised *to him and King Alcfrid.* Of this Roetbert history leaves us no record, which appears rather strange if he was so eminent a personage as to be considered worthy of sharing the monument with King Alcfride. From what I have previously said on this word, however, a doubt may be fairly entertained whether the word 'Roetbert' ever was placed on the monument.

He alters the word 'umæ' into 'ymb,' which signifies 'about,'—'around,' *i. e.,* something winding about or compassing. It is very evident, however, that a stone pillar (although it is fifteen feet in length) would be a very unsuitable winding-sheet for the corpse of King Alcfrid. Its use on this monument, signifying 'in memory of,' seems rather a forced one. Besides, its proper position should have been *before* both the words 'Roetbert' and 'Alcfrid,' *and not between them,* as it has reference to both words.

The word 'gicegæd' appears to have some remarkable transformations rendering it what may be termed a 'far fetched' word. I presume that it is originally derived from the verb 'biddan'—'to pray,' which, in the imperative mood, plural number, is thus formed 'biddath'—'pray ye.' In the first transformation, then, we have the word 'biddath' changed into 'biddæd.' In the second transformation we have 'biddæd' changed into 'bigæd.' In the third we have 'bigæd' changed into 'cegæd.' In the fourth we have the expletive 'ge' changed into 'gi.' Besides these transformations, which appear very forced and unwarrantable, very grave doubts may be entertained whether such Runic characters can be really traced on the stone. I have not seen Mr. Haigh's second readings of the other parts of the stone.

After examining the chief inscription Mr. Haigh inquired if there were any traces of letters on any other part of the Cross. I directed his attention to the flat space near the top on the north side, where I had observed some traces. He mounted a ladder, and soon found the letters to which I had directed him. After a little examination with his finger—scratching among the moss with the point of his knife—and then taking a rubbing, he made out the word 'Gessu,' as he supposed, and satisfied himself that there was nothing besides. I afterwards cleared the stone from its thick coat of lichens and moss, took careful rubbings, and painted the stone, [37] and I ascertained that the inscription consisted of three crosses and the word 'Gessus,' as I have previously stated.

He then set the ladder against the west side, and examined the plain surface near the top, but soon pronounced it barren, and that the inscription on this side (if ever there was one) was totally broken off. By careful examination I found remains of the word 'Kristtus.' In a letter which I have since received from him, he stated that he had found the letter A on the west side, when he examined it (of which, however, I heard nothing said at the time), and that he suspected it was the first letter of the word 'Alpha,' and that the word 'Omega' would have been on the east side, which is now totally gone. He read the inscriptions on these plain surfaces thus : 'Gessu' on the north side ; 'Kriste' on the south side ; 'Alpha' on the west side ; and 'Omega' on the east side ; making the sentence 'Jesu Christ, the beginning and the ending.' This certainly is a very ingenious reading, but it is not confirmed by the existing traces of the letters.

He then examined the south side, and soon found what he had anticipated, namely, the word, or at least a part of the word, 'Kristte,' to correspond, as he said at the time, with the two lines on the west side, which I had discovered long before. After partly clearing away the moss with the point of his knife, and taking a rubbing, he was convinced that he had found the characters—

C R I S

very distinct, forming part of the word CRISTE. On a more careful examination, however, I found the letters to be LICE. These letters are now, when cleaned, very perfect, will receive the end of the finger very easily, and are quite visible to the eye. There fortunately cannot now be two opinions about them.

He next proceeded to inspect the other single lines on the south side of the pillar. *He examined the top line, and concluded that there had been nothing there.* He then came down to the next one, and after rubbing it a while with his finger, he fancied there *might be letters*. After a little further examination, he said he could find the words 'Ecgfrid Cyng,' 'King Egfrid.'

He then scraped the moss with the point of his knife in the places where he fancied the letters were lurking, and afterwards took a rubbing on strong dry paper (rubbing both ways across the stone, and then up and down) which rubbing, as a matter of course, gave him a faint trace—at least of the letter or marks which he had scratched in the lichen—if of nothing else. He was not long till he satisfied himself perfectly on this point, *i. e.* as to the words 'Ecgfrid Cyng' having once occupied a place there. This is the line which I read 'Rices thæs'—'of this kingdom.'

His next step was to the line below, where, after a process something similar to the one already described, he found the word 'Cyniburug,' the name of Alcfrid's queen.

This word I read 'kyninges,'—'king.' In one of his earliest letters to me he stated that he expected

to find the word ' Cyneburg' on one of the single
lines on the south side to correspond with the same
name on the north side.

In the bottom line he readily found the words ' Oswu
Cyning elt,'—' Oswy King the elder, as he had previously given them. These words I read thus—'+
fruman gear'—' in the first year.'

He then said that there was one name which be
should have liked better to have seen than any of
them, and that was the name of Queen Eanfleda. I
suggested that it might perhaps be found on the top
line if it were more strictly examined. He remounted
the ladder, and after a few rubs with his finger across
the stone he said—'I do believe here is a letter.'
After a few more rubs with his finger he again said—
'I do believe the name is here.' He then applied the
knife awhile, and [38] took a rubbing as before, and
found the word ' Eanflad,' in

the first part of the line, and pronounced the remainder
of the line blank. He was quite delighted with this
discovery, and more especially with the particular form
of the letter ᛉ (EA). In fact, so overjoyed was he
with the discovery of this interesting family tree (which
he had possibly found in his own imagination before
he left home) that he quite forgot to look at the lines
on the north side of the monument. With more careful tests I have been induced to read this line—'Ecgfrithu,' ' of Ecgfrid.'

Thus clouded is the origin of the version with which
Mr. Haigh has ventured to honour the members of the
Newcastle Society of Antiquarians. He did not give

his version to the Society with a hood over his eyes, for he no sooner informed me of his intentions than I informed him of the true character of the rubbings which I had sent him. He however persisted in the correctness and accuracy of his version, *stating that he had not only inspected the monument, but made rubbings of it, and traced the letters with his finger, and thus assured himself of its accuracy.* I have also examined the monument and fingered the Runes many scores of times, and scores of times I have come to the conclusion that the decipherings were not correct on which on a former inspection I had not the least doubt or scruple. It is only by very slow steps, and by carefully examining and re-examining, that I have arrived at the conclusion that my version accords with the original. Mr. Haigh's inspection of the several parts of the monument, tracing the letters with his finger, scratching marks in the moss, and taking rubbings of them, was limited to about two hours ; my examinations of the Cross have extended over twice the number of years.

I have thought it necessary to enter into these minute details, and thus to put my readers in possession of every fact and circumstance connected with this version, in order that they may have sufficient data on which to form their own judgment as to the merits of the respective readings of the inscriptions on this important Memorial.

XIV. HAIGH'S SECOND ACCOUNT, 1861.

[This is taken from Haigh's *Conquest of Britain by the Saxons*, pp. 37, 39—41. The runes at the end are from Plate II, at the beginning of the volume.]

[37] Two of them are of particular interest, as being of greater length than others, and presenting us with specimens of the Anglian dialect, as spoken in Northumbria in the seventh century. The first, on the western face of the cross at Bewcastle in Cumberland, is simply a memorial of Alcfrid, who was associated by his father Oswiu with himself in the kingdom of Northumbria, and died probably in A. D. 664.[1] It gives us (Pl. I. fig. 2) three couplets[2] of alliterative verse, thus[3]:—

✠ THIS SIGBECUN	This memorial
SETTÆ HWÆTRED	Hwætred set
ĒM GÆRFÆ BOLDU	and carved this monument
ÆFTÆR BARÆ	after the prince,
YMB CYNING ALCFRIDÆ	after the King Alcfrid,
GICEGÆD HEOSUM SAWLUM	pray for their souls.

Other inscriptions on the same monument present merely names of some of Alcfrid's kindred, in which, however, some additional characters occur.

The second inscription, on two sides of a similar cross at Ruthwell, in Annandale, which may possibly have been brought from Bewcastle, and once have stood at the other end of Alcfrid's grave,[4] consists, etc. ...

[39] The poem of which these are fragments was probably one of those which Cædmon, who was living at the time when these monuments were erected, composed.[5] That they belong to the seventh century cannot be doubted; they contain forms of the language which are evidently earlier even than those which occur in the contemporary version of Bæda's verses in

a MS. at S. Gallen, and the copy of Cædmon's first song at the end of the MS. of the 'Historia Ecclesiastica,' which was completed two years after its author's death.   Thus *hifun* (ana[40]logous to the Gothic *sibun* for *seofen*) is certainly an earlier form than *hefaen* and *heben*, which we find in the latter of these little poems.   *Em* in the Bewcastle inscription is *efen* contracted.   *Boldu*,[1] *galgu*, and *dalgu*, present a form of nouns which later would be monosyllabic.   *Heosum*,[1] the dative plural of the possessive pronoun of the third person, regularly formed, like *usum*, from the genitive of the personal, (*hire, úre*), occurs only in the Bewcastle inscription ; *ungcet*, the dual of the first personal pronoun, only in that at Ruthwell.   *Gærfæ*[1] is a strange instance of a strong verb [41] taking an additional syllable in the præterite ; but it seems to be warranted by *scopa* in Cædmon's song, and even by *ahofe* in the Durham ritual ; and the analogy of the Sanscrit præterite (*tutôpa, tutôpa*), and the Greek (τέτυφα, τέτυφε), shows that such forms as these, not only for the third person, but for the first also, are more ancient than *cearf, scóp,* and *ahóf.*

NOTES

This edition has been repaginated. Therefore, in using these Notes, convert the page number of the note as follows:

1	-	131	40	- 174	78	-	212
2	-	132	41	- -175	80	-	214
3	-	133	42	- -176	81	-	215
4	-	134	43	-177	82	-	216
5	-	135	44	-178	83	-	217
6	-	136	45	-179	84	-	218
8	-	138	46	-180	85	-	219
9	-	139	47	-181	86	-	220
10	-	140	48	-182	87	-	221
12	-	142	51	-185	88	-	222
13	-	143	52	-186	89	-	223
14	-	144	53	-187	90	-	224
15	-	145	54	-188	91	-	225
16	-	146	55	-189	92	-	226
17	-	147	56	-190	94	-	228
20	-	150	57	-191	96	-	230
21	-	151	58	-192	97	-	231
22	-	152	59	-193	98	-	232
23	-	153	60	-194	99	-	233
24	-	154	61	-195	100	-	234
25	-	157	63	-197	101	-	235
28	-	160	64	-198	102	-	236
30	-	164	67	-201	103	-	237
31	-	165	68	-202	105	-	239
32	-	166	70	-204	106	-	240
33	-	167	71	-205	108	-	242
35	-	169	72	-206	110	-	244
36	-	170	73	-207	116	-	250
38	-	172	74	-208	123	-	257
39	-	173	75	-209	124	-	258

NOTES

[The references are to page and note. *Date* signifies *The Date of the Ruthwell and Bewcastle Crosses* (*Trans. Conn. Acad. Arts and Sciences* 17. 213—361), which may be consulted for photographs of the crosses, as well as the discussion of details.]

1 1. *Buechastell.* For the derivation and various spellings of this name, see *Date*, pp. 96—8; and compare instances below.

1 2. Hubert de Vaux received the barony of Gil(le)sland from Henry II in 1158 (*Date*, p. 100). His son, Robert de Vaux, founded the priory of Lanercost in 1169 (*Date*, p. 98). The inscription must have been that now read as *Cynnburug* (*Date*, p. 26).

1 3. The 'checky coate' in the panel of chequers (*Date*, p. 26), thought of as a coat of arms.

1 4. Does 'other' here mean the *south* face?

1 5. B and R are much alike in Runic and Roman. By beginning at the B of CYNNBURUG (as commonly read), taking the first U as a somewhat angular O (see *Date*, Fig. 26), and the second U as a battered A, one might possibly, considering the defaced condition of the final letter, arrive at BORAX; the E would occasion more difficulty, and one would have to disregard the previous letters. As for VAUX, one might take the first U for Roman V, regard the R as A, deal boldly with the second U, and again take the final letter as X; HUBERT DE would require more conjuring. (A convenient table of 'commoner Anglian runes' may be found in Wyatt's *Old English Riddles*, opposite p. xxviii.)

2 1. *Vaulx.* It seems as though Camden had adopted Roscarrock's suggestion (see p. 1). See note on p. 148.

3 1. *untoward part.* Cf. pp. 12, 23, and *Date*, pp. 147—8. If we may believe Hutchinson (*Hist. Cumb.* 1. 78), Bewcastle was not always a tiny hamlet : 'Bewcastle seems to have

anciently been an extensive town, by the scites and ruins of houses, which yet remain.'

3 2. *Curate.* See p. 10.

3 3. *Communicated.* On April 18, 1629, Sir Henry Spelman (1564 ?–1641) wrote a letter from London to Palæmon (or Palle) Rosencrantz, the Danish ambassador to England, in which, among other things, he refers to a recent book of the runologist Olaus Worm (1588–1654), who, after occupying successively the chairs of belles lettres (1613–5) and Greek (1615–1624) at Copenhagen, had been made Professor of Medicine in 1624. Spelman would like to learn whence runes derive their name, and to what country and people they properly belong. In particular, he submits a runic inscription for Worm to interpret. This, he says, came from the epistyle of a stone cross at Bewcastle, in the north of England, where the Danes had been numerous. The inscription had been shown by Lord William Howard to Camden and himself together, in 1618, eleven years before. In his Latin this runs: 'Sculpta fuit hæc Inscriptio Epistylio crucis lapideæ, Beucastri partibus Angliæ borealibus (ubi Dani plurimum versabantur) Cambdenoque & mihi simul exhibita Anno Domini 1618, ab Antiquitatum inter proceres Angliæ peritissimo Domino Guilielmo Howard novissimi Ducis Norfolciæ filio' (Worm, *Danicorum Monumentorum Libri Sex*, p. 161).

The inscription is printed by Worm as follows:

ᚱᛁᛚᚠᛡᛞᚱᛆᚻᛏᛣ ᚠᛡ·

On July 18 of the same year Worm replies. The inscription is indeed runic, but the copy, made by an unskilful person, is incomplete, and wrong in the case of at least five letters. He proposes to make the necessary corrections, and so to read: *Rino satu runa stina d* (the *d* being for *þ*); that is, 'Rino set runic stones these.' The Latin is (p. 168): 'Inscriptio epistilii crucis lapideæ Beucastriensis verè Gothica seu Runica est, sed ab imperito haud planè descripta; nam nec integra est, nec 4, 5, 7, 8, 12 notæ confusionem & depravationem effugêre. . . . Quod si ita legendum?' After giving his conjectural runes, their transliteration, and the Latin,

Rino lapides hos runicos posuit, he proceeds to express the wish that Spelman would have the inscription more accurately copied by some one not wholly ignorant of the literature, in which case he would do what he could with it.

The explanation of Worm's extraordinary answer is to be found, as Wilhelm Grimm long afterwards saw (*Ueber Deutsche Runen,* Göttingen, 1821, pp. 165–6) in the fact that the Scandinavian runes differ in some respects from the Old English ones, and that Worm was unfamiliar with the latter (for instance, he reads as N the Old English rune for C). Accordingly, he made various arbitrary changes, provided a plural verb for a singular nominative, and used the plural, 'stones,' where evidently only one stone is in question.

According to an entry in the British Museum Cottonian MS. Domitian A. 18, fol. 37, the inscription was on a cross-head (Spelman's *epistylium crucis*) found at Bewcastle in 1615. The entry, which I suspect to be in the hand of Sir Robert Cotton, follows:

Cotton MS. Julius F. 6 has a similar entry on fol. 313 (formerly 297), *recto*, which looks like a rough draft, on a torn and mended sheet, of that in the Domitian MS. The runes (at the left) are of the same form, but larger. The English (at the right) is in a ruder hand; it omits the first two lines, and reads 'bringe', 'a crosse', '....deth', and '.....nes'. In a print-hand, at right angles to the foregoing: 'Bucastle inscription | For Mr. Clarenceaulx'.

But the runes are again recorded on a slip of paper between pages 643 and 644 of Bodleian MS. Smith I, Camden's copy of his Britannia. There is no doubt, according to Sir George Frederic Warner, that the entry which follows is in Cotton's own hand:

received this morning a Ston from my Lord of Arundell sent him from my Lord william it was the head of a Cross at Bewcastell All the letters legable ar thes in one Line And I have sett to them such as I can gather out of my Alphabett that lyk an A I can find in non But whether thes be only letters or words I somwhatt dout I had sent you before this some but that I am not able to walk I am so sorru with the Emrrodi from a car of your health for welk you the Gift of our understanding is Gyk to point I have yett sent I send you many thanks amonghst them I have an Æthelwoldi Story fair and ancient

For convenience, I print the part of the entry which concerns us, supplying punctuation:

'I receaued this morning a ston from my lord of Arundell sent him from my lord William; it was the head of a Cross at Bewcastell. All the lettres legable ar thes in on[e] line. And I have sett to them such as I can gather out of my Alphabetts: that lyk an A I can find in non. But wether thes be only lettres or words I somwhatt dout.'

The purport I take to be this: Lord William Howard, who in 1618 had shown the cross-head to Camden and Spelman (see above), sent it, at some time between this and 1623 (when Camden died) to Thomas Howard (1586–1646), second Earl of Arundel, the collector of the Arundel marbles and other works of art, who (promptly?) turned it over to Cotton. Some of the letters were legible, others not; such as were legible were in a single line. Cotton searched in his runic alphabets to find how these letters should be transliterated. R he seems at first sight to have mistaken for V, but his small r's much resemble v's, so possibly it is R. C (K) he misreads as N, as did Worm. About D he is uncertain whether it may not be an M—pardonable enough. Y he gives up. T he reads as F. The other letters he interprets correctly.

Cotton, immediately upon receipt of the stone, sends a note from his house at Westminster, on the site of the present House of Lords, to his former teacher and constant friend, Camden, then probably residing at Chislehurst, eleven miles southeast of London; and afterwards sees to it that the particulars concerning the inscription shall be preserved, by inserting them in one of his manuscripts.

Thus, in the first quarter of the seventeenth century, there were (and are still) extant four copies of the same inscription—that printed in Worm's book, and three in manuscript. Of the three, two are now in Cotton manuscripts of the British Museum, and another in the Bodleian library. These all agree, save that those in Worm and the Bodleian slip have Y as the 8th letter, while the two of the British Museum read U, as the result of omitting an interior stroke.

In 1703 Hickes (*Thesaurus*, Præf., p. XII) and Wanley (*Catalogus*, p. 248) read (with help from the Bodleian copy?) *rynas Dryhtnes* (Hickes, *Drithnes!*), 'mysteries of the Lord,' and Wanley reproduces the Domitian copy of runes.

In 1741, Pontoppidan, in his *Gesta et Vestigia Danorum extra Daniam* 2. 14, reproduces Spelman's runes from Worm (somewhat toppling to the right the twelfth letter), and gives a new rendering, furnished by Christian Helverschov, formerly Counsellor of Justice and Provincial Judge in Denmark. Helverschov supposes the runes to represent an utterance of Christ on the cross—*Vilos ero ateos*—which he takes to be vile Latin for *Vilis ero atheis*: 'I shall be vile to the godless'; whereupon Pontoppidan gravely doubts whether the initial letters of these three words have been quite correctly read. He ends with a copy of Worm's emended line.

In 1821, Wilhelm Grimm (*op. cit.*, p. 167), takes up the matter of the inscription at Bevercastle (*sic*), near Nottingham (there is a Bevercoates near Tuxford), reproduces it from Worm, and renders it as *rices Dryhtnes*, observing at the same time that the *e* of the ending is not represented by the usual rune. He interprets the Old English as 'of the realm's dominion,' namely (p. 168), 'the rule of heaven over earth'; or, 'the power of the earthly realm through the acceptance of the cross'; or, most probably, 'the sway of the jurisdiction,' according to which the cross would have served to mark the boundary of a district.

In 1840, Kemble (*Archæologia* 28. 346) reproduces the Spelman inscription, and renders by *ricæs Dryhtnæs*, 'Domini potentis,' for '[signum] Domini potentis.'

But what bearing has all this upon the Bewcastle Cross? 'On the head of a· cross found at Beucastell in 1615,' says the Domitian MS. Sent (between 1618 and 1623) by Belted Will to his half-nephew, says Cotton's slip. Was the *cross* found in 1615? Then it was not our cross, written about in 1607 by a member of Belted Will's household (see p. 1, above). Was it the cross-*head* that was found in 1615? Then it could not have been on our cross in 1607. Was it disinterred in 1615, having originally belonged to our cross? If so, was it the cross-beam, or the portion immediately above? It has neither the shape nor the dimensions which fit either of these suppositions (*Date*, p. 122). Then it is not a part of our cross, but of some other cross. But if it was the portion above the cross-beam, and stood upon its edge, the cross must have been at once broader and thinner than the present. (Few of the Scottish slabs were so thin as 4 inches, but there is one at Brodie (Allen, *Early Christ. Mon.* 3. 132), not far from Forres in Elgin, which tapers upward from 5 inches to 4, its height being 5 feet 4 inches, and its breadth, 3 feet 5 inches to 3 feet 2 inches. Significant in this connection is the one at Keills in Argyll pictured by Allen (between pp. 390 and 391), 7 feet 4 inches high, 1 foot 9 inches across the arms, and $6^1/_2$ inches thick.) And if it was the cross-beam itself, and lay upon its broader face (a rather improbable supposition), the cross must have been much shorter than the present one, in order that the thickness of four inches should bear some due proportion to the height of the cross.

Observing, too, that the ending -*æs* (as Kemble has told us : *op. cit.*, p. 346) is a mark of antiquity, why may we not assume that this was the head of an older cross, of quite different shape, fallen, perhaps overthrown and covered with earth, and with some of the letters illegible. Might not such an older cross have been removed when the newer, and perhaps more highly ornamented one, was erected? In thus superseding the older one, the sculptor of the present cross might or might not have adapted the work of his prede cessor. If so, an older *Cyniburg* might in this way have become *Cynnburug*.

It will be evident that *epistylium crucis*, in the light of Cotton's entries, must mean *cross-head* (Wilhelm Grimm said 'Queerstück,' cross-beam, transverse piece), and that all attempts to make the phrase mean the existing shaft, the lowest inscription on the south face, etc., are due to misapprehension.

4 1. Nicolson here assumed that the inscription sent to Worm was part of that on the west face.

4 2. *Epystilium* signified to Nicolson the whole cross. See note on 3 3.

4 3. *five yards.* Cf. pp. 12, 17, 25.

4 4. *white oyly Cement.* Frequently transcribed by later writers.

4 5. *two foot.* Compare the figures on pp. 12, 25.

4 6. Here is the first decipherment of this line, and clearly *Cynnburug.* See *Date*, pp. 12, 26, 37, 43–44, and above, pp. 10, 11.

5 1. Interpreting *Ryn-* as 'runes,' and *-buru* as 'burial.'

6 1. The last two letters are meant for NN.

6 2. *More antient date.* See note on 1 2.

8 1. Compare these with the previous reading, p. 7.

9 1. Cf. *Date*, pp. 98–9 (note).

9 2. Perhaps properly *Tonge*; cf. p. 10, and *Miscellany Accounts*, p. 163.

9 3. *Benson.* Mentioned in Nicolson's Diary, under 1704; see *Pub. Mod. Lang. Assoc. of America* 17. 371.

9 4. As it does now.

9 5. Cf. note on 3 3.

10 1. 1695.

10 2. Again *Cynnburug.*

10 3. *Thistle.* The topmost vine? Or the sundial?

12 1. *Obelisk.* The first time it is so called. See *Date*, pp. 121–3.

12 2. Cf. Nicolson, p. 4.

12 3. Cf. Nicolson, p. 4.

12 4. *Cross.* The first suggestion of this.

13. For the third and fourth letters of *Cynnburug*, cf. pp. 4, 10, 11.

14. The inscription at the left is intended to reproduce the lowest one visible; cf. p. 8.

15 1. Southern Baltic, east of Jutland.

15 2. Note the advance in the interpretation.

15 3. The Massagetæ inhabited what is now northern Khiva. For a so-called Massagetic alphabet, see Hickes, *Thesaurus, Gram. Isl.*, Tabella I, bottom.

15 4. Not the European Don.

16 1. *Buchanan.* George Buchanan (1506–1582), *Rer. Scot. Hist.* 6. 74.

16 2. Died 900.

16 3. Never published.

16 4. Cf. Nicolson's view, p. 6.

16 5. *Bride-Kirk.* Cf. pp. 3, 7, 22, 24.

17 1. Cf. p. 12.

17 2. Cf. note on 12 4.

17 3. *Dial.* The earliest mention.

17 4. The earliest mention.

20 1. The reading of *Cynnburug*.

21 1. Cf. p. 7.

21 2. *Eleventh century.* A new date, unless this was what Nicolson had in mind; see note on 6 2, p. 30, and p. 97, note 40.

21 3. *Pomegranet.* The dial?

21 4. Cf. note on 12 4.

22 1. *Effigies.* Note the fulness of the descriptions of the figures.

23 1. Cf. p. 4.

23 2. Cf. p. 5.

24 (plate, fig. 3). The stroke of the second N in CYNN-BURUG is here faint.

25 1. See note on 4 5.

25 2. Cf. note on 12 4.
25 3. *Working.* Cf. p. 21.
25 4. Cf. note on 24.
28 1. *Holy lamb.* Here first identified.
28 2. Cf. note on 14.
30 1. Again *Cynnburug.*
31 1. Cf. note on 14.
32 1. *Baptist.* Here first identified; cf. p. 23.
32 2. *Hawk.* Cf. pp. 4, 17, 22, 32.
32 3. Cf. note on 17 3.
32 4. *Ed.* Perhaps Albert Way (1805—1874); see pp. 69, 72.
33 1. *Mr. Smith.* Rather Hutchinson; see p. 22.
35 1. The first mention of Dunstan in connection with the Cross.
36 1. An abstract of Dr. Edward Charlton's paper (read Jan. 2, 1856) is contained in the rare Vol. 1 (no more published) of the *Proceedings of the Society of Antiquaries of Newcastle upon Tyne* (1856), pp. 75—7. Dr. Charlton follows the readings, now of Maughan, whom he calls 'the zealous incumbent of Bewcastle,' and now of Haigh (I owe my information to the transcript obligingly made for me by Robert Blair, Esq., F. S. A., Secretary of the Society). Dr. Charlton says: 'Having with great care, cleansed the stone of its lichen and moss [cf. pp. 70, 118], Mr. Maughan took careful casts of the characters, and communicated copies to several archæologists, amongst others, to the Rev. Daniel Haigh. ... On the north side of the cross is inscribed, very plainly, "Kyniburuk" [cf. pp. 15, 99], or "Cyneburg," the name of a queen of Northumbria, being the wife of Alchfrid, son of Oswiu, king of Northumberland. On the western face, the inscription, as deciphered, is "THIS SIGBECUN SETTAE HWÆTRED, WITGAER, FELWOLD & ROETBERT, UMÆ KYNING ALCFRITHÆ GEBIDÆD HISSUM SAULA"—intimating that the four persons first named had set up this cross to King Alcfrith, and requested prayers for his soul. Roetbert is commemorated in the Falstone inscription, as dead.' Here Charlton follows Haigh (see pp. 107, 110, 111). He proceeds: ...'On the south face is a Runic inscription, interpreted by Mr. Haigh—"OSWU

KYNING ELT,"—or Oswy the King. "Elt" may possibly refer to his being the elder (or head) of the family [see p. 109]. This inscription confirms the supposition that the cross was reared in the lifetime of Oswy. No prayers being asked for the souls of Oswy and Cyneburga, as for the soul of Alchfrid, it may be inferred that they were still living. If so, the memorial must have been erected between 664, when we last hear of Alchfrid, and 670, when Oswy died.' . . . In a note to his paper, Dr. Charlton refers to a new version of the Bewcastle inscription, published by Mr. Maughan in December, viz.: "This sigbeacithon saetta Hwaetred, Withgar, Aalewolthu, aft Alcfrithu, ean Kunig eak Oswiuing. Igebid heo sinna sawhula." "Hwaetred, Withgar, and Alfwold, erected this little beacon in memory of Alfrid, at one time king with, and son of, Oswy. Pray for them, their sins and their souls." The Doctor thinks the version of Mr. Haigh, the more probable of the two, and nearer the truth.

'The chairman [Mr. John Hodgson Hinde] said, the paper was very interesting. At the same time, it would have been more conclusive if "Cyneburga" had not been deciphered first. Assuming the accuracy of the conclusions now before the meeting, it would seem that, contrary to the historians, the Anglo-Saxons had written characters before their conversion to Christianity.'

36 2. *Penrith.* See Collingwood's *Early Sculptured Crosses,* pp. 240 ff.

36 3. *Camden.* Rather, Cotton; see note on 3 3.

38 1. See note on 3 3.

38 2. This is taken from Worm's conjectural emendation (*Dan. Mon.,* p. 168).

38 3. Cf. p. 119.

39 1. These variants occur in the form presented by Dr. Charlton on March 2, 1856 (*Newcastle Proc.,* p. 98, as communicated by Mr. Blair): line 1, DIS; 2, VN SÆT-; V ROETBERT. See pp. 110, 116.

39 2. Here, as in *Ecgfrid* (below) and *Alcfridæ* (next page), the *d* is a Latinization of *þ*, and would not occur in a runic inscription.

39 3. His plate reads distinctly *Cynn-*.

40 1. Cf. *Date*, pp. 93—4.

41 1. *Rit.* 68. 11—12.

42 1. *ahofe*. Rather, *ahof*, *Rit.* 61. 15.

42 2. *gicegath*. Normally, *giceigað* (see *Rit.* 173. 9, and cf. 175.21); but *gicegað* occurs 54. 3. The sense is 'call upon.'

42 3. It is hardly necessary to comment upon these conjectures and assumptions.

42 4. *hiora*. And *hiara* (3).

43 1. See note on 42 3.

44 1. Cf. pp. 100, 102.

45 1. But Wilfrith went abroad to be consecrated in 664, and did not return till 666 (Bede, *Op. Hist.*, ed. Plummer, 2. 317).

46 1. See my edition of *The Dream of the Rood*, pp. xi ff.

46 2. See *Date*, pp. 53—5.

47 1. Cf. note on 40 1.

48 1. Cf. p. 36, and *Date*, p. 75.

48 2. From Bewcastle?

51 1. See *Date*, pp. 111—3.

52 1. See p. 31.

52 2. See *Date*, pp. 121—3.

53 1. Rather, p. 318; see p. 13.

53 2. See p. 18.

53 3. See p. 24.

54 1. See p. 24.

54 2. See p. 20.

54 3. See plate opposite p. 28.

54 4. See p. 2. Note the variations.

55 1. Cf. *Date*, p. 122.

55 2. 2. 478—9. They say the stone is 'about five feet and a half high.'

55 3. See note on 3 3.

55 4. Omit *in*.

55 5. See note on 3 3.

55 6. This comes ultimately from Worm's p. 162, but with two important changes. The eighth letter (= Y) is properly an inverted v, with an oblique downward stroke from the

inside of the left leg. This Worm represents almost as in Maughan's plate, which makes it resemble an Æ, the fourth and twelfth letters, only tilted instead of upright. Maughan tilts all three; hence we should either read RICÆS DRÆHTNÆS, or RICYS DRYHTNYS; but this Maughan does not see.

55 7. This is not Spelman's reading; Spelman could not read it, and therefore sent it to Worm; see below.

55 8. From Kemble.

55 9. Read *Dryhtnes*.

55 10. See note on 3 3.

56 1. Rather Spelman.

56 2. See note on 55 4.

56 3. Here there are various deviations from Worm's runes.

56 4. Worm has *stina d*—'these stones'; for 'made,' Worm has *posuit*, 'placed.'

56 5. *Roden Dryhtness.* I do not find this. Hickes says (Præfatio, p. XIII): 'Inveni *Saxonicam* crucis epigraphen, nempe, Rynas Drithnes [*sic*], *mysteria domini, literis Runicis* descriptam.' He then refers to Wanley (p. 248).

56 6. For *Nicolson.*

56 7. Maughan seems to have followed the copy in Hutchinson's *Hist. Cumb.* 1. 82–3.

56 8. For *erlat.*

56 9. Which Maughan has not reproduced (see p. 7).

56 10. Published 1840.

57 1. Kemble's words are (p. 346): 'There has, therefore, been either a portion of the inscription lost, or the cross or pillar on which it stood was meant to be taken as part of the legend:—thus, Signum Domini Potentis.'

57 2. Pp. 346–7.

57 3. This is still unpublished; it was compiled by Jonathan Boucher (1738–1804), a friend of Washington's, for whom see *Dict. Nat. Biog.*

57 4. Omit 'the reader.'

57 5. This is from Nicolson.

58 1. See p. 24.

58 2. *Robert White.* At the meeting of the Society of

Antiquaries of Newcastle on October 1, 1856, Mr. White said that, ' being recently in the neighbourhood of Bewcastle, he stepped aside to view the famous cross which had so repeatedly been brought under their observation, and, to his astonishment, found that the portions containing the long-studied inscriptions had been painted!—painted blue! The Runic letters were indicated by black lines upon the blue, the painter tracing the lines as he himself deciphered them; and even where there were no letters decipherable at all, Runes were painted. To satisfy himself of this fact, he drew his finger over the painted characters, and found no corresponding hollows in the stone. . . . Dr. Charlton said, he had no doubt the paint had been applied with a commendable object—to preserve the cross from further injury; but the Runes, of course, should have been left to speak for themselves, instead of being made to favour any particular reading. Mr. Henry Turner said, the paint would preserve the stone; and the black lines, legitimate or not, would not affect the substance of the cross ' (*Proc.* 1. 165–6).

In a letter to the *Gateshead Observer* of October 18, 1856, Mr. Maughan replied: ' My motive for so doing was neither to disfigure, to injure, nor to preserve the Cross, but merely to secure as much accuracy as possible in deciphering the inscriptions. A stone which has retained its inscriptions for twelve hundred years requires no such adventitious aid as a coat of paint, and it is difficult to conceive how such a puerile idea can have found a lodgment in the cranium of the antiquated patriarchs of such a renowned Society. . . . My object in painting those parts of the Cross where I had reason to suspect the existence of inscriptions, was simply to obtain every vestige, however obscure it might be; and I have been gratified by thus recovering several traces which it was impossible for the eye to detect before. The process is most unquestionably a good one, and the result has been satisfactory. The paint has not done the slightest injury to the stone, and in a few winters will entirely disappear. . . . The paint was a mixture of white and brown, and, when first applied, was as near as possible of the same grey colour

as the old mossy covering with which the stone was coated
Since the application the brown has rather predominated
over the white, and it has now a darker appearance. . . .
I am ready to admit that there are black marks on the
South and the North Sides of the Cross, where the letters
have partly disappeared. I feel firmly convinced, however,
that there is not a black mark in the chief inscription
without its corresponding depression on the stone, although
some of the tracings were all but obliterated. It was only
by thus tracing the letters in black that I was able to arrive
at the full and the clear conviction that my decipherings
are probably correct '.

At a meeting of the Society on August 5, 1857, there was
'a short conversation on the Bewcastle cross ' and 'a joke
or two on the recent controversy thereon and on the Rev.
Mr. Maughan's latest pamphlet ' (*Proc.*, p. 263). On September
2, 1857, a member said 'the cross had received a second
coat of paint of a puce colour, over its former covering of
blue (blue-blue, such as carts are painted with) and as these
portions of the pillar which were not inscribed had been
spared by the brush, it had a strange, motley aspect '
(p. 266).

59 1. I can not find that Mr. Howard ever made any such
suggestion, but he had published (*Archæologia* 13 (1800).
309—312) a paper read on March 29, 1798, entitled, 'En-
quiries concerning the Tomb of King Alfred at Hyde Abbey,
near Winchester '; and he began his letter (p. 24, above)
with a reference to the former article: 'The Society of Antiquaries have honoured a communication of mine, respecting
the tomb of Alfred, in a manner far beyond its deserts.'
Maughan apparently confuses Alcfrith with Alfred the Great,
who flourished more than two centuries later.

59 2. Referring to the plate on p. 15.

59 3. See note on 3 3.

59 4. See note on 3 3.

60 1. But see Anderson, *Early Christ. Mon. of Scotland*
1. xxviii—ix.

61 1. See *Date*, p. 123.

63 1. See *Date*, p. 25.

64 1. See note on 36 1, end.

67 1. See *Date*, p. 37.

68 1. Properly, Verelius.

70 1. See *Date*, p. 58.

71 1. George Stephens (1813—1895) accepted, for the most part, Maughan's readings, and from him they were taken by Henry Sweet (*Oldest English Texts*, 1885, p. 124) and others. Stephens explains (*Old-Northern Runic Monuments* 1 (1866—7). 398) that his pictures of the cross (p. 399) were founded on Maughan's sketches, photographs, and rubbings, assisted by his *Memoir*, and that the completed drawings were again checked and corrected by Maughan from the stone itself. It is therefore not surprising that all Maughan's readings of illegible runes appear on the stone itself in Stephens' two pictures of the cross, except that in the long inscription in Stephens' plate *o* is sometimes reproduced by *a*, etc. In this (p. 402) the differences are (Stephens' readings in parenthesis): *beacn* (*becn*); *Wæthgar* (*Wothgar*); *Alwfwolþu* (*Olwfwolthu*); *-ing* (*-ng*); *heo sinna* (*heo-sinna*); *sawhula* (*sowhula*); and, in translation: *Pray thou for them, their sins, their souls* (*Pray for the crime* (*high sin*) *of his soul*). On the south face, he reads *thæes* for Maughan's *thæs*, and after *lice* he conjectures *he*. At the top of the east face (p. 403) he conjectures a former *frithes*. On the north face he reads *Kynnburug*, and the rest on this face as Maughan does.

As to Stephens' trustworthiness, I quote from Wimmer (*Die Runenschrift*, pp. XV, XVI, translated): 'In everything for which runology is indebted to this man, a fantastic enthusiasm for the subject is coupled with the most amazing lack of insight into the questions dealt with, and with utter contempt for all scientific method. . . . My judgment also holds with reference to the treatment of Old English inscriptions, though here the author is concerned with his mother-tongue, and one can allow him a certain authority in virtue of his position. But where he can not depend upon the thorough work of predecessors, which he was fortunately able to do in the case of the larger inscriptions, but had to strike out for himself, he is capable of reaching incredible results, as in his interpretation of the Brough stone in West-morland, where on ten folio pages he renders a Greek in-scription as Old English, in a dialect which he invented for the occasion.' Add Henry Bradley's opinion (*Dict. Nat. Biog.* 54. 173—4): 'His own contributions to the interpre-tation of the inscriptions are almost worthless, owing to his want of accurate philological knowledge. His method of translation consisted in identifying the words of the in-scriptions with any words of similar appearance that he could discover in the dictionaries of ancient or modern Scandi-navian languages, and then forming them into some plausible meaning without regard to grammar.... A ludicrous illustra-tion of the worthlessness of his principles of decipherment is afforded by his treatment of the inscription found at Brough in Westmoreland, which he declared to be written in Anglian runes, and translated in accordance with that supposition. When it was pointed out that the inscription consisted of five Greek hexameters, Stephens frankly acknowledged his blunder, though the acknowledgment involved the con-demnation of nearly all that he had done in the decipherment of the inscriptions.'

Stephens' views concerning the Brough inscription (the stone, discovered in 1879, is now in the Fitzwilliam Museum, Cambridge) will be found in *Trans. Cumb. and Westm. Antiq. and Arch. Soc.*, Vol. 5 (1881); his reprint (from *Mém. de la Soc. Royale des Antiquaires du Nord*, Copenhagen, 1882—4) of lectures delivered in the spring of 1881, entitled, *Prof. S. Bugge's Studies in Northern Mythology* (London, 1883), pp. 377—380 (with plate); and his *Runic Monuments* 3 (1884). 169—179 (with plate). For the discussion by Sayce, Ridge-way, Bradley, and various other scholars, see *Academy* 25 (1884). 421—2, 440, 458; 26 (1884). 10, 28, 47—8, 62, 77—8, 94—5, 137—9, 173; 27 (1885). 170, 336—7; *Athenæum* for 1884[2]. 664 (with plate), 741, 777, 813; *Camb. Univ. Reporter* for March 3, 1885 (pp. 495—8); *Camb. Antiq. Soc. Report and Communications*, No. 27 (Vol. 6, No. 1, 1887), pp. xxiii—xxix (read Feb. 23, 1885). The authoritative form of the Greek inscription will be found in Kaibel, *Inscr. Græcæ, Siciliæ, et Italiæ, additis* . . . *Britanniæ* (1890), p. 671. Stephens had rendered it (*Camb. Antiq. Soc.*, as above, p. xxvii); 'Ingalang in Buckenhome bigged this gravekist of Cimokom, Ahl's wife but born in Ecby at Ackleigh. Holy into destruction walked she. The mound Oscil, Osbiol, Cuhl, Oeki made. The body all-friend Christ, young, reaches after death; eke sorrow's cry never moves me more.' Professor E. C. Clark thus rendered the Greek in a free metrical paraphrase (same page):

> Hermes of Commagene here—
> Young Hermes, in his sixteenth year—
> Entombed by fate before his day
> Beholding, let the traveller say:—
> Fair youth, my greeting to thy shrine
> Though but a mortal course be thine,
> Since all too soon thou wing'dst thy flight
> From realms of speech to realm of night;
> Yet no misnomer art thou shewn,
> Who with thy namesake God art flown.

71 2. The character which, with Maughan, represents Æ in HWÆTRED, WÆTHGAR (p. 110), represents A in BEACN (110), FRUMAN, GEAR (96), KYNESWITHA (102), MYRCNA (102), WÆTHGAR, ALWFWOLTHU, AFT, ALCFRITHU, EAN, EAC, SINNA, SAWHULA, twice (110), and O in SETTON, ALWFWOLTHU, OSWIUING, HEO (110). With Haigh, it represents O in FLWOLDU (110), HEOSUM (116). With Stephens, it represents O in SETTON, WOTHGAR, OLWF-WOLTHU, OSWIUING, HEO-, SOWHULA (402). The true value of this rune is O.

The character which, with Haigh, represents Æ in SETTÆ, HWÆTRED, WITGÆR, GEBIDÆD (so for GEGIDÆD), ALC-FRITHÆ (110), represents A in ALCFRITHÆ, SAWLUM (110; cf. also 116), EANFLAD (121), and O in OSWU (109). With Stephens, it represents Æ in HWÆTRED (402), THÆES (403). Its true value is Æ.

The character which, with Haigh, represents O in ROETBERT (110), with Stephens represents A in WOTHGAR, AFT,

ALCFRITHU, EAN, EAC, SINNA, SOWHULA (402), FRUMAN, GEAR (403), KYNESWITHA, MYRCNA (404). Its true value is A.

The character which, with Maughan, represents Æ in THÆS (95), with Stephens represents ÆE in THÆES (403).

EA is written with two characters in BEACN, EAN, EAC by Maughan (110) and Stephens (402), and by Maughan in GEAR (97), but as one character by Haigh in EANFLÆD, PREASTER (39), EANFLAD (121). It is properly written as one.

Two runes are written in combination by Maughan (called by Maughan 'trirunor,' and by Stephens 'bind-stave' or 'tie') for Æ (95), MA (96), EA, ON, ÆT, ÆTH, HU (110), THU (94, 110); ER is thus written by Haigh (110). These seem to be otherwise unexampled in Old English runes (cf. Stephens, pp. 401, 403). The reading of THU in CYNNBURTHUG (99) makes nonsense of the word.

NG is represented as two characters by Maughan in KYNINGES (96), KYNG (102), and by Haigh in KYNG (120); but as one character by Haigh in CYNING (39 (3), 109, 110), CYNGN, twice (39), and by Maughan (for ING) in CYNIING, OSWIUING (110). It is properly written as one (see Hickes, *Thesaurus, Gram. Isl.*, Tabella II).

72₁. See p. 32.

72₂. Not in Nicolson's letter; cf. p. 22.

73₁. Never.

73₂. There is no OE. word *thun*; the nearest approach to it is *ðyn(ne)*, *ðin(ne)*, 'thin.'

74₁. There is no *ean* in OE.

74₂. In the seventh century, *ge-* would have been *gi-*; see Cædmon's *Hymn*.

74₃. 'To pray for' is regularly *(ge)biddan for*, with the accusative or (less often) dative.

74₄. A Celtic, not an OE. word.

75₁. Wrong.

75₂. Impossible.

78₁. Wrong.

80₁. See *Date*, pp. 42–3.

80₂. As a Latin genitive: *Signum manus Alhfriþi*.

80 3. Properly, Riemmelth.

81 1. *Stephenson's.* Properly, Stevenson's.

81 2. Published 1838.

81 3. *Aldfrid.* There was a tenth-century Aldred, the provost, who transcribed four collects in the *Durham Ritual*; cf. Stevenson's preface to his edition, pp. ix, x.

82 1. As late as 1911, we find such a scholar as Dalton saying (*Byzantine Art and Archæology*, p. 236, note 3): 'The Bewcastle and Ruthwell crosses are of the same age, and the former is dated by the mention of Alcfrith.' And in 1912 Prior and Gardner say (*Mediæval Figure-Sculpture in England*, p. 117), referring to Maughan's views concerning Ecgfrith (p. 94, above): 'It is true the last important word [Ecgfrith] is much defaced. But doubt is set at rest by the runes in other parts of the inscriptions—said to be quite distinct—of recorded contemporaries, one of these being Alcfrith.' Prior and Gardner, it may be said in passing, by referring the Bridekirk Font to the twelfth century (p. 94), weaken the force of Dalton's statement (*loc. cit.*): 'Runes would have been unintelligible in the twelfth century.' Cf. Collingwood, *Early Sculpt. Crosses*, pp. 68 ff.

Collingwood, in the *Victoria History of Cumberland* (1901), 1. 277–8, (cf. pp. 256–7), says of the inscriptions on the Bewcastle Cross : 'The reading which may be called the *Textus Receptus*, though not without difficulties, we owe mainly to the late Rev. J. Maughan of Bewcastle. It is as follows. . . . The main purport of the [long] inscription seems to be fairly clear. If the Bewcastle cross is to be dated 671, as its inscription and ornament seem to suggest, these runes are the earliest dated piece of English writing in existence'; cf. his *Early Sculpt. Crosses*, pp. 44–47.

Dr. Thomas Hodgkin, Fellow of the British Academy, speaking of the Bewcastle Cross in 1906 (Hunt and Poole, *Pol. Hist. Eng.* 1. 172), called it 'a monument raised to his [Alchfrith's] memory.' He referred to the 'inscription which, though not yet deciphered beyond dispute, certainly says that the stone was raised as a memorial of "Alchfrith, son of Oswy, and aforetime King."' . . . An inscription seems to record that it was reared in the first year of his brother Egfrid, that is in 670.' To him 'the standing figure of a man with a bird on his wrist' was 'perhaps King Alchfrid himself with his falcon.' He thought it possible, however, that 'the reading of one line of the inscription, "Pray for his soul's great sin"' might 'prove too fanciful to be accepted by future students.'

83 1. Bede merely says that Oswy held the kingdom for 28 years with great difficulty, being warred upon by the heathen Mercians, Alchfrith, and Ethelwald.

84 1. Rather 651 (Bede 5. 24).

84 2. Late in 665 or early in 666 (Bright, *Early Eng. Church Hist.*, p. 213), Chad was sent to Canterbury by Oswy to be consecrated bishop of York, as Wilfrith, at Alcfrith's instance, had been consecrated in France a year or so earlier. Plummer says (2. 198): 'It is certain that at this point he [Alcfrith] disappears from history; and probable that that disappearance, whether by death or exile, was due to his rebellion against his father;' cf. Bright, p. 212.

84 3. Bede's mention in 3. 14 is nothing to the purpose; but cf. 3. 21.

84 4. Misprint for 'reigned.'

85 1. Bede and Eddi agree.

86 1. Cuthbert was not consecrated bishop till 685; it was Ecgfrith who was instrumental in having Cuthbert called (Bede 4. 28).

86 2. John was made bishop in 687, under king Aldfrith.

86 3. At the Synod of Whitby, 664.

87 1. Rather, Iona.

88 1. Bede distinctly says Oswy (3. 28).

88 2. Chad.

89 1. Misprint for 664.

89 2. 664, according to Plummer (Bede, *Op. Hist.* 2. 317).

90 1. Properly, Ettmüller.

91 1. Soon after 642, and not later than 645 (Plummer 2. 165).

91 2. As he died in 725 (Bede 5. 23), he must indeed have been young in 645, or earlier.

92 1. This Alfwold died in 749 (Plummer 2. 107).

92 2. Kemble, *Cod. Dipl.* 2. 337.

94 1. Rather, *lichama, lichoma.*

96 1. Such forms in *-es* (instead of *-æs*), did they exist on the stone, would prove that the inscriptions were not of the 7th century; see *Cædmon's Hymn*; Sievers, *Gram.* 237, note 1; Kemble, *Archæologia* 28. 346).

96 2. This word, if it could be so read, would end in *-e* (or very early *-i*: Sievers, *Gram.* 237, note 2); see Wülfing, *Syntax* 125.

96 3. See *Date*, p. 42, note 1.

97 1. Read 'Nicolson.'

98 1. Rather *-buru*; the error is from Hutchinson, like 'Nicholson' for 'Nicolson.'

98 2. Aldhelm's. Anselm of Canterbury lived 1033—1109.

99 1. Cf. p. 25.

99 2. The two readings are exactly the same.

99 3. *Arch.* 28. 347, and Pl. 16. 15.

99 4. *Cyniburuh.*

99 5. See p. 57.

99 6. 3. 21.

100 1. But Bede died in 735.

101 1. It was Osric, King of the Hwiccas, who founded the monastery of St. Peter's at Gloucester, and he surely was not the son of the Mercian Penda, nor, consequently, the brother of Cyniburg.

102 1. In the seventh century, this would be *Cyni-* (*Kyni-*); see Bede, ed. Plummer, 2. 446—7.

102 2. See the Saxon *Chronicle* (Laud MS.) under 656 and 963. Both she and Cyniburg were buried at Caistor.

102 3. These are impossible as seventh-century forms.

103 1. In the seventh century, this word would have been *Wulfheri* (Sievers, *Gram.* 246, note 1; Bede, ed. Plummer, 1. 141, 199, 206, 207, 354).

105 1. *White.* See p. 58.

105 2. See note on 36 1.

106 1. See note on 59 1.

106 2. See pp. 96, 108, 121.

108₁. No such rune is known to me.

110₁. UMÆ should have been transliterated UME, and the last two lines should read:

EBIDÆD : HE

OSUM : SAWLUM,

allowing the Æ of the first line to be identical with the A of the second.

116₁. *hissum* and *heosum* are equally impossible.

123₁. See p. 43.

123₂. See pp. 40, 76.

123₃. See pp. 39, 41.

123₄. See pp. 36, 48.

123₅. See pp. 45, 46.

124₁. See p. 42.

Supplementary note on 2₁.

The nucleus of Camden's statement is to be found in a communication made to him by Mr. Bainbrigg, schoolmaster at Appleby, who made a tour in 1601 (Camden was never in Cumberland save in 1599), in the interest of the *Britannia*. His words are (Cott. Julius F. 6, fol. 321): 'Crux quæ est in cæmiterio est viginti fere pedum, ex uno quadrato lapide graphice exciso cum hac inscriptione :

D†BOROX.*

Talem Edwardus primus in Alienoræ conjugis memoriam posuit, vel qualem Roisia mulier eo tempore celeberrima ad Roistone statuit.' This is apparently the very first mention of the Bewcastle Cross, and accounts for Roscarrock's statement about *Eborax.* See Professor F. Haverfield's communication in *Trans. Cumb. and Westm. Antiq. and Archæol. Assoc.*, N. S. 11 (1911). 355 (cf. 349, 376, 377).

* In Bainbrigg's manuscript the D has a vertical stroke in the middle.